Second Workshop on Storytelling 2019

Florence, Italy
1 August 2019

ISBN: 978-1-5108-9110-4

ACL 2019

Storytelling

Proceedings of the Second Workshop

August 1, 2019
Florence, Italy

Introduction

Welcome to the second *ACL workshop on Storytelling!

Human storytelling has existed for as far back as we can trace, and is thought to be fundamental to being human. Stories help share ideas, histories, and common ground. This workshop examines what storytelling is, its structure and components, and how it is expressed, with respect to state of the art in language and computation.

Part of grounding artificial intelligence work in human experience can involve the generation, understanding, and sharing of stories. This workshop highlights the diverse work being done in storytelling and AI across different fields. Papers at this workshop are multi-disciplinary, including work on neural and linguistic approaches to understanding and generating stories in narrative texts, social media, and visual narratives.

The second workshop of Storytelling received 22 submissions. We accepted 14 submissions into the proceedings, 6 of which were presented as oral presentations, and 8 as posters. We accepted 3 of the submitted papers as non-archival works to be presented during the poster session. We are pleased to host an invited talk from Melissa Roemmele.

We hope you enjoy the workshop!
The Storytelling Workshop Organizers

Organizers:

Francis Ferraro, University of Maryland Baltimore County
Ting-Hao (Kenneth) Huang, Pennsylvania State University
Stephanie M. Lukin, U.S. Army Research Laboratory
Margaret Mitchell, Google

Program Committee:

Snigdha Chaturvedi*, University of California, Santa Cruz
Elizabeth Clark, University of Washington
David Elson, Google
Drew Farris*, Booz Allen Hamilton
Mark Finlayson*, Florida International University
Jon Gillick, University of California, Berkeley
Andrew Gordon, University of Southern California
Daphne Ippolito*, University of Pennsylvania
Anna Kasunic, Carnegie Mellon University
Lun-Wei Ku*, Academia Sinica
Boyang "Albert" Li*, Baidu Research
Joao Magalhaes, Universidade Nova de Lisboa
Ramesh Manuvinakurike*, University of Southern California
Lara Martin, Georgia Institute of Technology
Cynthia Matuszek*, University of Maryland Baltimore County
Nanyun Peng, University of Southern California
Eli Pincus*, University of Southern California
Elahe Rahimtoroghi, Google
Melissa Roemmele, SDL
Mark Riedl, Georgia Institute of Technology
Mariët Theune*, University of Twente

An immense thank you to all our reviewers, especially these last-minute reviewers (*). We could not have put together our program without everyone's help!

Invited Speaker:

Melissa Roemmele, SDL

Table of Contents

Composing a Picture Book by Automatic Story Understanding and Visualization
Xiaoyu Qi, Ruihua Song, Chunting Wang, Jin Zhou and Tetsuya Sakai 1

"My Way of Telling a Story": Persona based Grounded Story Generation
Khyathi Chandu, Shrimai Prabhumoye, Ruslan Salakhutdinov and Alan W Black 11

Using Functional Schemas to Understand Social Media Narratives
Xinru Yan, Aakanksha Naik, Yohan Jo and Carolyn Rose 22

A Hybrid Model for Globally Coherent Story Generation
Fangzhou Zhai, Vera Demberg, Pavel Shkadzko, Wei Shi and Asad Sayeed 34

Guided Neural Language Generation for Automated Storytelling
Prithviraj Ammanabrolu, Ethan Tien, Wesley Cheung, Zhaochen Luo, William Ma, Lara Martin
and Mark Riedl 46

An Analysis of Emotion Communication Channels in Fan-Fiction: Towards Emotional Storytelling
Evgeny Kim and Roman Klinger 56

Narrative Generation in the Wild: Methods from NaNoGenMo
Judith van Stegeren and Mariët Theune 65

Lexical concreteness in narrative
Michael Flor and Swapna Somasundaran 75

A Simple Approach to Classify Fictional and Non-Fictional Genres
Mohammed Rameez Qureshi, Sidharth Ranjan, Rajakrishnan Rajkumar and Kushal Shah 81

Detecting Everyday Scenarios in Narrative Texts
Lilian Diana Awuor Wanzare, Michael Roth and Manfred Pinkal 90

Personality Traits Recognition in Literary Texts
Daniele Pizzolli and Carlo Strapparava 107

Winter is here: Summarizing Twitter Streams related to Pre-Scheduled Events
Anietie Andy, Derry Tanti Wijaya and Chris Callison-Burch 112

WriterForcing: Generating more interesting story endings
Prakhar Gupta, Vinayshekhar Bannihatti Kumar, Mukul Bhutani and Alan W Black 117

Prediction of a Movie's Success From Plot Summaries Using Deep Learning Models
You Jin Kim, Yun Gyung Cheong and Jung Hoon Lee 127

Conference Program

Thursday, August 1, 2019

08:45–09:00   *Opening Remarks*

Morning Session 1

09:00–10:00   *Invited Talk*
Melissa Roemmele

10:00–10:30   *Composing a Picture Book by Automatic Story Understanding and Visualization*
Xiaoyu Qi, Ruihua Song, Chunting Wang, Jin Zhou and Tetsuya Sakai

10:30–11:00   *Morning Break*

Morning Session 2

11:00–11:30   *"My Way of Telling a Story": Persona based Grounded Story Generation*
Khyathi Chandu, Shrimai Prabhumoye, Ruslan Salakhutdinov and Alan W Black

11:30–12:00   *Using Functional Schemas to Understand Social Media Narratives*
Xinru Yan, Aakanksha Naik, Yohan Jo and Carolyn Rose

12:00–12:30   *A Hybrid Model for Globally Coherent Story Generation*
Fangzhou Zhai, Vera Demberg, Pavel Shkadzko, Wei Shi and Asad Sayeed

12:30–14:00   *Lunch*

Afternoon Session

14:00–14:30   *Guided Neural Language Generation for Automated Storytelling*
Prithviraj Ammanabrolu, Ethan Tien, Wesley Cheung, Zhaochen Luo, William Ma,
Lara Martin and Mark Riedl

14:30–15:00   *An Analysis of Emotion Communication Channels in Fan-Fiction: Towards Emotional Storytelling*
Evgeny Kim and Roman Klinger

15:00–15:30   *Poster Lightning Talks*

15:30–16:00   *Afternoon Break*

Thursday, August 1, 2019 (continued)

16:00–17:30   *Poster Session*

Adversarial Generation and Encoding of Nested Texts
Alon Rozental

Narrative Generation in the Wild: Methods from NaNoGenMo
Judith van Stegeren and Mariët Theune

Lexical concreteness in narrative
Michael Flor and Swapna Somasundaran

A Simple Approach to Classify Fictional and Non-Fictional Genres
Mohammed Rameez Qureshi, Sidharth Ranjan, Rajakrishnan Rajkumar and Kushal Shah

DREAMT - Embodied Motivational Conversational Storytelling
David Powers

Detecting Everyday Scenarios in Narrative Texts
Lilian Diana Awuor Wanzare, Michael Roth and Manfred Pinkal

Personality Traits Recognition in Literary Texts
Daniele Pizzolli and Carlo Strapparava

Winter is here: Summarizing Twitter Streams related to Pre-Scheduled Events
Anietie Andy, Derry Tanti Wijaya and Chris Callison-Burch

WriterForcing: Generating more interesting story endings
Prakhar Gupta, Vinayshekhar Bannihatti Kumar, Mukul Bhutani and Alan Black

Prediction of a Movie's Success From Plot Summaries Using Deep Learning Models
You Jin Kim, Yun Gyung Cheong and Jung Hoon Lee

Character-Centric Storytelling
Aditya Surikuchi and Jorma Laaksonen

17:30–17:45   *Closing Remarks*

Composing a Picture Book
by Automatic Story Understanding and Visualization

Xiaoyu Qi[1], Ruihua Song[1], Chunting Wang[2] , Jin Zhou[2], Tetsuya Sakai[3]
[1]Microsoft, Beijing, China
[2]Beijing Film Academy, Beijing, China
[3]Waseda University, Tokyo, Japan
`{xiaqi, rsong}@microsoft.com, 04172154@mail.bfa.edu.cn`
`whitezj@vip.sina.com, tetsuyasakai@acm.org`

Abstract

Pictures can enrich storytelling experiences. We propose a framework that can automatically compose a picture book by understanding story text and visualizing it with painting elements, i.e., characters and backgrounds. For story understanding, we extract key information from a story on both sentence level and paragraph level, including characters, scenes and actions. These concepts are organized and visualized in a way that depicts the development of a story. We collect a set of Chinese stories for children and apply our approach to compose pictures for stories. Extensive experiments are conducted towards story event extraction for visualization to demonstrate the effectiveness of our method.

1 Introduction

A story is an ordered sequence of steps, each of which can contain words, images, visualizations, video, or any combination thereof (Kosara and Mackinlay, 2013). There exist vast amounts of story materials on the Internet, while few of them include visual data. Among the few presented to audience, some include illustrations to make the stories more vivid; others are converted to video forms such as cartoons and films, of which the production consumes a lot of time and human efforts. Although visualized stories are difficult to generate, they are more comprehensible, memorable and attractive. Thus, automatic story understanding and visualization has a broad application prospect in storytelling.

As an initial study, we aim to analyze events of a story and visualize them by combining painting elements, i.e., characters and backgrounds. Story understanding has been a challenging task in Natural Language Processing area for a long time (Charniak, 1972). In order to understand a story, we need to tackle the problem of event extraction in a story. A story usually consists of several plots, where characters appear and make actions. We define event keywords of a story as: scene (where), character (who, to whom) and action (what). We extract events from story on both sentence level and paragraph level, so as to make use of the information in each sentence and the context of the full story.

As for story visualization, the most challenging problem is stage directing. We need to organize the events following certain spatial distribution rules. Although literary devices might be used e.g. flashbacks, the order in a story plot roughly corresponds with time (Kosara and Mackinlay, 2013). We arrange the extracted events in a screen along the story timeline. Positions of elements on the screen are determined according to both current and past events. Finally, with audio track added, simple animations could be generated. These simple animations are like storyboards, in which each image represents a major event that correspond to a sentence or a group of consecutive sentences in the story text.

Regarding storytelling, we need to first know our audiences, assess their level of domain knowledge and familiarity with visualization conventions (Ma et al., 2012). In this paper, our target is to understand and visualize Chinese stories for children. We collect children's stories from the Internet. (The sources are described in Section 7.1.) Then, we extract events and prepare visualization materials and style for children. The framework we proposed, however, has wide extensibility, since it does not depend on domain specific knowledge. It could serve as an automatic picture book composition solution to other fields and target audience.

Our contributions are threefold. 1) We propose an end-to-end framework to automatically generate a sequence of pictures that represent major

1

Proceedings of the Second Storytelling Workshop, pages 1–10
Florence, Italy, August 1, 2019. ©2019 Association for Computational Linguistics

events in a story text. 2) New formulation of story event extraction from sentence level to paragraph level to align the events in a temporal order. 3) We propose using a neural encoder-decoder model to extract story events and present empirical results with significant improvements over the baseline.

The paper is organized as follows: In Section 2 we introduce related work. Then we formulate the problem and overview our proposed solution in Section 3. Details of different modules are provided in Section 4, 5 and 6. We describe our data and experiments in Section 7. In Section 8 we make conclusion and present our future work.

2 Related Work

2.1 Story Event Extraction

Event extraction is to automatically identify events from text about what happened, when, where, to whom, and why (Zhou et al., 2014). Previous work on event extraction mainly focuses on sentence-level event extraction driven by data or knowledge.

Data-driven event extraction methods rely on quantitative methods to discover relations (Hogenboom et al., 2011). Term frequency-inverse document frequency (TF-IDF) (Salton and McGill, 1986) and clustering (Tanev et al., 2008) are widely used. Okamoto et al. (2009) use hierarchical clustering to extract local events. Liu et al. (2008) employ weighted undirected bipartite graphs and clustering methods to extract events from news. Lei et al. (2005) propose using support vector machines for news event extraction.

Knowledge-driven approaches take advantages of domain knowledge, using lexical and syntactical parsers to extract target information. McClosky et al. (2011) convert text to a dependency tree and use dependency parsing to solve the problem. Aone et al. (2009) and Nishihara et al. (2009) focus on designed patterns to parse text. Zhou et al. (2014) propose a Bayesian model to extract structured representation of events from Twitter in an unsupervised way. Different frameworks are designed for specific domains, such as the work in (Yakushiji et al., 2000), (Cohen et al., 2009) and (Li et al., 2002)). Although there is less demand of training data for knowledge-driven approaches, knowledge acquisition and pattern design remain difficult.

In order to deal with the disadvantages of both methods, researchers work on combining them.

At the training stages of data-driven methods, initial bootstrapppings with dependency parser (Lee et al., 2003) and clustering techniques (Piskorski et al., 2007) are used for better semantic understanding. Chun et al. (2004) combine lexicon syntactic parser and term co-occurrences to extract biomedical events while Jungermann et al. (2008) combine a parser with undirected graphs. The only trial of neural network on this task is the work in (Tozzo et al., 2018), where they employ RNN with dependency parser as training initialization.

We propose a hybrid encoder-decoder approach for story event extraction to avoid human-knowledge requirement and better utilize the neural network. Moreover, previous work focus on sentence-level event extraction, which has a gap to apply to full story visualization due to the loss of event continuity. Thus, we extend event extraction to paragraph level so that it is possible to visualize a story coherently in a time sequence.

2.2 Story Visualization

Previous work mainly focuses on narrative visualization (Segel and Heer, 2010), where the visualization intention is deeper understanding of the data and the logic inside. Valls et al. (2017) extract story graphs a formalism that captures the events (e.g., characters, locations) and their interactions in a story. Zitnick et al. (2013) and Zeng et al. (2009) interpret sentences and visualize scenes. There also exists visual storytelling task (Huang et al., 2016).

The most relevant work to ours is that of Shimazu et al. (1988), where they outlined a story driven animation system and presented story understanding mechanism for creating animations. They mainly targeted on interpretations of three kinds of actions: action causality check, action continuity beyond a sentence and hidden actions between neighbouring sentences. The key solution was a Truth Maintenance System proposed in (Doyle, 1979), which relies on pre-defined constrains from human knowledge. Understanding a story with a TMS system would cost a lot of manual efforts. In light of this, we propose an approach to story understanding that automatically learns from labelled story data.

Different from previous work, we propose new story visualization techniques, including temporal and spatial arrangement for screen view. Our

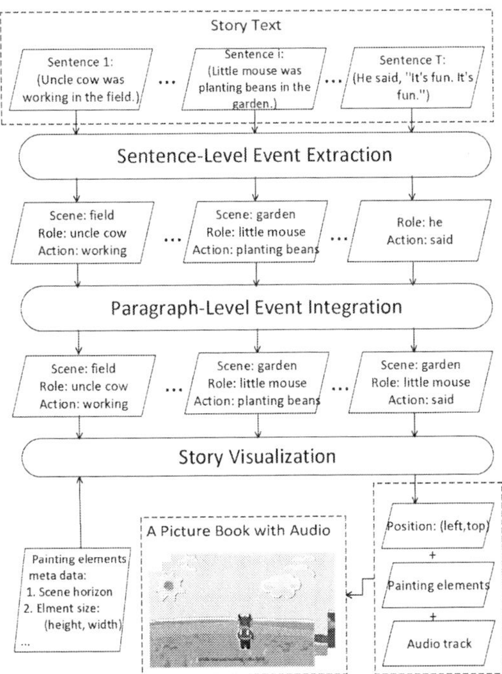

Figure 1: A flowchart for story understanding and visualization

framework generates story animations automatically from end to end. Moreover, it is based on event extraction on both sentence level and paragraph level.

3   Problem Formulation and System Overview

We formulate the problem as follows: the input is a story that contains m paragraphs and each paragraph p contains n sentences, which are composed of several words. The output is a series of images that correspond to the story. An image I is composed by some prepared painting elements (30 scenes, such as sea, and 600 characters, such as fox and rabbit, with different actions in our experiment). As it is costly to prepare painting elements, given a number of stories to visualize, we hope that the fewer elements are prepared the better.

We show the flowchart of our proposed solution in Figure 1. Given a story text, we first split it into a sequence of narrative sentences. Story event extraction is conducted within each sentence independently. Then events are integrated on paragraph level and fed into the visualization stage, where they are distributed temporally and spatially on the screen. The visualization part determines what to be shown on the screen, when and where they should be arranged. Finally, painting elements are displayed on the screen and audio track is added to make a picture book with audio.

4   Sentence-Level Event Extraction

We start from event extraction on sentence-level. Given a sentence $s = (x_1, x_2, ..., x_T)$ of length T, we intend to get a label sequence $y = (y_1, y_2, ..., y_T)$, where $y_i \in scene, character, action, others, i \in [1, T]$. We propose using a neural encoder-decoder model to extract events from a story.

4.1   BiLSTM-CRF

BiLSTM-CRF is the state-of-the-art method to solve the sequence labeling problem. Thus we apply this model to extract events in sentence level.

We can encode the story sentence with a Bidirectional LSTM (Graves and Schmidhuber, 2005), which processes each training sequence forwards and backwards. A Conditional Random Fields (CRF) (Ratinov and Roth, 2009) layer is used as the decoder to overcome label-bias problem .

Given a sentence $s = (x_1, x_2, ..., x_T)$ of length T, we annotate each word and get a ground-truth label sequence $l = (l_1, l_2, ..., l_T)$. Every word $x_i (i \in [1, T])$ is converted into a real-valued vector $e_i (i \in [1, T])$ with a word-embedding dictionary pre-trained from Wikipedia Chinese corpus. Then the sentence is represented as $E = (e_1, e_2, ..., e_T)$, where each e_i is padded to a fixed-length. We set the embedding length to 100 in our experiment. The embedded sentence vector E is fed into a BiLSTM neural network. The hidden state h_i of the network is calculated in the same way as in (Graves and Schmidhuber, 2005).

Different from standard LSTM, Bidirectional LSTM introduces a second hidden layer that processes data flow in the opposite direction. Therefore, it is able to extract information from both the previous and latter knowledge. Each final hidden state is the concatenation of the forward and backward hidden states:

$$h_t = [\overleftarrow{h_t}; \overrightarrow{h_t}] \tag{1}$$

Instead of adding a softmax classification layer after the hidden states, we employ CRF (Ratinov and Roth, 2009) to take the label correlations into consideration. The hidden layer $h = (h_1, h_2, ..., h_T)$ is fed into the CRF layer. We intend to get the predicted label sequence $y = (y_1, y_2, ..., y_T)$. The conditional probability is defined as:

$$f(y, h) = \sum_{i=1}^{T} W_{y_i}^{T} h_i + \sum_{i=0}^{T} A_{y_i, y_{i+1}}$$

$$P(y|h) = \frac{\exp(f(y, h))}{\sum_{y'} \exp(f(y', h))} \quad (2)$$

where T is the length of the output sequence. $W_{y_i}^{T}$ is weight matrix. $A_{y_i, y_{i+1}}$ represents the transitioning score from label y_i to label y_{i+1}. And y' stands for any possible output label sequence. Our training objective is minimizing the negative log likelihood of $P(y|h)$.

4.2 Model Variants

Recently, a new pre-trained model BERT obtains new state-of-the-art results on a variety of natural language processing tasks (Devlin et al., 2018). We apply this model to our story event extraction. We input a sentence to the BERT base model released by Devlin et al. The last layer of BERT serves as word embedding and input of the BiLSTM model. The other parts of the model remain the same for comparison. We refer to this variant as BERT-BiLSTM-CRF.

We also experiment with IDCNN model (Strubell et al., 2017) and fix the parameter setting for comparison. IDCNN model leverages convolutional neural network instead of recurrent one to accelerate the training process.

5 Paragraph-Level Event Integration

When generating a story animation, we need to take consideration of the full paragraph, so that the events could be continuous in temporary order. (A story might consists of one or multiple paragraphs.) In this part, we integrate sentence-level story events to paragraph-level ones. Given a story paragraph $p = (s_1, s_2, ..., s_n)$ of length n, where sentence $s = (x_1, x_2, ..., x_T)$ has corresponding label sequence $y = (y_1, y_2, ..., y_T)$, we integrate the label information and get a refined event keyword set for each sentence, denoted as $\hat{y} = (scene, character, action)$. $\hat{y}$ indicates the events in the current sentence.

A story paragraph example is presented in Table 1. The sentence-level detection results are listed. Event detection results of a story vary in different sentences and they are quite unbalanced. Only the

1st, the 8th and the 14th sentence have tokens indicating the story scenes. We need to infer that the first scene "field" should cover the sentence spans from the 1st to the 7th. And the scene changes to "river" in the 8th sentence and remains until the 13th one. Then it turns to "garden" and keeps the same until the end of the story. Similarly, we have to decide which character and action should appear in a sentence time span according to the paragraph information, even if nothing is detected in a specific sentence.

We mainly consider scene and character detection. An action may last from when it last emerged until the next action, such as running or driving. While it could also be short and happens within a sentence time (e.g. He sits down.). The determination of action continuity requires significantly more human knowledge and is beyond this paper's scope.

Extracted scene of a sentence is expanded to its neighbours in both forward and backward directions. At the scene boundaries, we follow the newly detected one. In this way, the story is divided into several scenes. Then we deal with characters within scenes. Normally, a character emerges at the first detected sentence and remains on the screen until the current plot ends.

6 Story Visualization

In this part, we calculate positions on the screen for each element. We define the position as $[left, top]$ in percentage relative to the top-left corner of the screen. Elements' positions are determined according to three constraints: 1) Meta data of the painting elements for the characters; 2) character number and significance in current time span; 3) history positions of the elements. The painting meta data of all elements include the following information:

- $(height, width)$: size of an element

The additional meta data of a painting scene are:

- $horizon$: distance from the horizontal line in a scene to the scene bottom. We use it as a safe line to arrange the feet of our characters; otherwise, a bear might float above the grassland, for example.

- point A: left point on the screen where we can locate a character.

story sentence (actions denoted with underlines)	scene	character
1. The sun beat down on the earth.	/	sun
2. Uncle cow was working in the field.	field	uncle cow
3. Beads of sweat were pattering down.	/	/
4. Seeing this, little elephant Lala quickly went to his side.	/	little elephant Lala, his
5. He fanned up big ears, and sent cool wind for uncle cow.	/	He, uncle cow
6. Uncle cow said with a smile:"Its so cool, thank you."	/	uncle cow
7. Lala replied happily:"No worries. No worries."	/	Lala
8. Grandma bear was washing clothes by the river,	river	Grandma bear
9. She was wiping sweat from time to time.	/	She
10. Lala saw it and fanned his big ears.	/	Lala
11. Grandma bear was not hot.	/	Grandma bear
12. She smiled kindly and said, "Good boy, thank you."	/	She
13. Lala replied:"No worries, no worries."	/	Lala
14. Little mouse was planting beans in the garden.	garden	Little mouse
15. Lala walked forward with enthusiasm and said,	/	Lala
16. "Little mouse, let me help you fan the wind."	/	Little mouse
17. "Thank you very much." said the mouse gratefully.	/	the mouse
18. Lala fanned her big ears again.	/	Lala
19. Suddenly he fanned the little mouse against the plantain leaf.	/	he, little mouse
20. Lala scratched her head shyly and said, "I'm really sorry."	/	Lala
21. Little mouse snort a laugh, and he said, "It's fun. It's fun."	/	Little mouse

Table 1: Example of extracted results for story "Big ears of the little elephant". (We have translated the Chinese story into English.)

- point B: right point on the screen where we can locate a character.

We calculate the character number to show on the screen in a time span and evenly distribute their positions based on the painting elements size and the horizon of the scene. Characters with high significance (talking ones or newly emerged ones) are placed near point A or B. If the character appeared in previous time spans, its position keeps the same or changes by minimal distance. The position should follow the equations:

$$top \leq 1 - height - horizon \qquad (3)$$

$$left \leq 1 - width \qquad (4)$$

$$\min \|top - top'\| \qquad (5)$$

$$\min \|left - left'\| \qquad (6)$$

where top' and $left'$ stand for previous position of an element. If the element appears for the first time, Equation 6 and 7 are ignored.

As to the orientation setting, we initialize each character with an orientation facing towards the middle of the screen. Those who are talking or interacting with each other are set face to face.

Finally, we add a timeline to the story. Each event in the text is assigned a start time and an end time, so that it appears in the screen accordingly. Along with an audio track, the static images are combined to generate a story animation. The characters are mapped to corresponding elements with the detected actions if they are available (e.g., we have the elements when a character is saying). Dialogue boxes are added to show which character is saying. The painting elements are prepared in clip art style to make it more flexible to change them, as shown in Figure 2.

7 Experiment and Discussion

7.1 Experiment Setup

Data Collection: We collect 3,680 Chinese stories for children from the Internet[1]. The stories include 47 sentences on average. We randomly sample $10,000$ sentences from the stories and split them into three parts: training set (80%), testing set

[1] http://www.tom61.com
http://www.cnfla.com
http://story.beva.com
http://www.61ertong.com
(Our data are public copyrighted.)

Dataset	Train	Test	Dev
#sentences	8,000	1,000	1,000
#scene	5,896	711	664
#character	10,073	1,376	1,497
#action	15,231	1,949	2,023

Table 2: Dataset statistics.

Event	scene	character	action
Example	sea, forest...	fox, bear...	cry, run...

Table 3: Story events examples.

Event	Method	Precision	Recall	F1
scene	Parser	0.585	0.728	0.649
scene	IDCNN	0.968	0.968	0.968
scene	BiLSTM	**0.973**	**0.974**	**0.973**
scene	BERT	0.931	0.918	0.924
chara	Parser	0.514	0.475	0.494
chara	IDCNN	0.829	0.758	0.792
chara	BiLSTM	0.831	0.758	0.793
chara	BERT	**0.833**	**0.853**	**0.843**
action	Parser	0.373	0.377	0.375
action	IDCNN	0.423	0.375	0.395
action	BiLSTM	0.442	0.400	0.420
action	BERT	**0.500**	**0.499**	**0.499**

Table 4: Sentence-level results comparison. (chara is short for character. BiLSTM and BERT represent BiLSTM-CRF and BERT-BiLSTM-CRF respectively.) We report the mean scores and conduct Tukey's HSD test. For scene extraction, the F1 score differences of all method pairs are statistically significant. So are that on character extraction (except the difference between BiLSTM and IDCNN). For action extraction, only the difference between BERT and Parser is significant.

(10%), and development set (10%). We hired four experienced annotators to provide story events annotations. For each sentence, the annotators select event keywords and give them a category label of scene, character, or action. The words rather than event keywords are regarded as "others". We present the statistics of the collected corpus in Table 2.

Each sentence in the training and development set was annotated by one annotator for the sake of saving cost. But each sentence in the testing sets was annotated by three annotators independently. We calculate Fleiss' Kappa (Viera et al., 2005) to evaluate the agreement among annotators. For each token in a sentence, it is annotated as $y(y \in scene, character, action, others)$ by 3 annotators. The Fleiss' Kappa value is 0.580, which shows that the annotations have moderate agreement.

For story visualization, we hire two designers to design elements for storytelling. The elements include story scenes and characters (with different actions). Each frame of an animation consists of several elements. This mechanism is flexible for element switch and story plot development. We prepared 30 scenes and 600 characters, which have high frequencies in the collected stories. Some example animation elements are shown in Table 3.

Training Details: In the neural based methods, the word embedding size is 100. The LSTM model contains 100 hidden units and trains with a learning rate of 0.001 and Adam (Kingma and Ba, 2014) optimizer. The batch size is set to 20 and 50% dropout is used to avoid overfitting. We train the model for 100 epochs although it converges quickly.

7.2 Sentence-Level Evaluation

We compare the neural based models with a baseline based on parser. We first conduct word segmentation with Jieba (Sun, 2012) and part of speech (POS) annotation using Stanford CoreNLP Toolkit (Manning et al., 2014). Then we use dependency parser to extract events. For scene extraction, we find that most scenes in the childrens' stories are common places with few specific names or actions. Thus, we construct a common place dictionary with 778 scene tokens. We keep NP, NR, NT and NN (Klein and Manning, 2003) of POS tagging results and filter the scene tokens according to the scene dictionary. Dependency parser is employed to extract characters and actions. The subjects and objects in a sentence are denoted as the current story characters. The predicates (usually in terms of verbs or verb phrases) in the dependency tree are considered to contain actions of the corresponding characters.

The mean evaluation results over the test sets are shown in Table 4. The result shows that the BiLSTM-CRF method can achieve as high as 0.973 $F1$ score in scene extraction. The BERT-BiLSTM-CRF method can achieve 0.843 $F1$ score in character extraction, which is high too. But action extraction is the most difficult. Even

Sentence (actions denoted with underlines)	Scene	character
1. The chicken and duck <u>walked happily</u> by the lake.	lake	chicken,duck
2. The chicken and duck <u>walked happily</u> by the lake.	lake	chicken,duck
1. The rabbit's father and mother are <u>in a hurry</u> at home.	home	rabbit's father,mother
2. The rabbit's father and mother are <u>in a hurry</u> at home.	home	rabbit,father,mother
1. He <u>walked into</u> the big forest with his mother's words.	forest	He
2. He <u>walked into</u> the big forest with his mother's words.	forest	He,his mother
1. He said that he once <u>donated money</u> to mountain children.	/	he,children
2. He said that he once <u>donated money</u> to mountain children.	mountain	he,children
1. The rabbit walked and suddenly <u>heard</u> a deafening help.	/	rabbit
2. The rabbit walked and suddenly heard a <u>deafening</u> help.	/	rabbit

Table 5: Case study of sentence-level event extraction results.(1:Annotation, 2:Detection)

Event	Method	Precision	Recall	F1
scene	sentence	0.694	0.581	0.632
scene	paragraph	**0.878***	**0.837†**	**0.857†**
chara	sentence	0.705	0.763	0.733
chara	paragraph	**0.846†**	**0.987***	**0.911†**

Table 6: Paragraph-level event integration results. (chara is short for character.) † and ⋆ denote our improvements are significant in t-test with $p \leq 0.01$ and $p \leq 0.10$ respectively.

the best method BERT-BiLSTM-CRF can achieve 0.499 $F1$ score only, which is too low to use.

We conduct Tukey HSD significant test over all method pairs too. The results indicate that the neural methods are significantly better than the baseline based on parser in scene and character extraction. BERT-BiLSTM-CRF also significantly beats the parser baseline in action extraction. Among three neural methods, BERT brings significant improvements over the BiLSTM-CRF method in scene and character extraction. Only in scene extraction, BiLSTM-CRF is the best and the differences are significant.

Table 5 illustrates sample event extraction results. We can find that most of the story events are correctly extracted while there still exist a lot of biases. For example, some detected events do not actually happen in real but merely appear in the imagination or dialogues. (e.g. In verb phrase "heard a deafening help", the action is "heard", not "deafening".) Some serves as an adjective that modifies an character. (e.g. In noun phrase "mountain children", "mountain" does not indicate the current scene, but the children's hometown.)

7.3 Paragraph-Level Evaluation

In this evaluation, we focus on event switch detection. Take paragraph-level scene detection as an example. The story in Table 1 includes three scenes: field, river and garden, starting from the 1st, the 8th and the 14th sentence respectively. Paragraph-level event extraction is required to find the correct switch time and the event content. We compare simple extension of sentence-level results and paragraph-level event integration results (denoted as base and ours in Table 6).

We randomly selected 20 stories from the collected corpus and manually annotated the scene and character spans. Scene keywords are mapped into 30 categories of painting scenes. Sentence-level scene results are extended in a way where the first sentence including the keyword is regarded as the start of the scene span and the previous sentence of next scene is denoted as the span end. For paragraph level scene integration, scene spans are extended both in forward and backward orientation. Moreover, the dialogue contexts are ignored because the scene in a dialogue might not be the current one. It might be imagination or merely action of the past or the future. Other event information is also utilized as supplement, as the characters keywords might indicate specific scenes.

We calculate precision, recall and $F1$ value for event detection. A correct hit should detect both the event switch time and the right content. The results are listed in Table 6. As we can see, about 0.878% of scene switches are correctly detected. After story scene switch information extracted, it is used in paragraph-level character detection. Character switch is defined as the appearance and disappearance of a single character. The first time

(a) First scene: field

(b) Second scene: river

(c) Third scene: garden

(d) Painting elements

Figure 2: Visualized scenes and painting elements of story "Big ears of the little elephant"

when a character keyword is detected is denoted as the switch time of appearance. Scene switch is used as an indication of disappearance of the characters in that scene. Paragraph-level character detection reaches relatively higher accuracy than sentence-level character detection, with $F1$ score of over 0.91. T-test results indicate that our improvements are statistically significant.

7.4 Visualization Demonstration

Using the prepared 30 painting scenes and 600 characters, we are able to generate picture books for the collected 3680 stories, with 1.42 scenes and 2.71 characters in each story on average.

Figure 2 shows some story pictures and painting elements. More examples of video visualization results could be found on our website[2].

8 Conclusion and Future Work

In this paper, we propose a framework to address the problem of automatic story understanding and visualization. Story event extraction is extended from sentence level to paragraph level for continuous visualization. We collect children's story from the Internet and apply our framework to generate simple story picture books with audio.

Currently, our story events include scenes, characters and actions. There is room for event extraction improvement. Furthermore, it is difficult to enumerate and compose an intimate action between characters, such as "hug", or a complex action, such as "kneeling on the ground". We plan to learn the various actions from examples, such as movies, in the future.

Acknowledgments

We would like to thank Qingcai Cui from Microsoft and Yahui Chen from Beijing Film Academy for providing helpful ideas, data and resources.

References

Eugene Charniak. 1972. *Toward a model of children's story comprehension.* Ph.D. thesis, Massachusetts Institute of Technology.

Hong-Woo Chun, Young-Sook Hwang, and Hae-Chang Rim. 2004. Unsupervised event extraction from biomedical literature using co-occurrence information and basic patterns. In *International Conference on Natural Language Processing*, pages 777–786. Springer.

K Bretonnel Cohen, Karin Verspoor, Helen L Johnson, Chris Roeder, Philip V Ogren, William A Baumgartner Jr, Elizabeth White, Hannah Tipney, and

---

[2]https://github.com/StoryVisualization/Demos

Lawrence Hunter. 2009. High-precision biological event extraction with a concept recognizer. In *Proceedings of the Workshop on Current Trends in Biomedical Natural Language Processing: Shared Task*, pages 50–58. Association for Computational Linguistics.

Jacob Devlin, Ming-Wei Chang, Kenton Lee, and Kristina Toutanova. 2018. Bert: Pre-training of deep bidirectional transformers for language understanding. *arXiv preprint arXiv:1810.04805*.

Jon Doyle. 1979. A truth maintenance system. *Artificial intelligence*, 12(3):231–272.

Alex Graves and Jürgen Schmidhuber. 2005. Framewise phoneme classification with bidirectional lstm and other neural network architectures. *Neural Networks*, 18(5-6):602–610.

Frederik Hogenboom, Flavius Frasincar, Uzay Kaymak, and Franciska De Jong. 2011. An overview of event extraction from text. In *Workshop on Detection, Representation, and Exploitation of Events in the Semantic Web (DeRiVE 2011) at Tenth International Semantic Web Conference (ISWC 2011)*, volume 779, pages 48–57. Citeseer.

Ting-Hao Kenneth Huang, Francis Ferraro, Nasrin Mostafazadeh, Ishan Misra, Aishwarya Agrawal, Jacob Devlin, Ross Girshick, Xiaodong He, Pushmeet Kohli, Dhruv Batra, et al. 2016. Visual storytelling. In *Proceedings of the 2016 Conference of the North American Chapter of the Association for Computational Linguistics: Human Language Technologies*, pages 1233–1239.

Felix Jungermann and Katharina Morik. 2008. Enhanced services for targeted information retrieval by event extraction and data mining. In *International Conference on Application of Natural Language to Information Systems*, pages 335–336. Springer.

Diederik P Kingma and Jimmy Ba. 2014. Adam: A method for stochastic optimization. *arXiv preprint arXiv:1412.6980*.

Dan Klein and Christopher D Manning. 2003. Accurate unlexicalized parsing. In *Proceedings of the 41st Annual Meeting on Association for Computational Linguistics-Volume 1*, pages 423–430. Association for Computational Linguistics.

Robert Kosara and Jock Mackinlay. 2013. Storytelling: The next step for visualization. *Computer*, 46(5):44–50.

Chang-Shing Lee, Yea-Juan Chen, and Zhi-Wei Jian. 2003. Ontology-based fuzzy event extraction agent for chinese e-news summarization. *Expert Systems with Applications*, 25(3):431–447.

Zhen Lei, Ying Zhang, Yu-chi Liu, et al. 2005. A system for detecting and tracking internet news event. In *Pacific-Rim Conference on Multimedia*, pages 754–764. Springer.

Fang Li, Huanye Sheng, and Dongmo Zhang. 2002. Event pattern discovery from the stock market bulletin. In *International Conference on Discovery Science*, pages 310–315. Springer.

Mingrong Liu, Yicen Liu, Liang Xiang, Xing Chen, and Qing Yang. 2008. Extracting key entities and significant events from online daily news. In *International Conference on Intelligent Data Engineering and Automated Learning*, pages 201–209. Springer.

Kwan-Liu Ma, Isaac Liao, Jennifer Frazier, Helwig Hauser, and Helen-Nicole Kostis. 2012. Scientific storytelling using visualization. *IEEE Computer Graphics and Applications*, 32(1):12–19.

Christopher D. Manning, Mihai Surdeanu, John Bauer, Jenny Finkel, Steven J. Bethard, and David McClosky. 2014. The Stanford CoreNLP natural language processing toolkit. In *Association for Computational Linguistics (ACL) System Demonstrations*, pages 55–60.

David McClosky, Mihai Surdeanu, and Christopher D Manning. 2011. Event extraction as dependency parsing. In *Proceedings of the 49th Annual Meeting of the Association for Computational Linguistics: Human Language Technologies-Volume 1*, pages 1626–1635. Association for Computational Linguistics.

Yoko Nishihara, Keita Sato, and Wataru Sunayama. 2009. Event extraction and visualization for obtaining personal experiences from blogs. In *Symposium on Human Interface*, pages 315–324. Springer.

Masayuki Okamoto and Masaaki Kikuchi. 2009. Discovering volatile events in your neighborhood: Local-area topic extraction from blog entries. In *Asia Information Retrieval Symposium*, pages 181–192. Springer.

Jakub Piskorski, Hristo Tanev, and Pinar Oezden Wennerberg. 2007. Extracting violent events from online news for ontology population. In *International Conference on Business Information Systems*, pages 287–300. Springer.

Lev Ratinov and Dan Roth. 2009. Design challenges and misconceptions in named entity recognition. In *Proceedings of the thirteenth conference on computational natural language learning*, pages 147–155. Association for Computational Linguistics.

Gerard Salton and Michael J McGill. 1986. Introduction to modern information retrieval.

Edward Segel and Jeffrey Heer. 2010. Narrative visualization: Telling stories with data. *IEEE transactions on visualization and computer graphics*, 16(6):1139–1148.

Hideo Shimazu, Yosuke Takashima, and Masahiro Tomono. 1988. Understanding of stories for animation. In *Proceedings of the 12th conference on Computational linguistics-Volume 2*, pages 620–625. Association for Computational Linguistics.

Emma Strubell, Patrick Verga, David Belanger, and Andrew McCallum. 2017. Fast and accurate entity recognition with iterated dilated convolutions. *arXiv preprint arXiv:1702.02098*.

J Sun. 2012. jiebachinese word segmentation tool.

Hristo Tanev, Jakub Piskorski, and Martin Atkinson. 2008. Real-time news event extraction for global crisis monitoring. In *International Conference on Application of Natural Language to Information Systems*, pages 207–218. Springer.

Alex Tozzo, Dejan Jovanovic, and Mohamed Amer. 2018. Neural event extraction from movies description. In *Proceedings of the First Workshop on Storytelling*, pages 60–66.

Josep Valls-Vargas, Jichen Zhu, and Santiago Ontañón. 2017. Towards automatically extracting story graphs from natural language stories. In *Workshops at the Thirty-First AAAI Conference on Artificial Intelligence*.

Anthony J Viera, Joanne M Garrett, et al. 2005. Understanding interobserver agreement: the kappa statistic. *Fam med*, 37(5):360–363.

Akane Yakushiji, Yuka Tateisi, Yusuke Miyao, and Jun-ichi Tsujii. 2000. Event extraction from biomedical papers using a full parser. In *Biocomputing 2001*, pages 408–419. World Scientific.

Xin Zeng and Tan Mling. 2009. A review of scene visualization based on language descriptions. In *2009 Sixth International Conference on Computer Graphics, Imaging and Visualization*, pages 429–433. IEEE.

Deyu Zhou, Liangyu Chen, and Yulan He. 2014. A simple bayesian modelling approach to event extraction from twitter. In *Proceedings of the 52nd Annual Meeting of the Association for Computational Linguistics (Volume 2: Short Papers)*, volume 2, pages 700–705.

C Lawrence Zitnick, Devi Parikh, and Lucy Vanderwende. 2013. Learning the visual interpretation of sentences. In *Proceedings of the IEEE International Conference on Computer Vision*, pages 1681–1688.

"My Way of Telling a Story": Persona based Grounded Story Generation

Khyathi Raghavi Chandu[*], **Shrimai Prabhumoye**[*],
Ruslan Salakhutdinov, Alan W Black
Language Technologies Institute, Carnegie Mellon University
Pittsburgh, PA, USA
{kchandu, sprabhum, rsalakhu, awb}@cs.cmu.edu

Abstract

Visual storytelling is the task of generating stories based on a sequence of images. Inspired by the recent works in neural generation focusing on controlling the *form* of text, this paper explores the idea of generating these stories in different personas. However, one of the main challenges of performing this task is the lack of a dataset of visual stories in different personas. Having said that, there are independent datasets for both visual storytelling and annotated sentences for various persona. In this paper we describe an approach to overcome this by getting labelled persona data from a different task and leveraging those annotations to perform persona based story generation. We inspect various ways of incorporating personality in both the encoder and the decoder representations to steer the generation in the target direction. To this end, we propose five models which are incremental extensions to the baseline model to perform the task at hand. In our experiments we use five different personas to guide the generation process. We find that the models based on our hypotheses perform better at capturing words while generating stories in the target persona.

1 Introduction

Storytelling through pictures has been dated back to prehistoric times – around 30,000 years ago, paintings of herds of animals like bisons, rhinos and gazelles were made in a cave in Southern France. However, these were not merely paintings, they were stories about the heroic adventures of humans. Since then visual storytelling has evolved from paintings to photography to motion pictures to video games. With respect to its timeline, neural generative storytelling has gained traction only recently. Recent research has focused on challenges in generating longer documents (Wiseman et al., 2017; Lau and Baldwin, 2016) as well as on predicting the next events in the story (Martin et al., 2018). Contemporary research has focused on using deep generative models to capture high-level plots and structures in stories (Fan et al., 2018). Recent years have also seen some work hinging on the event structures and scripts (Mostafazadeh et al., 2016; Rishes et al., 2013; Peng et al., 2018). Generating an appropriate ending of a story was also studied by Guan et al. (2018) and Sharma et al. (2018). Research on generating stories from a sequence of images is anew (Peng et al., 2018; Lukin et al., 2018; Kim et al., 2018; Hsu et al., 2018; Gonzalez-Rico and Fuentes-Pineda, 2018).

Cavazza et al. (2009) have stressed the importance of expressing emotions in the believability of the automated storytelling system. Adapting a personality trait hence becomes crucial to capture and maintain interest of the audience. Associating the narrative to a personality instigates a sense of empathy and relatedness. Although there has been research in generating persona based dialog responses and generating stylistic sentences (Shuster et al., 2018; Fu et al., 2018; Prabhumoye et al., 2018; Shen et al., 2017), generating persona based stories with different personality types narrating them has been unexplored. In this paper, we focus on generating a story from a sequence of images as if the agent belongs to a particular personality type. In specific, we choose to perform experimentations on visual story telling (Huang et al., 2016).

This paper introduces a novel approach to generating visual stories in five different personality types. A key challenge to this end is the lack

---

Both authors contributed equally to this work.

Proceedings of the Second Storytelling Workshop, pages 11–21
Florence, Italy, August 1, 2019. ©2019 Association for Computational Linguistics

of large scale persona annotated stories. We address this by transferring knowledge from annotated data in dialog domain to the storytelling domain. We base our visual story generator model on Kim et al. (2018) and propose multiple techniques to induce the personalities in the latent representations of both the encoder and the decoder. The goal of our work is to learn the mapping between the latent representations of the images and the tokens of the story such that we encourage our generative model to generate tokens of a particular personality. We evaluate our generative models using the automatic metric of ROUGE (Lin, 2004) which takes into account the sentence level similarity in structure and thus roughly evaluates the matching of content. We acknowledge that there is a drop in this metric since our model is not trying to optimize generation alone but also adapt personality from a different dataset.

We also evaluate the success of generating the story in the target personality type using automatic and qualitative analysis. The automatic metrics comprise of the classification accuracies rooted from the annotated data. We observe that one of the proposed models (LEPC, described in Section 3 performs slightly better at classification accuracies for most of the personas while retaining similar ROUGE scores.

The main contribution of this paper is showing simple yet effective approaches to narrative visual stories in different personality types. The paper also displays an effective way of using annotated data in the dialog domain to guide the generative models to a specified target personality.

2 Related Work

Visual Story Telling: Last decade witnessed enormous interest in research at the intersection of multiple modalities, especially vision and language. Mature efforts in image captioning (Hossain et al., 2019) paved way into more advanced tasks like visual question answering (Wu et al., 2017) and visual dialog (Das et al., 2017) , (Mostafazadeh et al., 2017). As an obvious next step from single shot image captioning lies the task of describing a sequence of images which are related to one another to form a story like narrative. This task was introduced as visual story telling by Huang et al. (2016), differentiating de-

scriptions of images in isolation (image captions) and stories in sequences. The baseline model that we are leveraging to generate personality conditioned story generation is based on the model proposed by Kim et al. (2018) for the visual story telling challenge. Another simple yet effective technique is late fusion model by Smilevski et al. (2018). In addition to static images, Gella et al. (2018) have also collected a dataset of describing stories from videos uploaded on social media. Chandu et al. (2019) recently introduced a dataset for generating textual cooking recipes from a sequence of images and proposed two models to incorporate structure in procedural text generation from images.

Style Transfer: One line of research that is closely related to our task is style transfer in text. Recently generative models have gained popularity in attempting to solve style transfer in text with non-parallel data (Hu et al., 2017; Shen et al., 2017; Li et al., 2018). Some of this work has also focused on transferring author attributes (Prabhumoye et al., 2018), transferring multiple attributes (Lample et al., 2019; Logeswaran et al., 2018) and collecting parallel dataset for formality (Rao and Tetreault, 2018). Although our work can be viewed as another facet of style transfer, we have strong grounding of the stories in the sequence of images.

Persona Based Dialog: Persona based generation of responses has been studied by NLP community in dialog domain. (Li et al., 2016) encoded personas of individuals in contextualized embeddings that capture the background information and style to maintain consistency in the responses given. The embeddings for the speaker information are learnt jointly with the word embeddings. Following this work, (Zhou et al., 2018) proposed Emotional Chatting Machine that generates responses in an emotional tone in addition to conditioning the content. The key difference between former and latter work is that the latter captures dynamic change in emotion as the conversation proceeds, while the user persona remains the same in the former case. (Zhang et al., 2018) release a huge dataset of conversations conditioned on the persona of the two people interacting. This work shows that conditioning on the profile information improves the dialogues which is measured by next utterance prediction. In these works, the gold value of the target response was known. For our work, we do not have gold values of stories in different personas. Hence we leverage annotated data from a different task and transfer that knowledge to steer our generation process.

Multimodal domain: With the interplay between visual and textual modalities, an obvious downstream application for persona based text generation is image captioning. Chandrasekaran et al. (2018) worked on generating witty captions for images by both retrieving and generating with an encoder-decoder architecture. This work used external resources to gather a list of words that are related to puns from web which the decoder attempts to generate conditioned on phonological similarity. Wang and Wen (2015) studied the statistical correlation of words associated with specific memes. These ideas have also recently penetrated into visual dialog setting. Shuster et al. (2018) have collected a grounded conversational dataset with 202k dialogs where humans are asked to portray a personality in the collection process. They have also set up various baselines with different techniques to fuse the modalities including multimodal sum combiner and multimodal attention combiner. We use this dataset to learn personas which are adapted to our storytelling model.

3   Models

We have a dataset of visual stories $S = \{S_1, \ldots, S_n\}$. Each story S_i is a set of sequence of five images and the corresponding text of the story $S_i = \{(I_i^{(1)}, x_i^{(1)}), \ldots, (I_i^{(5)}, x_i^{(5)})\}$. Our task is to generate the story based on not only the sequence of the images but also closely following the narrative style of a personality type. We have five personality types (described in Section 4) $P = \{p_1, \ldots, p_5\}$ and each story is assigned one of these five personalities as their target persona. Here, each p_i represents the one-hot encoding of the target personality for story i.e $p_1 = [1, 0, 0, 0, 0]$ and so on till $p_5 = [0, 0, 0, 0, 1]$. Hence, we create a dataset such that for each story, we also have a specified target personality type $S_i = \{(I_i^{(1)}, x_i^{(1)}), \ldots, (I_i^{(5)}, x_i^{(5)}); p_i\}$. The inputs to our models are the sequence of images and

the target personality type. We build generative models such that they are able to generate stories in the specified target personality type from the images. In this section, we first briefly describe classifiers that are trained discriminatively to identify each of the personalities and then move on to the story generation models that make use of these classifiers.

Here is an overview of the differences in the six models that we describe next.

1. The baseline model (Glocal) is a sequence to sequence model with global and local contexts for generating story sentence corresponding to each image.

2. The Multitask Personality Prediction (MPP) model is equipped with predicting the personality in addition to generating the sentences of the story. This model also incorporates binary encoding of personality.

3. The Latent Encoding of Personality in Context (LEPC) model incorporates an embedding of the personality as opposed to binary encoding.

4. The Latent Encoding of Personality in Decoder (LEPD) model augments personality embedding at each step in the decoder, where each step generates a token.

5. Stripped Encoding of Personality in Context (SEPC) is similar to LEPC but encodes personality embedding after stripping the mean of the story representation.

6. Stripped Encoding of Personality in Decoder (SEPD) is similar to LEPD but encodes personality embedding after stripping the mean of the story representation. This is similar to the intuition behind SEPC.

3.1   Classification

We use convolutional neural network (CNN) architecture to train our classifiers. We train five separate binary classifiers for each of the personality types. The classifiers are trained to predict whether a sentence belongs to a particular personality or not. We train the classifiers in a supervised manner. We need labeled data to train each of the classifiers. Each sample of text x in the respective datasets of each of the five personality types has a label in the set $\{0,1\}$. Let $\theta_C^{p_j}$ denote the parameters of the classifier for personality p_j where $j \in \{1,\ldots,5\}$. Each classifier is trained with the following objective:

$$\mathcal{L}(\theta_C^{p_j}) = \mathbb{E}_X[\log q_C(p_j|x)] \qquad (1)$$

We use cross entropy loss to calculate $\mathcal{L}_C^{p_j}$ for each of the five classifiers. The classifiers accept continuous representations of tokens as input.

3.2 Story Generation

We present five extensions to incorporate personality based features in the generation of stories.

(1) Baseline model (Glocal): We first describe the baseline model that is used for visual story telling. This is based on the model (Kim et al., 2018) that attained better scores on human evaluation metrics. It follows an encoder-decoder framework translating a sequence of images into a story. From here on, we refer to this model as *glocal* through the rest of the paper owing to the global and local features in the generation of story sequence at each step (described in this section).

The image features for each of the steps are extracted with a ResNet-152 (He et al., 2016) post resizing to 224 X 224. The features are taken from the penultimate layer of this pretrained model and the gradients are not propagated through this layer during optimization. These features are passed through a fully connected layer to obtain the final image features. In order to obtain an overall context of the story, the sequence of the image features are passed through a Bi-LSTM. This represents the global context of the story. For each step in the generation of the story, the local context corresponding to the specificity of that particular image is obtained by augmenting the image features (local context) to the context features from the Bi-LSTM (global context). These *glocal features* are used to decode the story sentence at each step. This concludes the encoder part of the story. The decoder of each step in the story also uses an LSTM which takes the same glocal feature for that particular step at each time step. Hence there are 5 glocal features feeding into each time step in the decoder.

For simplicity in understanding, we use the following notations throughout model descriptions to represent mathematical formulation of the generation models. Subscript k indicates the kth step or sentence in a story. Subscript i indicates the ith story example. The story encoder is represented as *Encoder* which comprises of the features extracted from the penultimate layer of ResNet-152 concatenated with the global context features from the Bi-LSTM. The entirety of this representation in encoder and the glocal features obtained is represented using z_k for the k_{th} step or sentence in the story.

$$z_k = Encoder(I_k) \qquad (2)$$

Now, the generation of a sentence in the story is represented as follows:

$$\hat{x}_k \sim \prod_t Pr(\hat{x}_k^t|\hat{x}_k^{<t}, z_k) \qquad (3)$$

The generated sentence $\hat{x}_k$ is obtained from each of the output words $\hat{x}_k^t$ which is generated by conditioning on all of the prior words $\hat{x}_k^{<t}$ and the glocal feature obtained as z_k.

Personality based Generation: In the rest of the section, we are going to describe the incremental extensions to the baseline to adapt the model to perform persona based story generation.

(2) Multitask Personality Prediction (MPP): The intuition behind the hypothesis here is to provide the personality information to the model and also enable it to predict the personality along with the generation of the story. The obvious extension to provide personality information is to incorporate the one-hot encoding $p_i \in P$ of the five personas in the context before the decoder. The visual story telling data is split into five predetermined personalities as described in Section 4. For each story, the corresponding personality is encoded in a one hot representation and is augmented to the glocal context features. These features are then given to the decoder to produce each step in the story. The model is enabled to perform two tasks: the primary task is to generate the story and the secondary task is to predict the personality of the story. The classifiers described in Section 3.1 are used to perform personality prediction. Formally, the generation process is represented by:

$$\hat{x}_k \sim \prod_t Pr(\hat{x}_k^t | \hat{x}_k^{<t}, z_k, p_i) \qquad (4)$$

Here, we condition the generation of each word on the glocal context features z_k, binary encoding of the personality p_i and the words generated till that point.

The cross entropy loss for generation is $\mathcal{L}_g$ and the loss for the prediction of each of the personalities is $L_C^{p_j}$ given by Eq 1. The overall loss optimized for this model is:

$$\mathcal{L}_{total} = \alpha \cdot \mathcal{L}_g + \frac{(1-\alpha)}{5} \cdot \sum_{j=1}^{5} \mathcal{L}_C^{p_j}$$

The overall model is optimized on this total loss. We use cross entropy loss for each of the individual losses. We give a higher weight α to the story generation and equally distribute the remaining $(1-\alpha)$ among each of the 5 personalities.

(3) Latent Encoding of Personality in Context (LEPC): This model is an incremental improvement over MPP model. The key difference is the incorporation of personality as an embedding that captures more centralized traits in the words belonging to that particular personality. For each of the five personality types, we have a latent representation of the personality ($\mathcal{P}$), as opposed to the binary encoding in MPP model. Similar to the earlier setting, this average personality feature vector is concatenated with the glocal context vector The generation step is formally represented as:

$$\hat{x}_k \sim \prod_t Pr(\hat{x}_k^t | \hat{x}_k^{<t}, [z_k; \mathcal{P}], p_i) \qquad (5)$$

This means that z_k is concatenated with $\mathcal{P}$ to give personality informed representation; and the generation of each word is conditioned on these concatenated features z_k, binary encoding of the personality p_i and the words generated so far.

(4) Latent Encoding of Personality in Decoder (LEPD): Instead of augmenting the personality traits to the context as done in LEPC model, they could be explicitly used in each step of decoding. The latent representation of the personality ($\mathcal{P}$) is concatenated with the word embedding for each

time step in the decoder.

$$\hat{x}_k \sim \prod_t Pr(\hat{x}_k^t | [\hat{x}_k^{<t}; \mathcal{P}], z_k, p_i) \qquad (6)$$

The generation of each of the words is conditioned on the words generated so far that are already concatenated with the average vector for the corresponding personality, and the glocal features along with the binary encoding of the personality.

(5) Stripped Encoding of Personality in Context (SEPC): In order to orient the generation more towards the personality, we need to go beyond simple augmentation of personality. Deriving motivation from neural storytelling[1], we use a similar approach to subtract central characteristics of words in a story and add the characteristics of the personality. Along the same lines of calculating an average representation for each of the personalities, we also obtain an average representation of the story $\mathcal{S}$. This average representation $\mathcal{S}$ intuitively captures the style of the story. Essentially, the story style is being stripped off the context and personality style is incorporated. The modified glocal feature that is given to the decoder is obtained as $m = z_k - \mathcal{S} + \mathcal{P}$. The generation process is now conditioned on m instead of z_k. Hence, the generation of each word in decoding is conditioned on the words generated so far ($\hat{x}_k^{<t}$), the binary encoding of the personality (p_i) and the modified representation of the context features (m).

$$\hat{x}_k \sim \prod_t Pr(\hat{x}_k^t | \hat{x}_k^{<t}, m, p_i) \qquad (7)$$

Here, note that the context features obtained thus far are from the visual data and performing this operation is attempting to associate the visual data with the central textual representations of the personalities and the stories.

(6) Stripped Encoding of Personality in Decoder (SEPD): This model is similar to SEPC with the modification of performing the stripping at each word embedding in the decoder as opposed to the context level stripping. The time steps to strip features is at the sentence level in SEPC and is at word level in SEPD model. The LSTM based

---

[1] https://github.com/ryankiros/neural-storyteller

decoder decodes one word at a time. At each of these time steps, the word embedding feature $\mathcal{E}$ is modified as $e_k = \mathcal{E} - \mathcal{S} + \mathcal{P}$. This modification is performed in each step of the decoding process. These modified features are used to generate each sentence in the full story. The model is trained to generate a sentence in the story as described below:

$$\hat{x}_k \sim \prod_t Pr(\hat{x}_k^t | e_k^{<t}, z_k, p_i) \qquad (8)$$

The generation of each word is conditioned on the modified word embeddings using the aforementioned transformation ($e_k^{<t}$), the binary encodings of the personalities (p_i) and the glocal context features.

4   Datasets

Coalescing the segments of personality and sequential generation together, our task is to generate a grounded sequential story from the view of a personality. To bring this to action, we describe the two sources of data we use to generate personality based stories in this section. The first source of data is focussed on generic story generation from a sequence of images and the second source of data includes annotations for personality types for sentences. We tailor a composition of these two sources to obtain a dataset for personality based visual storytelling. Here, we note that the techniques described above can be applied for unimodal story generation as well.

Visual Story Telling: Visual Storytelling is the task of generating stories from a sequence of images. A dataset for this grounded sequential generation problem was collected by Huang et al. (2016) and an effort for a shared task [2] was led in 2018. The dataset includes 40,155 training sequences of stories. It comprises of a sequence of images, descriptions of images in isolation and stories of images in sequences. We randomly divide the dataset into 5 segments (comprising of 8031 stories each) and each segment is associated with a personality.

Personality Dialog: Shuster et al. (2018) have provided a dataset of 401k dialog utterances, each

of which belong to one of 215 different personalities. The dataset was collected through image grounded human-human conversations. Humans were asked to play the role of a given personality. This makes this dataset very pertinent for our task as it was collected through engaging image chat between two humans enacting their personalities.

For our task, we wanted to choose a set of five distinct personality types. Let the set of utterances that belong to each personality type be $U_p = \{u_p^1, \ldots, u_p^n\}$ where $p \in \{1, \ldots, 215\}$. We first calculate the pooled BERT representation (Devlin et al., 2018) of each of the utterances. To get the representation of the personality $\mathcal{P}$, we simply average the BERT representations of all the utterances that belong to that personality. The representation of each personality is given by:

$$\mathcal{P}_p = \frac{\Sigma_{k=1}^n BERT(u_p^k)}{n} \qquad (9)$$

This representation is calculated only on the train set of (Shuster et al., 2018).

Since our goal is to pick five most distinct personality types, we have the daunting task of filtering the 215 personality types to 5. To make our task easier we want to group similar personalities together. Hence, we use K-Means Clustering to cluster the representations of the personalities into 40 clusters [3]. We get well formed and meaningful clusters which look like [Impersonal, Aloof (Detached, Distant), Apathetic (Uncaring, Disinterested), Blunt, Cold, Stiff]; [Practical, Rational, Realistic, Businesslike]; [Empathetic, Sympathetic, Emotional]; [Calm, Gentle, Peaceful, Relaxed, Mellow (Soothing, Sweet)] etc. We then build a classifier using the technique described in Section 3.1 to classify the utterances to belong to one of the 40 clusters. We pick the top five clusters that give the highest accuracy for the 40-way classification.

The five personality clusters selected are:

- Cluster 1 **(C1)**: Arrogant, Conceited, Egocentric, Lazy, Money-minded, Narcissistic, Pompous and Resentful

- Cluster 2 **(C2)**: Skeptical and Paranoid

---

[3]We do not perform exhaustive search on the number of clusters. We tried k values of 5, 20 and 40 and selected 40 as the ideal value based on manual inspection of the clusters.

- Cluster 3 (**C3**): Energetic, Enthusiastic, Exciting, Happy, Vivacious, Excitable

- Cluster 4 (**C4**): Bland and Uncreative

- Cluster 5 (**C5**): Patriotic

We build five separate classifiers, one for each personality cluster. Note that these clusters are also associated with personalities and hence are later referred as P followed by the cluster id in the following sections. To build the five binary classifiers, we create label balanced datasets for each cluster i.e we randomly select as many negative samples from the remaining 4 clusters as there are positive samples in that cluster. We use the train, dev and test split as is from (Shuster et al., 2018). The dataset statistics for each of the five clusters is provided in Table 1.

Cluster Type	Train	Dev	Test
Cluster 1	26538	1132	2294
Cluster 2	6614	266	608
Cluster 3	19784	898	1646
Cluster 4	6646	266	576
Cluster 5	3262	138	314

Table 1: Statistics of data belonging to each of the persona clusters

Note that all the datasets have a balanced distribution of labels 0 and 1. For our experiments it does not matter that distribution of the number of samples is different because we build separate classifiers for each of the cluster and their output is treated as independent from one another.

As seen in Table 2, all the classifiers attain good accuracies and F-scores on the test set.

	C1	C2	C3	C4	C5
Acc.	79.12	81.09	83.17	77.95	84.08
F1	0.79	0.81	0.83	0.78	0.84

Table 2: Performance of classifiers for each of the persona clusters

We finally calculate the representation $\mathcal{P}$ for each of the five clusters and the representation $\mathcal{S}$ of stories using equation 9. Note that $\mathcal{S}$ is calculated over the visual story tellind dataset. These representations are used by our generative models **LEPC**, **LEPD**, **SEPC**, and **SEPD**.

5 Experiments and Results

This section presents the experimental setup for the models described in Section 3. Each of the models are incremental extensions over the baseline glocal model. The hyperparameters used for this are as follows.

Hyperparameters: The hidden size of the Bi-LSTM encoder of the story to capture context is 1024. The dimensionality of the glocal context vector z_k is 2048. A dropout layer of 50% is applied post the fully connected layer to obtain the image features and after the global features obtained from Bi-LSTM which is 2 layered. The word embedding dimension used is 256. The learning rate is 1e-3 with a weight decay of 1e-5. Adam optimizer is used with batch normalization and a momentum of 0.01. Weighting the loss functions differently is done to penalize the model more if the decoding is at fault as compared to not predicting the personality of the story. α is set to 0.5 and each of the individual personality losses are weighted by a factor of 0.1.

The rest of the 5 models use the same hyperparameter setting with an exception to word embedding dimension. The average personality ($\mathcal{P}$) and the average story ($\mathcal{S}$) representations are obtained from pre-trained BERT model.Hence this is a 768 dimensional vector. In order to perform the stripping of the story feature and adding the personality features to the word embeddings in the decoder, the word embedding dimension is matched to 768 in the SEPD model.

Model	C1	C2	C3	C4	C5
Glocal	69.90	73.29	51.55	34.91	65.86
MPP	69.35	72.44	47.54	33.83	58.49
LEPC	70.10	73.24	52.13	34.59	66.42
LEPD	76.44	79.20	33.71	34.02	67.13
SEPC	76.76	77.00	32.84	44.53	60.08
SEPD	78.14	79.44	31.33	34.99	73.88

Table 3: Performance (in terms of accuracy) of generated stories to capture persona

5.1 Quantitative Results

We perform two sets of experiments: (1) evaluating the performance of the models on capturing the personalities in the story and (2) performance

Original	grandma loves when all the kids come over to visit .	she will pick them them up and put them on her lap even though it <unk> .	the kids love each other as well giving lots of hugs and love .	grandma can not forget her little girl and gives her some love as well .	grandpa says it 's time for cake .
Glocal	the family is having a great time .	they are playing with each other .	he is happy to see his grandson .	she is being silly	the birthday girl is eating a cake .
MPP	[male] and his friends are having a great time .	they are all smiles for the camera .	everyone is enjoying their new family .	[female] is so excited to be there .	she is very happy about her birthday .
LEPC	the family was having a great time .	they were so happy to be together .	they were having a good time with grandson .	she was very excited to play with a kid .	he was surprised by all of his friends .
LEPD	the family was ready to see a lot of a party .	they had a great time .	they were having a lot of fun .	we had a great day .	he was happy to eat cake .
SEPC	the parade was very beautiful .	there were a lot of people there .	we were so happy to be a great time .	i had a great time .	this was a picture of a little girl .
SEPD	the family is a great time .	it was a lot of a big .	there were a lot .	i had a picture .	they were a very .

Figure 1: Comparison of generated *stories* from all the described models.

Model	ROUGE_L
Glocal	0.1805
MPP	0.1713
LEPC	0.1814
LEPD	0.1731
SEPC	0.1665
SEPD	0.1689

Table 4: ROUGE_L scores for the generated stories by each of our models

of story generation. The former evaluation is performed using the pre-trained classifiers (3.1) on the personality dataset. We calculate the classification accuracy of the generated stories of the test set for the desired target personality. However, we need to note that the classification error of the models trained is reflected in this result as well. This evaluation is done at a sentence level i.e accuracy is calculated over each sentence of the story (each sentence of the story has the same target personality as that of the entire story). The performance of the generation is evaluated using the ROUGE score [4]. Although this captures the generic aspect of generation, the metric explicitly does not evaluate whether the story is generated on a conditioned personality. In future, we would also like to look at automatic evaluation of the generated stories with respect to incorporation of personalities.

Table 3 shows the results of classification accuracy for each of the five personalities. Table 4 shows the results of ROUGE_L evaluation. We acknowledge that there would be a deviation to this automatic score since optimizing the gold standard generation of story from training data is not our end goal. Rather our models make use of two distinct datasets and learn to transfer the traits annotated in personality dialog dataset into the visual story telling dataset.

Despite this, we notice that LEPC model gives comparative results to that of the glocal model in terms of story generation. It is noticed that LEPC

[4]We use the implementation from `https://github.com/Maluuba/nlg-eval`

model also gives slight improvement on the classification accuracies for most of the clusters (each cluster representing a personality). However this is an insufficient result to generalize that incorporating personality at context level performs better than that at the word level since the inverted stance is observed in SEPC and SEPD models. We plan to investigate this further by performing ablations and examine which operation is causing these models to perform weakly. Note that the SEPC model performs the best in incorporating personality in three of the five personality types. But this model takes a hit in the automatic score. This is because our generative models are dealing with competing losses or reconstruction of classification.

5.2 Qualitative Results

We present an example of the story generated by each of the models proposed in Figure 1. This example belongs to persona in cluster **C3**. The words corresponding to this cluster are highlighted with blue color in the persona conditioned generation of the stories. The main observation is that all of the five sentences in the story contain a word relevant to *happiness* for each of the MPP, LEPC and LEPD models. SEPC and SEPD models capture these happiness features in only two and one sentences respectively. The glocal model does not cater explicitly to the personality while our proposed models attempt to capture the persona tone in generation. This is observed in the fourth generated sentence in the sequence by each of our proposed models. While the glocal model uses the word *'silly'*, our models capture the tone and generate *'excited'* and *'great'*. Similarly for the fifth sentence, MPP, LEPC and LEPD generate *'happy'*, *'surprised'* and *'happy'* respectively.

It is observed that in most generated stories, the language model has taken a rough hit in the SEPD model. This is also substantiated in Figure 1. This seems to be due to stripping away the essential word embedding features that contribute to linguistic priors or language model. This could be potentially corrected by retaining the word embedding feature as is and augmenting it with the stripped features. Having presented these results, we notice that there is a significant scope for improving the generation of the story while capturing

high level persona traits in generation.

6 Conclusions and Future Work

Automatic storytelling is a creative writing task that has long been the dream of text generation models. The voice conveying this story is the narrative style and this can be attributed to different personalities, moods, situations etc. In the case of persona based visual storytelling, this voice not only is aware of the grounded content to be conveyed in the images, but also has a model to steer the words in the narrative to characterize the persona.

A key challenge here is that there is no targeted data for this specific task. Hence we leverage annotations of persona from an external persona based dialog dataset and apply it on the visual storytelling dataset. We address this task of attribution of a personality while generating a grounded story by simple techniques of incorporating persona information in our encoder-decoder architecture. We propose five simple incremental extensions to the baseline model that captures the personality. Quantitatively, our results show that the LEPC model is improving upon the accuracy while at the same time not dropping the automatic scores. We also observe that the persona induced models are generating at least one word per sentence in the story that belong to that particular persona. While automatically evaluating this can be tricky, we adapt a classification based evaluation of whether the generated output belongs to the persona class or not. In the future, we hope to also perform human evaluations for measuring both the target personality type of the generated and story and its coherence.

There is yet a lot of scope in incorporating the persona in the word embeddings. This is an ongoing work and we plan on investigating the relatively poor ROUGE performance of the SEPC and SEPD models and rectify them by equipping them with language model information. We also plan to work towards a stable evaluation protocol for this task in the future.

References

Marc Cavazza, David Pizzi, Fred Charles, Thurid Vogt, and Elisabeth André. 2009. Emotional input for character-based interactive storytelling. In *Proceedings of The 8th International Conference on Autonomous Agents and Multiagent Systems-Volume 1*, pages 313–320. International Foundation for Autonomous Agents and Multiagent Systems.

Arjun Chandrasekaran, Devi Parikh, and Mohit Bansal. 2018. Punny captions: Witty wordplay in image descriptions. In *Proceedings of the 2018 Conference of the North American Chapter of the Association for Computational Linguistics: Human Language Technologies, Volume 2 (Short Papers)*, pages 770–775.

Khyathi Chandu, Alan W Black, and Eric Nyberg. 2019. Storyboarding of recipes: Grounded contextual generation. In *Proceedings of the 57th Annual Meeting of the Association for Computational Linguistics*, Florence, Italy. Association for Computational Linguistics.

Abhishek Das, Satwik Kottur, Khushi Gupta, Avi Singh, Deshraj Yadav, José MF Moura, Devi Parikh, and Dhruv Batra. 2017. Visual dialog. In *Proceedings of the IEEE Conference on Computer Vision and Pattern Recognition*, volume 2.

Jacob Devlin, Ming-Wei Chang, Kenton Lee, and Kristina Toutanova. 2018. Bert: Pre-training of deep bidirectional transformers for language understanding. *arXiv preprint arXiv:1810.04805*.

Angela Fan, Mike Lewis, and Yann Dauphin. 2018. Hierarchical neural story generation. In *Proceedings of the 56th Annual Meeting of the Association for Computational Linguistics (Volume 1: Long Papers)*, pages 889–898.

Zhenxin Fu, Xiaoye Tan, Nanyun Peng, Dongyan Zhao, and Rui Yan. 2018. Style transfer in text: Exploration and evaluation. In *Thirty-Second AAAI Conference on Artificial Intelligence*.

Spandana Gella, Mike Lewis, and Marcus Rohrbach. 2018. A dataset for telling the stories of social media videos. In *Proceedings of the 2018 Conference on Empirical Methods in Natural Language Processing*, pages 968–974.

Diana Gonzalez-Rico and Gibran Fuentes-Pineda. 2018. Contextualize, show and tell: a neural visual storyteller. *arXiv preprint arXiv:1806.00738*.

Jian Guan, Yansen Wang, and Minlie Huang. 2018. Story ending generation with incremental encoding and commonsense knowledge. *arXiv preprint arXiv:1808.10113*.

Kaiming He, Xiangyu Zhang, Shaoqing Ren, and Jian Sun. 2016. Deep residual learning for image recognition. In *Proceedings of the IEEE conference on computer vision and pattern recognition*, pages 770–778.

MD Hossain, Ferdous Sohel, Mohd Fairuz Shiratuddin, and Hamid Laga. 2019. A comprehensive survey of deep learning for image captioning. *ACM Computing Surveys (CSUR)*, 51(6):118.

Chao-Chun Hsu, Szu-Min Chen, Ming-Hsun Hsieh, and Lun-Wei Ku. 2018. Using inter-sentence diverse beam search to reduce redundancy in visual storytelling. *arXiv preprint arXiv:1805.11867*.

Zhiting Hu, Zichao Yang, Xiaodan Liang, Ruslan Salakhutdinov, and Eric P Xing. 2017. Toward controlled generation of text. In *Proceedings of the 34th International Conference on Machine Learning-Volume 70*, pages 1587–1596. JMLR. org.

Ting-Hao Kenneth Huang, Francis Ferraro, Nasrin Mostafazadeh, Ishan Misra, Aishwarya Agrawal, Jacob Devlin, Ross Girshick, Xiaodong He, Pushmeet Kohli, Dhruv Batra, et al. 2016. Visual storytelling. In *Proceedings of the 2016 Conference of the North American Chapter of the Association for Computational Linguistics: Human Language Technologies*, pages 1233–1239.

Taehyeong Kim, Min-Oh Heo, Seonil Son, Kyoung-Wha Park, and Byoung-Tak Zhang. 2018. Glac net: Glocal attention cascading networks for multi-image cued story generation. *arXiv preprint arXiv:1805.10973*.

Guillaume Lample, Sandeep Subramanian, Eric Smith, Ludovic Denoyer, Marc'Aurelio Ranzato, and Y-Lan Boureau. 2019. Multiple-attribute text rewriting. In *International Conference on Learning Representations*.

Jey Han Lau and Timothy Baldwin. 2016. An empirical evaluation of doc2vec with practical insights into document embedding generation. *ACL 2016*, page 78.

Jiwei Li, Michel Galley, Chris Brockett, Georgios Spithourakis, Jianfeng Gao, and Bill Dolan. 2016. A persona-based neural conversation model. In *Proceedings of the 54th Annual Meeting of the Association for Computational Linguistics (Volume 1: Long Papers)*, volume 1, pages 994–1003.

Juncen Li, Robin Jia, He He, and Percy Liang. 2018. Delete, retrieve, generate: a simple approach to sentiment and style transfer. In *Proceedings of the 2018 Conference of the North American Chapter of the Association for Computational Linguistics: Human Language Technologies, Volume 1 (Long Papers)*, pages 1865–1874.

Chin-Yew Lin. 2004. Rouge: A package for automatic evaluation of summaries. *Text Summarization Branches Out*.

Lajanugen Logeswaran, Honglak Lee, and Samy Bengio. 2018. Content preserving text generation with attribute controls. In *Advances in Neural Information Processing Systems*, pages 5103–5113.

Stephanie Lukin, Reginald Hobbs, and Clare Voss. 2018. A pipeline for creative visual storytelling. In *Proceedings of the First Workshop on Storytelling*, pages 20–32.

Lara J Martin, Prithviraj Ammanabrolu, Xinyu Wang, William Hancock, Shruti Singh, Brent Harrison, and Mark O Riedl. 2018. Event representations for automated story generation with deep neural nets. In *Thirty-Second AAAI Conference on Artificial Intelligence*.

Nasrin Mostafazadeh, Chris Brockett, Bill Dolan, Michel Galley, Jianfeng Gao, Georgios P Spithourakis, and Lucy Vanderwende. 2017. Image-grounded conversations: Multimodal context for natural question and response generation. *arXiv preprint arXiv:1701.08251*.

Nasrin Mostafazadeh, Alyson Grealish, Nathanael Chambers, James Allen, and Lucy Vanderwende. 2016. Caters: Causal and temporal relation scheme for semantic annotation of event structures. In *Proceedings of the Fourth Workshop on Events*, pages 51–61.

Nanyun Peng, Marjan Ghazvininejad, Jonathan May, and Kevin Knight. 2018. Towards controllable story generation. In *Proceedings of the First Workshop on Storytelling*, pages 43–49.

Shrimai Prabhumoye, Yulia Tsvetkov, Ruslan Salakhutdinov, and Alan W Black. 2018. Style transfer through back-translation. In *Proceedings of the 56th Annual Meeting of the Association for Computational Linguistics (Volume 1: Long Papers)*, pages 866–876.

Sudha Rao and Joel Tetreault. 2018. Dear sir or madam, may i introduce the gyafc dataset: Corpus, benchmarks and metrics for formality style transfer. In *Proceedings of the 2018 Conference of the North American Chapter of the Association for Computational Linguistics: Human Language Technologies, Volume 1 (Long Papers)*, pages 129–140.

Elena Rishes, Stephanie M Lukin, David K Elson, and Marilyn A Walker. 2013. Generating different story tellings from semantic representations of narrative. In *International Conference on Interactive Digital Storytelling*, pages 192–204. Springer.

Rishi Sharma, James Allen, Omid Bakhshandeh, and Nasrin Mostafazadeh. 2018. Tackling the story ending biases in the story cloze test. In *Proceedings of the 56th Annual Meeting of the Association for Computational Linguistics (Volume 2: Short Papers)*, volume 2, pages 752–757.

Tianxiao Shen, Tao Lei, Regina Barzilay, and Tommi Jaakkola. 2017. Style transfer from non-parallel text by cross-alignment. In *Advances in neural information processing systems*, pages 6830–6841.

Kurt Shuster, Samuel Humeau, Antoine Bordes, and Jason Weston. 2018. Engaging image chat: Modeling personality in grounded dialogue. *arXiv preprint arXiv:1811.00945*.

Marko Smilevski, Ilija Lalkovski, and Gjorgi Madzarov. 2018. Stories for images-in-sequence by using visual and narrative components. *arXiv preprint arXiv:1805.05622*.

William Yang Wang and Miaomiao Wen. 2015. I can has cheezburger? a nonparanormal approach to combining textual and visual information for predicting and generating popular meme descriptions. In *Proceedings of the 2015 Conference of the North American Chapter of the Association for Computational Linguistics: Human Language Technologies*, pages 355–365.

Sam Wiseman, Stuart Shieber, and Alexander Rush. 2017. Challenges in data-to-document generation. In *Proceedings of the 2017 Conference on Empirical Methods in Natural Language Processing*, pages 2253–2263.

Qi Wu, Damien Teney, Peng Wang, Chunhua Shen, Anthony Dick, and Anton van den Hengel. 2017. Visual question answering: A survey of methods and datasets. *Computer Vision and Image Understanding*, 163:21–40.

Saizheng Zhang, Emily Dinan, Jack Urbanek, Arthur Szlam, Douwe Kiela, and Jason Weston. 2018. Personalizing dialogue agents: I have a dog, do you have pets too? *arXiv preprint arXiv:1801.07243*.

Hao Zhou, Minlie Huang, Tianyang Zhang, Xiaoyan Zhu, and Bing Liu. 2018. Emotional chatting machine: Emotional conversation generation with internal and external memory. In *Thirty-Second AAAI Conference on Artificial Intelligence*.

Using Functional Schemas to Understand Social Media Narratives

Xinru Yan   **Aakanksha Naik**   **Yohan Jo**   **Carolyn Rosé**
Language Technologies Institute
Carnegie Mellon University
{xinruyan, anaik, yohanj, cp3a}@cs.cmu.edu

Abstract

We propose a novel take on understanding narratives in social media, focusing on learning "functional story schemas", which consist of sets of stereotypical functional structures. We develop an unsupervised pipeline to extract schemas and apply our method to Reddit posts to detect schematic structures that are characteristic of different subreddits. We validate our schemas through human interpretation and evaluate their utility via a text classification task. Our experiments show that extracted schemas capture distinctive structural patterns in different subreddits, improving classification performance of several models by 2.4% on average. We also observe that these schemas serve as lenses that reveal community norms.

1 Introduction

Narrative understanding has long been considered a central, yet challenging task in natural language understanding (Winograd, 1972). Recent advances in NLP have revived interest in this area, especially the task of story understanding (Mostafazadeh et al., 2016a). Most computational work has focused on extracting structured story representations (often called "schemas") from literary novels, folktales, movie plots or news articles (Chambers and Jurafsky, 2009; Finlayson, 2012; Chaturvedi et al., 2018). In our work, we shift the focus to understanding the structure of stories from a different data source: narratives found on social media. Table 1 provides an example story from the popular online discussion forum Reddit [1]. Prior work has studied stories of personal experiences found on social media, identifying new storytelling patterns. However, these studies have focused on how storyteller identity is conveyed (Page, 2013). In our work, we instead

---

[1] https://www.reddit.com/

> *i was eating breakfast this morning while my stepfather was making his lunch to take to work. as he reached for the plastic wrap for his sandwich i subtly mentioned that he could use a reusable container. so he walked over to the container drawer and used a container realizing that it was the perfect size. i know its not much but hopefully he remembers this tomorrow when making his lunch...*

Table 1: Sample personal story from Reddit

aim to understand novel structural patterns exhibited by such stories.

Computational work in story understanding often attempts to construct structured representations revolving around specific narrative elements. Broadly, these approaches can be divided into two classes: *event-centric* techniques (Chambers and Jurafsky, 2008) and *character-centric* techniques (Bamman, 2015). We adopt a novel take that focuses instead on extracting the "functional structure" of stories. For example, a common story can have a functional structure consisting of phases such as character introduction, conflict setup and resolution. To represent such structure, we propose the paradigm of **functional story schemas**, which consist of stereotypical sets of functional structures. A major difference between our conceptualization of functional story schemas and prior approaches is the focus on high-level narrative structure, which reduces domain-specificity in the found schemas. Studies have shown that functional narrative structures are critical in forming stories and play an important role in story understanding (Brewer and Lichtenstein, 1980, 1982).

We develop a novel unsupervised pipeline to extract functional schemas (§3), which consists of two stages: *functional structure identification* and *structure grouping for schema formation*. The first stage uses the Content word filtering and

Proceedings of the Second Storytelling Workshop, pages 22–33
Florence, Italy, August 1, 2019. ©2019 Association for Computational Linguistics

Speaker preferences Model (CSM), a generative model originally applied to detect schematic progressions of speech-acts in conversations (Jo et al., 2017), while the second stage groups strongly co-occurring sets of structures using principal component analysis (PCA) (Jolliffe, 2011). To validate extracted schemas, we perform a two-phase evaluation: manual interpretation of schemas (§4.2) and automated evaluation in a downstream text classification task (§4.3).

Utilizing our pipeline to extract functional schemas from posts on three subreddits discussing environmental issues [2], namely */r/environment*, */r/ZeroWaste* and */r/Green*, we observe that our schema interpretations reflect typical posting strategies employed by users in each of these subreddits. Incorporating schema information into the feature space also boosts the performance of a variety of baseline text classification models on subreddit prediction by 2.4% on average. After validation, we use extracted schemas to gain further insight into how stories function in social media (§5). We discover that functional schemas reveal community norms, since they capture dominant and unique posting styles followed by users of each subreddit. We hope that our conceptualization of functional story schemas provides an interesting research direction for future work on story understanding, especially stories on social media.

2 Background & Related Work

2.1 Narrative Understanding

Much prior work on narrative understanding has focused on extracting structured knowledge representations ("templates" or "schemas") from narratives. These works can be divided into two major classes based on the narrative aspect they attend to: *event-centric* and *character-centric*.

Event-centric approaches primarily focus on learning "scripts", which are stereotypical sequences of events occurring in the narrative along with their participants (Schank and Abelson, 1977). While scripts were introduced in the 1970s, not much early work (with the exception of Mooney and DeJong (1985)) attempted to build models for this task due to its complexity. However, it has garnered more interest in recent years. Chambers and Jurafsky (2008) modeled scripts as narrative event chains, defined as partially ordered

sets of events related to a *single* common actor, and built an evaluation called the *narrative cloze* test aimed at predicting a missing event in the script given all other events. Chambers and Jurafsky (2009) broadened the scope of event chains by defining "narrative schemas" which model all actors involved in a set of events along with their *role*. These inspired several script learning approaches (Regneri et al., 2010; Balasubramanian et al., 2013). A related line of research focused on extracting "event schemas", which store *semantic roles* for typical entities involved in an event. Several works proposed unsupervised methods for this task (Chambers and Jurafsky, 2011; Cheung et al., 2013; Chambers, 2013; Nguyen et al., 2015). Recent research identified a key problem with the narrative cloze test, namely that language modeling approaches perform well without learning about events (Pichotta and Mooney, 2014; Rudinger et al., 2015). This drove the establishment of a new task: the *story cloze* test where the goal was to select the correct ending for a story given two endings (Mostafazadeh et al., 2016a; Sharma et al., 2018). Several works showed that incorporating event sequence information provides improvement in this task (Peng et al., 2017; Chaturvedi et al., 2017b). Additionally, some work has focused on defining new script annotation schemes (Mostafazadeh et al., 2016b; Wanzare et al., 2016; Modi et al., 2016) and domain-specific script-based story understanding (Mueller, 2004; McIntyre and Lapata, 2009).

Character-centric approaches adopt the outlook that *characters* make a narrative compelling and drive the story. While no standard paradigms have been established for character representation, a common approach concentrated on learning character types or *personas* (Bamman et al., 2013, 2014). Other work proposed to model inter-character relationships (Krishnan and Eisenstein, 2015; Chaturvedi et al., 2016, 2017a). Information about character types and their relationships has been demonstrated to be useful for story understanding tasks such as identifying incorrect narratives (e.g., reordered or reversed stories) (Elsner, 2012) and detecting narrative similarity (Chaturvedi et al., 2018). Finally, an interesting line of research has focused on constructing "plot units", which are story representations consisting of affect states of characters and tensions between them. Plot units were first proposed by

---

Lehnert (1981) and have recently attracted interest from the NLP community resulting in the development of computational approaches (Appling and Riedl, 2009; Goyal et al., 2010).

Our work takes a unique approach in that we propose a computational technique to learn *functional schemas* from stories. Functional schemas consist of stereotypical sets of functional structures observed in stories. The key difference between functional schemas and scripts is that scripts contain events present in the narrative, while functional schemas consist of phases in a story arc. For example, for a crime story, a script representation may contain a "murder" event, but a functional schema could represent that event as "inciting incident", based on its role in the arc. Functional structures are key to rhetorical structure theory for discourse analysis (Labov, 1996; Labov and Waletzky, 1997) and have been operationalized in discourse parsing (Li et al., 2014; Xue et al., 2015). However, not much work has explored their utility in uncovering novel narrative structures. One exception is Finlayson (2012), which learned functional structures from folktales, indicating that computational techniques could recover patterns described in Propp's theory of folktale structure (Propp, 2010). Our work differs since we aim to uncover new schemas instead of validating existing structural theories. We take this perspective because we are interested in studying stories told on social media which may not conform to existing theories of narrative structure.

2.2 Schema Induction via Topic Models

To computationally extract functional schemas, it is important to identify characteristic functional structures from stories. Topic models, such as Latent Dirichlet Allocation (LDA) (Blei et al., 2003), can be used for automatic induction of such structures since they identify latent themes, which may be treated as functions, from a set of documents. However, vanilla topic models do not model transitions between themes, whereas stories tend to follow stereotypical sequences of functional structures. For example, the conflict in a story must be set up before the resolution. Hence, to account for the order of functional structures, conversation models can be employed (Ritter et al., 2010; Lee et al., 2013; Ezen-Can and Boyer, 2015; Brychcín and Král, 2017; Joty and Mohiuddin, 2018; Paul, 2012; Wallace et al., 2013; Jo et al., 2017). These

models impose structure on transitions between latent themes, typically using an HMM. This uncovers latent themes that account for interactions among themselves, helping to identify dialogue acts, which these models aim to extract. A similar HMM-based framework has been used to extract story schemas from news articles (Barzilay and Lee, 2004).

Among many conversation models, we use the Content word filtering and Speaker preferences Model (CSM), which recently offered the best performance at unsupervised dialogue act identification (Jo et al., 2017). We choose this model because it has some characteristics which make it especially useful for capturing functional structures. Above all, it automatically distinguishes between topical themes and functional structures, which have different behavior. For example, a functional structure that represents asking a question would be characterized by wh-adverbs and question marks, rather than the specific content of questions. Being able to make this distinction between *topics* and *functional structures* is crucial to our task of extracting functional schemas.

3 Method

We use unsupervised algorithms to induce functional schemas from stories. More specifically our pipeline consists of the following stages:

1. **Functional Structure Identification:** We use CSM to identify typical sequences of functional structures.
2. **Story Schema Formation:** We perform PCA to form functional schemas.

3.1 Functional Structure Identification

The first step in our pipeline is to identify the typical sequences of functional structures in the corpus, which will then be clustered to form several functional schemas. Specifically, we utilize CSM to identify underlying functional structures from the corpus.

CSM is a generative model originally applied to conversation – a sequence of utterances by speakers. The model assumes that a corpus of conversations has a set of functional structures undertaken by individual sentences. Each structure is represented as a language model, i.e., a probability distribution over words. CSM can be seen as a combination of an HMM and a topic model but adopts a deliberate design choice different from other models that focus mainly on topical themes. It captures linguistic structures using multiple mechanisms. First, the model encodes that, in a conversation the content being discussed transitions more slowly than the structures that convey the content. Capturing the difference in transition paces allows the model to distinguish co-occurrence patterns of fast-changing words (functional structures) from words that occur consistently throughout (topical themes).

CSM also assumes that each utterance plays some functional role, indicated by structural elements found within it, and that the function is probabilistically conditioned on that of the preceding utterance. This captures dependencies between utterance-level functions and thus those between lower-level structural elements within sentences as well. We can see these dependencies in, for example, a tech forum, where a conversation begins with a user's utterance of "information seeking" comprising such functional structures as introduction, problem statement, and question. This utterance may be followed by another user's utterance of "providing solutions" comprising such functional structures as suggestions and references. Formally, an utterence-level function is represented as a "state", a probability distribution over functional structures.

Since each story in our task is a monologue rather than a conversation, we need to format our data in a way analogous to a conversation to apply CSM. Specifically, we treat each story as a "conversation", and each sentence in the story as an "utterance". Accordingly, each "conversation" has only one speaker. This way, we apply CSM to a corpus of stories, still benefiting from the model's ability to distinguish functional structures from topical themes and account for temporal dependencies between functional structures.

3.2 Functional Schema Formation

After determining functional structures, we identify sets of most strongly co-occurring structures to form functional story schemas. To identify co-occurring structures, we represent each story as a bag of functional structures and run PCA[3]. Each resultant principal component is treated as a

schema, consisting of functional structures which have a high loading value for that component. Since principal components are orthogonal, extracted schemas will be distinct. In addition, the set of extracted schemas will be representative of most stories, because PCA retains the variance of the original data. The functional structures present in each schema (based on loading) are treated as elements of that schema.

4 Experiments

4.1 Dataset

We demonstrate the utility of our schema extraction pipeline on Reddit posts[4]. We select three active subreddits to construct our dataset, */r/environment*, */r/ZeroWaste*, and */r/Green*, which cover issues from the environmental domain. We are interested in studying how people structure their experiences and stories differently in each subreddit, though all of them discuss similar topics, as well as the extent to which our extracted functional schemas capture such subtle structural differences. We collect all posts from these subreddits since their inception until Jan 2019. Table 2 summarizes statistics for our dataset.

Subreddit	# of Posts
environment	$3,785$
ZeroWaste	$2,944$
Green	305

Table 2: Dataset Statistics

Using our schema extraction pipeline, we first extract a set of 10 functional structures using CSM[5]. Then using PCA, we derive 10 sets of co-occurring structures as our candidate functional schemas. Next, we manually inspect each set of structures and select the most salient 4 sets as our functional schemas[6]. To validate these schemas, we perform a two-fold evaluation. First, we manually interpret extracted functional structures and schemas. Second, we demonstrate the utility of our schemas by incorporating them into a downstream task: text classification.

---

[3] Though using PCA in the next phase removes ordering from the final schemas constructed, incorporating ordering during functional structure estimation helps in detecting more salient structures.

[4] According to the Reddit User Agreement, users grant Reddit the right to make their content available to other organizations or individuals.

[5] For CSM specific parameter settings see A.

[6] During manual inspection, we also try to ensure diversity (each set contains different structures).

4.2 Manual Schema Interpretation

In order to interpret the schemas, we first need to label functional structures extracted by CSM. Labeling was performed independently by two annotators who looked at sample sentences assigned to each structure by the model and assigned structure name labels based on inspection. A consensus coding was assembled as the final interpretation after an adjudicating discussion. Table 3 gives a brief overview of the structure labels along with examples for each. We see that the detected structures indeed represent strategies commonly used by Reddit users.

Schemas can now be interpreted based on labels assigned to the structures they contain. Final schema interpretations, along with sample posts for each schema, are presented in table 4. We observe that schema 0 and schema 2 are news and fact oriented, whereas schema 1 and schema 3 include more personal experiences. Moreover, new posts can also be fit into these schemas. We assign a schema to each post P using the following formula:

$$schema(P) = \arg\max_{s \in S} \sum_{t \in s} l_t * \frac{n_t}{n_P} \quad (1)$$

Here, S is the set of schemas, s is a schema, t is a functional structure, n_t is the number of sentences assigned t in P, n_P is the total number of sentences in P, and l_t is the absolute value of the PCA loading for t.

Figure 1 shows the proportion of posts from each subreddit assigned to each schema. We clearly see that posts from different subreddits follow different schemas. Specifically, half of the posts in subreddit */r/environment* fit into schema 0 and about $1/4$ of the posts fit into schema 2; Schema 1 dominates posts in */r/ZeroWaste*; Posts in */r/Green* occupy schemas 0, 1, 2 and 3 in decreasing numbers. This demonstrates that our extracted schemas do capture typical structures present in Reddit posts and that posts in each subreddit indeed exhibit unique structures.

4.3 Using Schemas for Text Classification

In addition to manual interpretation, we demonstrate the practical utility of our schema extraction pipeline by applying it in a downstream task: multi-label text classification. In our task setup, we treat each post as a document and the subreddit it belongs to as the document label. Since

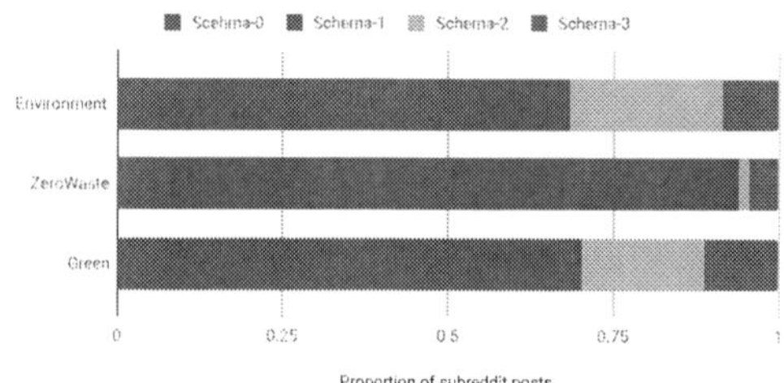

Figure 1: Proportion of schemas for each subreddit

all subreddits in our dataset focus on environmental issues, most posts discuss similar topics, making classification using only content information hard. However, as we observed in our schema interpretation, posts from different subreddits follow different schematic structures. Hence, we hypothesize that using schema information should help on this task. As a preliminary experiment, we construct a document representation using only schema-based features. Each document is represented as a 4-dimensional vector consisting of schema scores calculated per equation (1). The performance of logistic regression (**LR**) and support vector machine (**SVM**) classifiers using these feature representations is presented in table 5. These scores demonstrate that schema information is extremely predictive for the classification task in comparison to a majority vote baseline. Encouraged by this result, we conduct further experiments in which schema information is combined with word features. We experiment with both neural and non-neural baseline models for our task. Our models and results are described below.

4.3.1 Baseline Models

We set up the following baseline models, which use only word-level information, for text classification:

- **LR:** A logistic regression classifier with two feature settings (bag-of-words or tf-idf)
- **NB:** A naive bayes classifier with two feature settings (bag-of-words or tf-idf)
- **SVM:** A support vector machine classifier with unigram bag-of-word features
- **BiLSTM:** A bi-directional LSTM with mean-pooling (Yang et al., 2016), followed by an MLP classifier
- **CNN:** A CNN with filter sizes 3,4,5 and max-pooling (Kim, 2014), followed by an MLP

Structure	Label	Examples
0	Requesting help	*any advice would be appreciated* *any ideas on how i can do this*
1	Asking for feedback & thanking	*thanks in advance for your help* *if you want to help please send me a message here*
2	Disclosing personal stories	*i teach global environmental history...* *i'm trying to learn more about being eco-friendly...*
3	Presenting news/statements	*this is called economy of scale* *solar is unreliable expensive and imported*
4	Catch-all for questions	*how happy will we be when our wells are dry* *how do we make up for these losses*
5	Presenting news/facts (numbers)	*85 of our antibiotics come from ascomycetes fungi...* *reduce the global population of bears by two thirds...*
6	Expressing personal opinions	*now i think that landfills are the devil...* *i am sure something can be done with them...*
7	Providing motivation	*we r/environment need to be a vehicle for change...* *we need to engage learn share eulogize and inform*
8	Non-English sentences	*men data siden 2005 viste veksten av disse...* *durant ces cent dernires annes...*
9	Catch-all for personal story bits	*when i asked for a carafe of water he said...* *all i wanted to do was use a cup to get some coffee...*

Table 3: 10 functional structures extracted by CSM along with examples. These structures are more general than narrative primitives appearing in classic theoretical frameworks such as Propp's theory, but we believe that they provide a reasonable approximation.

classifier

For all models using bag-of-words or tf-idf features, we restrict the vocabulary to the most frequent $2,000$ words. All neural models use 300-dimensional GloVe embeddings (Pennington et al., 2014).

4.3.2   Schema-based Extension Models

To incorporate schema features alongside word-level features, we adopt a strategy inspired by domain adaptation techniques (Daume III, 2007; Kim et al., 2016). Daume III (2007) proposed a feature augmentation strategy for domain adaptation, which was extended to neural models by (Kim et al., 2016). It works as described: given two domains ("source" and "target"), each feature is duplicated thrice creating three versions – a general version, a source-specific version and a target-specific version. We follow the same intuition considering each schema to be a separate domain. Hence, we duplicate each feature 5 times (a general version and 4 schema-specific versions). For example, if a document contains the word "plastic", our feature space includes "general_plastic", "schema0_plastic", and so on. We experiment with several feature duplication strategies, resulting in the following settings for each model:

- **Vanilla:** Only the general domain features contain non-zero values. All schema domain features are set to zero, hence this setting contains no schema information.
- **AllSent:** Both general and schema domains contain non-zero feature values computed using sentences from the entire document. For each document, only one schema domain (i.e. assigned schema) contains non-zero values.
- **SchemaSent:** General domain feature values are computed using the entire document, while schema domain feature values are computed using only sentences which contain structures present in the assigned schema.

4.3.3   Results

To evaluate the performance of all models on our text classification task, we create a held-out test set using 10% of our data. The remaining data is divided into *train* and *dev* sets. To avoid double-dipping into the same data for both schema learning and subreddit prediction, we use *dev* set to learn schemas, and train **AllSent** and

Schema	Interpretation	Examples
0	Presenting news/facts, asking questions and providing motivation	*deforestation in the amazon can hardly be a headline for forty years running...how happy will we be when our wells are dry...right now the jaguars are on the rise and i have hope*
1	Disclosing personal problems or opinions, sharing story snippets and providing motivation	*i am not a techsavvy person...i literally know the bare minimum of how a computer works*
2	Presenting news/facts, asking questions and sharing story snippets	*the commission by environmental campaigners forecast 3 trillion euros would generate by 2050...it has yet to achieve agreement on binding targets beyond 2020...the crown report finds almost totally green energy would lead to half a million extra jobs*
3	Disclosing personal problems, presenting facts and requesting help	*i just got this job the only job i've been able to find for the last year...we work on different studies each week for the likes of bayer and monsanto...i know i should stop pestering the internet for help but you're so benevolent*

Table 4: Manual interpretation for 4 schemas extracted by PCA, along with example post sinppets. Note that the functional structures in each schema may appear in any order in the post, not necessarily the one presented here

Model	Accuracy
LR	83.64%
SVM	82.79%

Table 5: Accuracy of classifiers using only schema features for text classification. Majority vote accuracy is 53.34%

SchemaSent models on *train* data only. However for the **Vanilla** setting, we can use both *train* and *dev* sets for training since no schema information is used. Because we need a large dev set to learn good schemas, we perform a $50 : 50$ split to create train and dev sets. Exact statistics are provided in table 6.

Split	# of Posts
Train	3, 166
Dev	3, 165
Test	703

Table 6: Dataset split statistics

Table 7 shows the performance of all models in different settings on the text classification task. We observe that for both neural and non-neural models, incorporating schema information helps in all cases, the only exception being **NB-BoW**.

We also notice that neural and non-neural models achieved comparable performance which is surprising. To further investigate this, we look into precision recall and F1 scores of the best model for each type respectively i.e. **NB-BoW Vanilla** and **CNN AllSent**. Our investigation shows that unlike NB-BoW, the CNN model completely ignores the minority subreddit */r/Green*, which we believe could be due to the fact that our dataset is extremely small for neural models.

Model	Vanilla	AllSent	SchemaSent
LR-BoW	80.2%	**85.1%**	84.8%
LR-TfIdf	81.4%	80.7%	**81.7%**
NB-BoW	**86.9%**	78.0%	77.2%
NB-TfIdf	69.6%	**79.8%**	79.2%
SVM	77.8%	83.8%	**85.2%**
BiLSTM	82.4%	79.8%	**82.9%**
CNN	85.2%	**87.3%**	86.6%

Table 7: Accuracy of all models on text classification

5 Discussion

Our interpretation and experiments demonstrate that the extracted functional schemas uncover novel narrative structures employed by Reddit users. We also observe that functional schemas are differently distributed across subreddits, indicating that communities follow diverse story-telling practices, even when discussing similar topics. These subtle schema differences between narratives across subreddits can aid us in discerning how users structure stories differently when participating in different communities. In our case, extracted schemas show that users in subreddits */r/environment* and */r/Green* use more fact-oriented functions while telling stories (high abundance of stories fitting schemas 0 and 2), whereas users in subreddit */r/ZeroWaste* use more personal experience-oriented functions (high abundance of stories fitting schemas 1 and 3). We highlight this by giving prototypical example posts with assigned schema labels for each subreddit below:

> *...there is so many problems today with plastic strawsthe uk and the us use a combined total of 550 million plastic straws each day and unfortunately its safe to say that not all 550 million of these plastic items are recycled ...*
> (**/r/environment**, Schema 0)

> *...every single year plastic cards hotel key cards etc amount to 75 million pounds of pvc wasted or about 34000 tonsthe eiffel tower weighs just around 10000 tonsthis is the equivalent of burying around 3 eiffel towers a year just from used pvc cards...*
> (**/r/Green**, Schema 0)

> *...i had a few vegetables that were wilting and ready to be discarded...instead i made a soup with all of them and some broth and miso...it's good and isn't wasteful...*
> (**/r/ZeroWaste**, Schema 1)

More importantly, these narrative structures unique to each subreddit, as captured by functional schemas, can act as a lens and provide insight into community posting norms. This is analogous with previous work on computational sociolinguistics, where researchers have demonstrated that online discussion forums create community norms about language usage, and members adapt their language to conform to those norms (Nguyen et al., 2016). Especially on Reddit, language style is an essential indicator of community identity (Tran and Ostendorf, 2016; Chancellor et al., 2018). Our

schemas help us make similar observations, showing that dominant user posting styles in each subreddit seem to be ones that conform to subreddit descriptions. Figure 2 presents descriptions for all subreddits which we use in our dataset. We see */r/environment* and */r/Green* specifically position themselves as platforms to discuss news and current issues, which is also recovered by our functional schemas since they contain an abundance of news and fact related functions. On the other hand, */r/ZeroWaste* positions itself as a platform for like-minded people, resulting in dominant schemas demonstrating an abundance of functional structures related to describing personal experiences. This indicates that our technique of inducing functional schemas from social media posts is useful for drawing interesting insights about how narratives align to community norms in online discussion forums.

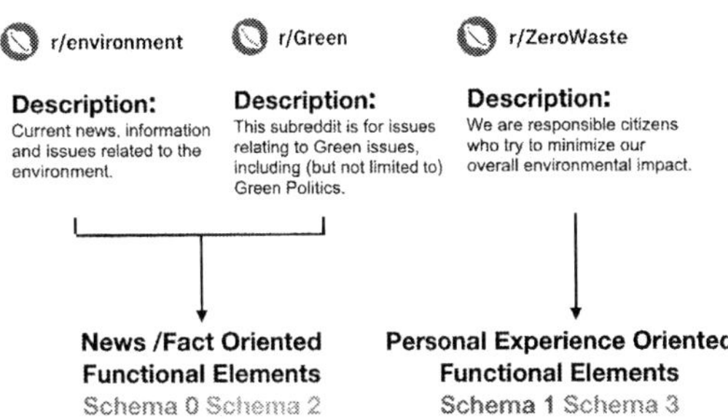

Figure 2: Subreddit description corresponding to schemas

6 Conclusion & Future Work

In this work we propose a novel computational approach to understand social media narratives. We present a unique take on story understanding, focusing on learning functional story schemas which are sets of typical functional structures. We first introduce a computational pipeline utilizing unsupervised methods such as CSM and PCA, to extract schemas and use it on social media data (posts from different communities on Reddit). We then validate learned schemas through human interpretation and a downstream text classification task. Our interpretation shows typical posting strategies used by community members and our experiments demonstrate that integrating schema information improves the performance of baseline models on subreddit prediction. Finally, we observe that functional schemas not only capture specific narrative structures existing in subreddits, but also reveal online community norms, which helps us better understand how stories function in social media.

A limitation of our work is that PCA-based grouping loses information about ordering of functional structures within each schema. Moving forward, we plan to tackle this to form ordered schemas. Possible applications of our work include using extracted schemas to study evolution of community norms and changes in user compliance to these norms over time.

7 Acknowledgements

This research was funded by Dow. The authors would like to thank the anonymous reviewers for their constructive feedback.

References

D Scott Appling and Mark O Riedl. 2009. Representations for learning to summarize plots. In *AAAI Spring Symposium: Intelligent Narrative Technologies II*, pages 1–4.

Niranjan Balasubramanian, Stephen Soderland, Mausam, and Oren Etzioni. 2013. Generating coherent event schemas at scale. In *Proceedings of the 2013 Conference on Empirical Methods in Natural Language Processing*, pages 1721–1731, Seattle, Washington, USA. Association for Computational Linguistics.

David Bamman. 2015. *People-Centric Natural Language Processing*. Ph.D. thesis, Carnegie Mellon University.

David Bamman, Brendan O'Connor, and Noah A. Smith. 2013. Learning latent personas of film characters. In *Proceedings of the 51st Annual Meeting of the Association for Computational Linguistics (Volume 1: Long Papers)*, pages 352–361, Sofia, Bulgaria. Association for Computational Linguistics.

David Bamman, Ted Underwood, and Noah A. Smith. 2014. A Bayesian mixed effects model of literary character. In *Proceedings of the 52nd Annual Meeting of the Association for Computational Linguistics (Volume 1: Long Papers)*, pages 370–379, Baltimore, Maryland. Association for Computational Linguistics.

Regina Barzilay and Lillian Lee. 2004. Catching the drift: Probabilistic content models, with applications to generation and summarization. In *HLT-NAACL 2004: Main Proceedings*, pages 113–120, Boston, Massachusetts, USA. Association for Computational Linguistics.

David M Blei, Andrew Y Ng, and Michael I Jordan. 2003. Latent dirichlet allocation. *Journal of machine Learning research*, 3(Jan):993–1022.

William F Brewer and Edward H Lichtenstein. 1980. Event schemas, story schemas, and story grammars. *Center for the Study of Reading Technical Report; no. 197*.

William F Brewer and Edward H Lichtenstein. 1982. Stories are to entertain: A structural-affect theory of stories. *Journal of pragmatics*, 6(5-6):473–486.

Tomáš Brychcín and Pavel Král. 2017. Unsupervised dialogue act induction using Gaussian mixtures. In *Proceedings of the 15th Conference of the European Chapter of the Association for Computational Linguistics: Volume 2, Short Papers*, pages 485–490, Valencia, Spain. Association for Computational Linguistics.

Nathanael Chambers. 2013. Event schema induction with a probabilistic entity-driven model. In *Proceedings of the 2013 Conference on Empirical Methods in Natural Language Processing*, pages 1797–1807, Seattle, Washington, USA. Association for Computational Linguistics.

Nathanael Chambers and Dan Jurafsky. 2008. Unsupervised learning of narrative event chains. In *Proceedings of ACL-08: HLT*, pages 789–797, Columbus, Ohio. Association for Computational Linguistics.

Nathanael Chambers and Dan Jurafsky. 2009. Unsupervised learning of narrative schemas and their participants. In *Proceedings of the Joint Conference of the 47th Annual Meeting of the ACL and the 4th International Joint Conference on Natural Language Processing of the AFNLP*, pages 602–610, Suntec, Singapore. Association for Computational Linguistics.

Nathanael Chambers and Dan Jurafsky. 2011. Template-based information extraction without the templates. In *Proceedings of the 49th Annual Meeting of the Association for Computational Linguistics: Human Language Technologies*, pages 976–986, Portland, Oregon, USA. Association for Computational Linguistics.

Stevie Chancellor, Andrea Hu, and Munmun De Choudhury. 2018. Norms matter: contrasting social support around behavior change in online weight loss communities. In *Proceedings of the 2018 CHI Conference on Human Factors in Computing Systems*, page 666. ACM.

Snigdha Chaturvedi, Mohit Iyyer, and Hal Daume III. 2017a. Unsupervised learning of evolving relationships between literary characters. In *Thirty-First AAAI Conference on Artificial Intelligence*.

Snigdha Chaturvedi, Haoruo Peng, and Dan Roth. 2017b. Story comprehension for predicting what happens next. In *Proceedings of the 2017 Conference on Empirical Methods in Natural Language Processing*, pages 1603–1614, Copenhagen, Denmark. Association for Computational Linguistics.

Snigdha Chaturvedi, Shashank Srivastava, Hal Daume III, and Chris Dyer. 2016. Modeling evolving relationships between characters in literary novels. In *Thirtieth AAAI Conference on Artificial Intelligence*.

Snigdha Chaturvedi, Shashank Srivastava, and Dan Roth. 2018. Where have I heard this story before? identifying narrative similarity in movie remakes. In *Proceedings of the 2018 Conference of the North American Chapter of the Association for Computational Linguistics: Human Language Technologies, Volume 2 (Short Papers)*, pages 673–678, New Orleans, Louisiana. Association for Computational Linguistics.

Jackie Chi Kit Cheung, Hoifung Poon, and Lucy Vanderwende. 2013. Probabilistic frame induction. In *Proceedings of the 2013 Conference of the North American Chapter of the Association for Computational Linguistics: Human Language Technologies*, pages 837–846, Atlanta, Georgia. Association for Computational Linguistics.

Hal Daume III. 2007. Frustratingly easy domain adaptation. In *Proceedings of the 45th Annual Meeting of the Association of Computational Linguistics*, pages 256–263, Prague, Czech Republic. Association for Computational Linguistics.

Micha Elsner. 2012. Character-based kernels for novelistic plot structure. In *Proceedings of the 13th Conference of the European Chapter of the Association for Computational Linguistics*, pages 634–644, Avignon, France. Association for Computational Linguistics.

Aysu Ezen-Can and Kristy Elizabeth Boyer. 2015. Understanding student language: An unsupervised dialogue act classification approach. *Journal of Educational Data Mining (JEDM)*, 7(1):51–78.

Mark Alan Finlayson. 2012. *Learning narrative structure from annotated folktales*. Ph.D. thesis, Massachusetts Institute of Technology.

Amit Goyal, Ellen Riloff, and Hal Daume III. 2010. Automatically producing plot unit representations for narrative text. In *Proceedings of the 2010 Conference on Empirical Methods in Natural Language Processing*, pages 77–86, Cambridge, MA. Association for Computational Linguistics.

Yohan Jo, Michael Yoder, Hyeju Jang, and Carolyn Rosé. 2017. Modeling dialogue acts with content word filtering and speaker preferences. In *Proceedings of the 2017 Conference on Empirical Methods in Natural Language Processing*, pages 2179–2189, Copenhagen, Denmark. Association for Computational Linguistics.

Ian Jolliffe. 2011. Principal component analysis. In *International encyclopedia of statistical science*, pages 1094–1096. Springer.

Shafiq Joty and Tasnim Mohiuddin. 2018. Modeling speech acts in asynchronous conversations: A neural-CRF approach. *Computational Linguistics*, 44(4):859–894.

Yoon Kim. 2014. Convolutional neural networks for sentence classification. In *Proceedings of the 2014 Conference on Empirical Methods in Natural Language Processing*, pages 1746–1751, Doha, Qatar. Association for Computational Linguistics.

Young-Bum Kim, Karl Stratos, and Ruhi Sarikaya. 2016. Frustratingly easy neural domain adaptation. In *Proceedings of COLING 2016, the 26th International Conference on Computational Linguistics: Technical Papers*, pages 387–396, Osaka, Japan. The COLING 2016 Organizing Committee.

Vinodh Krishnan and Jacob Eisenstein. 2015. "you're mr. lebowski, I'm the dude": Inducing address term formality in signed social networks. In *Proceedings of the 2015 Conference of the North American Chapter of the Association for Computational Linguistics: Human Language Technologies*, pages 1616–1626, Denver, Colorado. Association for Computational Linguistics.

William Labov. 1996. Some further steps in narrative analysis. *The Journal of Narrative and Life History. Special Issue: Oral Versions of Personal Experience: Three Decades of Narrative Analysis*, 7.

William Labov and Joshua Waletzky. 1997. Narrative analysis: oral versions of personal experience.

Donghyeon Lee, Minwoo Jeong, Kyungduk Kim, Seonghan Ryu, and Gary Geunbae Lee. 2013. Unsupervised Spoken Language Understanding for a Multi-Domain Dialog System. *IEEE Transactions on Audio, Speech, and Language Processing*, 21(11):2451–2464.

Wendy G Lehnert. 1981. Plot units and narrative summarization. *Cognitive science*, 5(4):293–331.

Jiwei Li, Rumeng Li, and Eduard Hovy. 2014. Recursive deep models for discourse parsing. In *Proceedings of the 2014 Conference on Empirical Methods in Natural Language Processing*, pages 2061–2069, Doha, Qatar. Association for Computational Linguistics.

Neil McIntyre and Mirella Lapata. 2009. Learning to tell tales: A data-driven approach to story generation. In *Proceedings of the Joint Conference of the 47th Annual Meeting of the ACL and the 4th International Joint Conference on Natural Language Processing of the AFNLP*, pages 217–225, Suntec, Singapore. Association for Computational Linguistics.

Ashutosh Modi, Tatjana Anikina, Simon Ostermann, and Manfred Pinkal. 2016. InScript: Narrative texts annotated with script information. In *Proceedings of the Tenth International Conference on Language Resources and Evaluation (LREC 2016)*, pages 3485–3493, Portorož, Slovenia. European Language Resources Association (ELRA).

Raymond J Mooney and Gerald DeJong. 1985. Learning schemata for natural language processing. In *IJCAI*, pages 681–687.

Nasrin Mostafazadeh, Nathanael Chambers, Xiaodong He, Devi Parikh, Dhruv Batra, Lucy Vanderwende, Pushmeet Kohli, and James Allen. 2016a. A corpus and cloze evaluation for deeper understanding of commonsense stories. In *Proceedings of the 2016 Conference of the North American Chapter of the Association for Computational Linguistics: Human Language Technologies*, pages 839–849, San Diego, California. Association for Computational Linguistics.

Nasrin Mostafazadeh, Alyson Grealish, Nathanael Chambers, James Allen, and Lucy Vanderwende. 2016b. CaTeRS: Causal and temporal relation scheme for semantic annotation of event structures. In *Proceedings of the Fourth Workshop on Events*, pages 51–61, San Diego, California. Association for Computational Linguistics.

Erik T Mueller. 2004. Understanding script-based stories using commonsense reasoning. *Cognitive Systems Research*, 5(4):307–340.

Dong Nguyen, A. Seza Doğruöz, Carolyn P. Rosé, and Franciska de Jong. 2016. Survey: Computational sociolinguistics: A Survey. *Computational Linguistics*, 42(3):537–593.

Kiem-Hieu Nguyen, Xavier Tannier, Olivier Ferret, and Romaric Besançon. 2015. Generative event schema induction with entity disambiguation. In *Proceedings of the 53rd Annual Meeting of the Association for Computational Linguistics and the 7th International Joint Conference on Natural Language Processing (Volume 1: Long Papers)*, pages 188–197, Beijing, China. Association for Computational Linguistics.

Ruth Page. 2013. *Stories and social media: Identities and interaction*. Routledge.

Michael J. Paul. 2012. Mixed membership Markov models for unsupervised conversation modeling. In *Proceedings of the 2012 Joint Conference on Empirical Methods in Natural Language Processing and Computational Natural Language Learning*, pages 94–104, Jeju Island, Korea. Association for Computational Linguistics.

Haoruo Peng, Snigdha Chaturvedi, and Dan Roth. 2017. A joint model for semantic sequences: Frames, entities, sentiments. In *Proceedings of the 21st Conference on Computational Natural Language Learning (CoNLL 2017)*, pages 173–183, Vancouver, Canada. Association for Computational Linguistics.

Jeffrey Pennington, Richard Socher, and Christopher Manning. 2014. Glove: Global vectors for word representation. In *Proceedings of the 2014 Conference on Empirical Methods in Natural Language Processing (EMNLP)*, pages 1532–1543, Doha, Qatar. Association for Computational Linguistics.

Karl Pichotta and Raymond Mooney. 2014. Statistical script learning with multi-argument events. In *Proceedings of the 14th Conference of the European Chapter of the Association for Computational Linguistics*, pages 220–229, Gothenburg, Sweden. Association for Computational Linguistics.

Vladimir Propp. 2010. *Morphology of the Folktale*, volume 9. University of Texas Press.

Michaela Regneri, Alexander Koller, and Manfred Pinkal. 2010. Learning script knowledge with web experiments. In *Proceedings of the 48th Annual Meeting of the Association for Computational Linguistics*, pages 979–988, Uppsala, Sweden. Association for Computational Linguistics.

Alan Ritter, Colin Cherry, and Bill Dolan. 2010. Unsupervised modeling of twitter conversations. In *Human Language Technologies: The 2010 Annual Conference of the North American Chapter of the Association for Computational Linguistics*, pages 172–180, Los Angeles, California. Association for Computational Linguistics.

Rachel Rudinger, Pushpendre Rastogi, Francis Ferraro, and Benjamin Van Durme. 2015. Script induction as language modeling. In *Proceedings of the 2015 Conference on Empirical Methods in Natural Language Processing*, pages 1681–1686, Lisbon, Portugal. Association for Computational Linguistics.

Roger C Schank and Robert P Abelson. 1977. Scripts. *Plans, Goals and Understanding*.

Rishi Sharma, James Allen, Omid Bakhshandeh, and Nasrin Mostafazadeh. 2018. Tackling the story ending biases in the story cloze test. In *Proceedings of the 56th Annual Meeting of the Association for Computational Linguistics (Volume 2: Short Papers)*, pages 752–757, Melbourne, Australia. Association for Computational Linguistics.

Trang Tran and Mari Ostendorf. 2016. Characterizing the language of online communities and its relation to community reception. In *Proceedings of the 2016 Conference on Empirical Methods in Natural Language Processing*, pages 1030–1035, Austin, Texas. Association for Computational Linguistics.

Byron C. Wallace, Thomas A. Trikalinos, M. Barton Laws, Ira B. Wilson, and Eugene Charniak. 2013. A generative joint, additive, sequential model of topics and speech acts in patient-doctor communication. In *Proceedings of the 2013 Conference on Empirical Methods in Natural Language Processing*, pages 1765–1775, Seattle, Washington, USA. Association for Computational Linguistics.

Lilian DA Wanzare, Alessandra Zarcone, Stefan Thater, and Manfred Pinkal. 2016. Descript: A crowdsourced corpus for the acquisition of high-quality script knowledge. In *Proceedings of the*

Tenth International Conference on Language Resources and Evaluation (LREC 2016), pages 3494–3501.

Terry Winograd. 1972. Understanding natural language. *Cognitive psychology*, 3(1):1–191.

Nianwen Xue, Hwee Tou Ng, Sameer Pradhan, Rashmi Prasad, Christopher Bryant, and Attapol Rutherford. 2015. The CoNLL-2015 shared task on shallow discourse parsing. In *Proceedings of the Nineteenth Conference on Computational Natural Language Learning - Shared Task*, pages 1–16, Beijing, China. Association for Computational Linguistics.

Zichao Yang, Diyi Yang, Chris Dyer, Xiaodong He, Alex Smola, and Eduard Hovy. 2016. Hierarchical attention networks for document classification. In *Proceedings of the 2016 Conference of the North American Chapter of the Association for Computational Linguistics: Human Language Technologies*, pages 1480–1489, San Diego, California. Association for Computational Linguistics.

A Appendices

A.1 CSM Parameter Values

Various parameter values were tested and the final parameter setting was chosen based on model performance and the parameter setting suggested in the original paper (Jo et al., 2017).

We found the optimal number of functional structures to be 10. Higher numbers tend to capture too content-specific structures, and lower numbers too general structures. The optimal number of content topics is 5, which indicates that the corpus is focused on environmental related issues and the content is relatively common across the corpus. The number of states reflects different patterns of structure composition within a post, and 5 states were found to be optimal. More states tend to capture too post-specific structures, and less states cannot account for the diversity of structures.

Parameter $\nu \in [0, 1]$ is the weight on state transition probabilities (as opposed to speaker preferences) for determining an utterance's state. 1 means only state transition probabilities are considered, and 0 means only speaker preferences are considered. In our study, we treat each post as a "conversation" that has only one speaker. Therefore, a low weight would identify functional structures that distinguish between posts rather than between sentences. We find a high weight ($\nu = 0.9$) drives the model to identify sentence structures well that also account for some consistency within each post. Parameter $\eta \in [0, 1]$ is the weight

on structure language models (as opposed to content topics) for generating words. 1 means that all words are generated from structure language models, and 0 means only from content topics. Our setting ($\eta = 0.8$) filters out 20% of words as content. This is quite a large proportion compared to the original paper, meaning that the corpus has a relatively large proportion of words that constitute functional structures.

Other hyperparameters for the model were set as per the original paper: $\alpha^F = \gamma^A = 0.1, \alpha^B = \gamma^S = 1, \beta = 0.001$.

A Hybrid Model for Globally Coherent Story Generation

Zhai Fangzhou[†], **Vera Demberg**[†,‡], **Pavel Shkadzko**[†], **Wei Shi**[†] and **Asad Sayeed**[*]
[†] Dept. of Language Science and Technology
[‡] Dept. of Mathematics and Computer Science, Saarland University
[*]Dept. of Philosophy, Linguistics and Theory of Science, University of Gothenburg
`{fzhai, vera, w.shi}@coli.uni-saarland.de`
`p.shkadzko@gmail.com, asad.sayeed@gu.se`

Abstract

Automatically generating globally coherent stories is a challenging problem. Neural text generation models have been shown to perform well at generating fluent sentences from data, but they usually fail to keep track of the overall coherence of the story after a couple of sentences. Existing work that incorporates a text planning module succeeded in generating recipes and dialogues, but appears quite data-demanding. We propose a novel story generation approach that generates globally coherent stories from a fairly small corpus. The model exploits a symbolic text planning module to produce text plans, thus reducing the demand of data; a neural surface realization module then generates fluent text conditioned on the text plan. Human evaluation showed that our model outperforms various baselines by a wide margin and generates stories which are fluent as well as globally coherent.

1 Introduction

Automatic story generation is the task of automatically determining the content and utilizing proper language to craft stories. One of the most important aspects of these stories is their coherence. The scope of global coherence includes arranging the contents in a plausible order, staying on topic, and creating cohesion through anaphoric expressions, etc.

Traditionally, story generation is performed with symbolic planning systems (see, e.g., Meehan, 1976; Riedl and Young, 2010; Busemann and Horacek, 1998). These systems often follow a hierarchical pipeline: higher level modules perform text planning, determine discourse relations and contents of each sentence; lower level modules account for surface realization accordingly. Although capable of producing impressive, coherent stories, these systems rely heavily on manual knowledge engineering to select actions, characters, etc., properly, therefore generalizing poorly to unseen domains.

Early NLG systems, on the other hand, excel at generating fluent on-topic utterances (see, e.g., Mei et al., 2015; Wen et al., 2015). These models are data-based, and therefore can be applied to new domains if data is available. However, these models struggle to keep track of longer story or dialog history, i.e., they may switch topics, repeat information or say things that are not consistent with sentences generated earlier (see, e.g., Vinyals and Le, 2015; Shang et al., 2015). Extra modelling efforts or knowledge input is required to improve global coherence.

Neural NLG systems that incorporate text planning efforts could improve global coherence, and grant some controllability over the contents, i.e. making it possible to generate stories given specific input of what should happen in the story. (Fan et al., 2019) uses a convolutional seq2seq model to generate a chain of predicate-argument structures from a prompt to sketch a story, and then uses another convolutional seq2seq model to convert the chain of predicate-argument structures to text. The *neural checklist* model (Kiddon et al., 2016) keeps track of the progress of recipe generation with the usage of ingredient words, to generate recipes from a bag of ingredients. If we consider the task of story generation, *events* ("script" events; scripts capture knowledge about "standardized sequences of events about daily activities such as going to a restaurant or visiting a doctor") are also fairly informative for the narration progress. Thus if one could identify events within surface texts, it is, in principle, possible to regard the events as indicators of the narration progress (just like the ingredients in a recipe) and apply the *neural checklist* model.

These requirements are fulfilled by the

Proceedings of the Second Storytelling Workshop, pages 34–45
Florence, Italy, August 1, 2019. ©2019 Association for Computational Linguistics

`InScript` (Modi et al., 2017a) corpus, a small corpus that contains a total of about 1000 stories about everyday events from 10 scenarios. Each story is annotated with script-relevant event types to align them with surface language. However, surprisingly, when we apply the *neural checklist* model on `InScript` to generate stories, the quality of the generated stories appears poor (see the second item in Table 1 for a sample generation).

We notice two possible reasons for why the *neural checklist* model does not perform well on the task: (1) the scale of `InScript` is less that 0.5% of the recipe task investigated in (Kiddon et al., 2016), thus the model may not be able to properly fit its complex structure and learn to plan the text; (2) each script event in our data corresponds to multiple possible surface realization options (e.g., both 'I went to the shop' and 'I drove to the supermarket' would be labeled as a `go_to_store` event), which makes the alignment between an event and the surface text inherently more complicated than that between ingredients and surface text.

To tackle these issues, we propose a new neural story generation model that exploits explicit, symbolic text planning. The model consists of two components: the ***agenda generator*** produces an agenda, a sequence of script events that would later be fleshed out to yield a story, by a neural ***surface realization module***; the neural surface realization module treats the events in the agenda as a latent variable that encodes the progress of story generation, and produces text conditioned on it. The outcome is a system that could be trained with much less data. To our knowledge, this is the first attempt to integrate a completely symbolic text planner with a neural surface realization component, to perform fully interpretable text planning. Human evaluation shows that our system significantly outperforms various baselines in terms of fluency and global coherence.

Our contributions are as follows:

- We develop a story generation model that generates globally coherent stories about daily activities.

- We propose a novel way to combine a neural story generation model with an explicit, symbolic text planning component; furthermore, we show that the design reduces the demand on training data.

- We illustrate the possibility of guiding the direction of story generation by conditioning the generation on a latent intention variable.

In the remainder of this paper, we start with a discussion of related research, and then introduce the `InScript` corpus. To follow is a detailed introduction of our model and the results from human evaluation. Analysis of the results and some discussions about future directions conclude the paper.

2   Related Work

NLG Conditioned on Latent Intention Variable

Incorporating a latent intention variable in NLG systems yields improved controllability over the content. It is proved effective in data-to-dialogue generation (see, e.g., Yarats and Lewis, 2017; Kiddon et al., 2016). In neural text generation, some domain-specific categories of words are also informative for the progress of generation. Kiddon et al. (2016) developed an end-to-end neural text generation model, which keeps track of the usage of the keywords (e.g. recipe ingredients) with attention mechanism, and conditions surface realization on the usage of these words.

NLG with Explicit Text Planning

Noting that RNN based language models could only account for local coherence, attempts have been made to perform text planning on a higher level (e.g. Jain et al., 2017; Peng et al., 2018). Puduppully et al. (2018) performs content selection and planning with attention based neural networks before surface realization, to generate specifically structured NBA game summaries. Martin et al. (2018) uses sequence to sequence neural network (*event2event*) to generate events (represented by a verb and its most important arguments) corresponding to consecutive sentences. A second sequence to sequence model (*event2sentence*) generates a sentence based on the event. Our method differs from that of Martin et al. (2018), mainly in that (1) we seek to implement text coherence on a document level whereas they mostly focused on consecutive sentence pairs; (2) we do not incorporate explicit sentence segmentation but leave the job to the surface realization component.

3 Data

Our work is based on the `InScript` corpus. We mainly utilized its event annotations and the ***temporal script graphs*** extracted from the corpus.

3.1 The `InScript` Corpus

The `InScript` corpus (Modi et al., 2017a) was designed for the investigation of script knowledge. The corpus includes around 100 stories for each of 10 common daily scenarios. These stories are annotated with event types as well as participant types. For this paper, we only exploit the event type annotations. An example is shown in Figure 1. The average story length is approximately 240 tokens; the corpus includes 238k tokens in total. We use the corpus to train the neural surface realization component.

3.2 The Temporal Script Graphs

Wanzare et al. (2017) compiled the `InScript` event annotations into *temporal script graphs* (see Figure 2). These directed graphs contain information on the typical temporal order of events in a script scenario, which is a crucial aspect of script knowledge. In our method, temporal script graphs are used to generate plausible sequences of events for building the agenda.

4 Our Model

Overview

Our model consists of three modules. Firstly, a symbolic ***agenda generator***, which is responsible for performing text planning. Given a specific scenario (e.g., `baking a cake`), it produces an agenda according its temporal script graph. Secondly, a neural ***surface realization module***, which performs two tasks: (1) it predicts the next word of the story conditioned on the text history and the event that needs to be realized at a specific point in the story; (2) it determines whether the current event has been completely realized so the generation could move to the next event in the agenda. Finally, a ***story generator*** which performs the following. (1) Calls the *agenda generator* to generate an agenda. (2) Creates a seed, a short, plausible beginning, to initialize surface realization, e.g., '*yesterday i went grocery shopping*'. (3) Iteratively calls the surface realization module to perform a beam search (see, e.g., Sutskever et al., 2014) and generate a complete story. (4) Removes occasional (approx. once per thousand to-

kens) excessive repetitions in the generated story. More precisely, when a word or phrase is repeated at least three times, the third repetition would be deleted. e.g., 'i like the tree very very very much' becomes 'i like the tree very very much'. The generation terminates when the agenda is exhausted and a sentence-terminating punctuation is generated.

4.1 The Agenda Generator

Given a scenario, the *agenda generator* goes through the temporal script graph and samples a path through it. For the example given in Figure 2, the path would start out with "choose recipe" and continue with either "get ingredients" or "buy ingredients", followed by "add ingredients", until the end of the graph is reached. The *agenda generator* also decides whether each event should be realized. In natural stories, narrators usually do not mention all of the events, and this component enables our model to mimic this behavior: the probability of event realization depends on the likelihood of the event given its predecessor $p(e|e')$, which is estimated on the training data using an event bigram model. To avoid excessive discontinuity in the realization, the *agenda generator* is prohibited to skip two consecutive events. The outcome of this process is an agenda, a plausible sequence of events.

Due to its symbolic nature, the *agenda generator* demands no extra training data, which is crucial for reducing the demand of data. Moreover, as the agenda generation is fully transparent and interpretable, we gain fair controllability over the content. For example, dropping a specific event from the agenda would cause the generation to skip it. Actually, it is also possible to use the surface realization module independently and generate a story from an event sequence as input.

4.2 The Neural Surface Realization Module

Our neural surface realization module is a GRU (Cho et al., 2014) language model, modified to enable two additional functionalities. (1) Conditioning the prediction of the successive word on the generation progress. (2) Determining whether the current event has been completely verbalized. If so, the surface realization module shifts its focus one event onward along the agenda and begins to instantiate the next event. See Figure 3 for a conceptual illustration.

(I)$^{(1)}$P_bather [decided]$_{E\_wash}$ to take a (bath)$^{(2)}$P_bath yesterday afternoon after working out . Once (I)$^{(1)}$P_bather got back home , (I)$^{(1)}$P_bather [walked]$_{E\_enter\_bathroom}$ to (my)$^{(1)}$P_bather (bathroom)$^{(3)}$P_bathroom and first quickly scrubbed the (bathroom tub)$^{(4)}$P_bathtub by [turning on]$_{E\_turn\_water\_on}$ the (water)$^{(5)}$P_water and rinsing (it)$^{(4)}$P_bathtub clean with a rag . After (I)$^{(1)}$P_bather finished , (I)$^{(1)}$P_bather [plugged]$_{E\_close\_drain}$ the (tub)$^{(4)}$P_bathtub and began [filling]$_{E\_fill\_water}$ (it)$^{(4)}$P_bathtub with warm (water)$^{(5)}$P_water set at about 98 (degrees)$^{(6)}$P_temperature .

Figure 1: An excerpt from a story on TAKING A BATH in the InScript corpus taken from Modi et al. (2017b). The referring expressions are in parentheses, and the corresponding discourse referent label is given by the superscript. Referring expressions of the same discourse referent have the same color and superscript number. Script-relevant events are in square brackets and colored in orange. Event types are indicated by the subscripts.

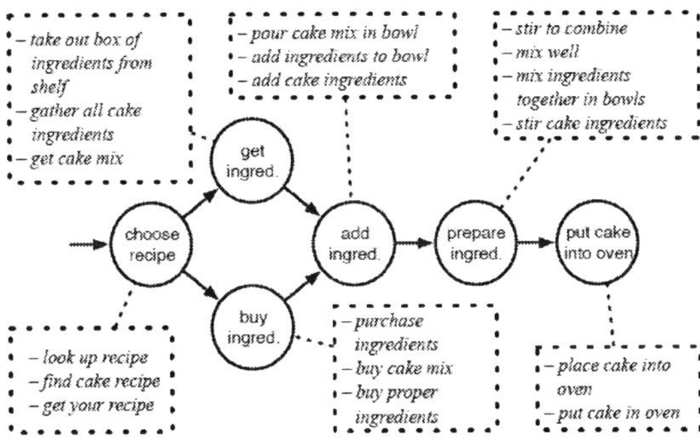

Figure 2: The *Temporal Script Graphs* for the BAKING A CAKE script induced from the InScript corpus, taken from (Wanzare et al., 2017). The nodes are the event clusters whereas the dashed boxes include some possible utterances that correspond to these clusters.

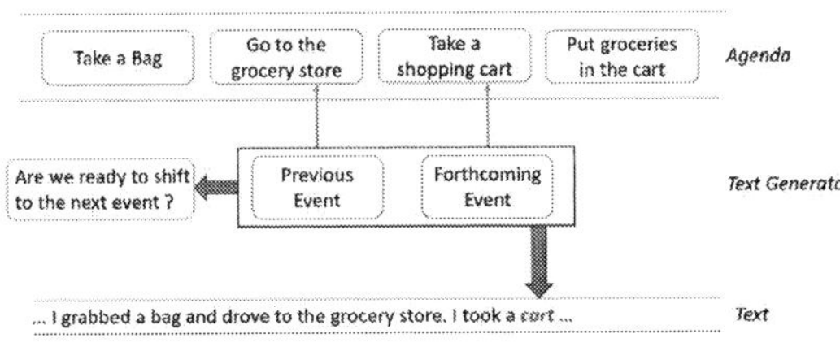

Figure 3: An illustration of the surface realization module. It produces two outputs: a distribution over the vocabulary that predicts the successive word, and a boolean-valued variable that indicates whether the generation should move to the next event.

For the first functionality (see Figure 4 for the model architecture), we condition the prediction of the next word on both the previously instantiated event (the ***preceding event***) and the event that should be verbalized now (the ***forthcoming event***). Intuitively, the surface realization module will be informed with something like '*I have taken a shopping cart, now tell me how to get my groceries*'. We train a dense vector representation for each event in the corpus, which we term ***event vectors***. To condition the surface realization on the events, we grant the generator access to the

event vectors e_t^p of the *preceding* event and e_t^f of the *forthcoming* event:

$$d_t = Softmax(D[o_t; e_t^p; e_t^f])$$

here d_t is the output distribution that predicts the successive word; D is an affine transformation; ';' stands for vector concatenation; $o_t = W h_t$ is the content from the GRU language model where h_t is the GRU cell states, and W is another affine transformation. To further relate the surface realization with the generation progress, we concatenate the event vectors with the embedding of previous word as the input to the GRUs:

$$h_t = GRU([x_{t-1}; e_{t-1}^p; e_{t-1}^f])$$

As a direct consequence, we need to train dense vector representations of all words in the vocabulary. This is quite ambitious, as the corpus is fairly small-scale (about 238k tokens). To alleviate this data sparsity issue, we initialize our word embeddings with Google's pre-trained word2vec vectors[1] (see, e.g., Mikolov et al., 2013). The effectiveness of this domain-adaptation method in language modelling is observed in Zhang et al. (2016). As a side effect, our word embedding dimensionality is fixed at 300.

To determine whether the *forthcoming event* has been instantiated, i.e. whether the model is ready to move onwards, we integrate a binary classifier into the architecture:

$$a_t = Softmax(A[h_t; e_t^p; e_t^f])$$

here A is a projection matrix; a_t is a 2-dimensional vector. If $a^1 > a^0$, the surface realization module decides that the *forthcoming event* has been completely narrated and it should move one event onwards to continue the generation; otherwise, it stick with the current *forthcoming event* to complete its instantiation.

[1]https://drive.google.com/file/d/0B7XkCwpI5KDYN1NUTT1SS21pQmM/edit

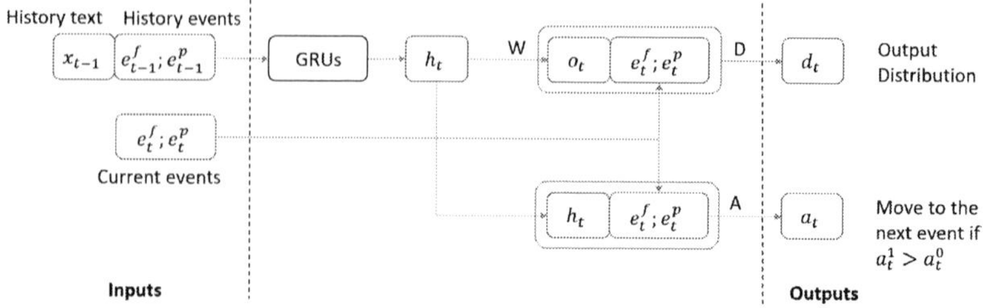

Figure 4: An illustration of the surface realization model architecture. It exploits a multi-task learning framework: it outputs the distribution over the next token d_t, as well as a_t, which determines whether to shift to the next event.

As there are more tokens than events in the corpus, the aforementioned binary classification is biased. The ratio between the categories is about $0.85 : 0.15$. To balance the performance on both categories, we apply greater weight on the loss of the less frequent category. More concretely, we measure a weighted cross-entropy loss on output a_t:

$$L_a(a_t, a_t^*; \gamma) = \begin{cases} -(1-\gamma)\log a_t^0, & a_t^* = (1,0) \\ -\gamma \cdot \log a_t^1, & a_t^* = (0,1) \end{cases}$$

here a_t^* is the ground truth; the weight coefficient γ is a hyper-parameter. All in all, the surface realization module exploits a multi-task learning architecture. The final loss function is

$$L(a_t, a_t^*, d_t, d_t^*; \gamma, \beta) = H(d_t, d_t^*) + \beta \cdot L_a(a_t, a_t^*; \gamma)$$

where $H(\cdot, \cdot)$ denotes the cross entropy between the parameters; d_t^* is the ground truth distribution of the next word (herein: a one-hot vector); β is another hyper-parameter.

It is worth noting that we did not incorporate explicit sentence planning, but completely rely on the surface realization module to perform sentence segmentation. The underlying reason is the absence of a clear correspondence between the agenda events and the sentences: multiple events could appear in a single sentence; likewise, multiple sentences could be devoted to one single event. We count on the surface realization module to punctuate correctly and generate syntactically correct sentences.

5 Experiments

5.1 Experimental Set-up and Optimization

2.5% of the data were randomly selected as the validation set; the rest was kept as the training set. As evaluation will be up to humans instead of any test set metric (see section 5.2), no test set is necessary.

The model was implemented with Python 3.5. The neural network part of the model was implemented with Keras 2.1.2 (Chollet et al., 2015). Optimization was performed with adam optimizer (Kingma and Ba, 2014) with gradient clipping to stabilize the training (see Pascanu et al., 2013). To regularize the model, dropout (Srivastava et al., 2014) was applied to all dense connections, including the explicit dense layers and the fully-connected layers within the GRU cells; besides, we applied early stopping, which monitors the loss function as is defined in section 4.2.

Hyper-parameters are tuned with a two-stage random hyper-parameter search, which is empirically proven more effective than grid search (see Bergstra and Bengio, 2012). On the validation set, the model yields a 0.90 accuracy and a 0.75 $F1$ score on the binary classification task concerning output a (whether to shift to the next event; see section 5.3.1 for some discussion on its consequences) and a 38.9 perplexity for predicting the next word. [2].

5.2 Evaluation

5.2.1 Model Variants

We re-implemented the neural checklist model by Kiddon et al. (2016) as a baseline. We decided not to use Martin et al. (2018) because the sentences it generates are not lexicalized, i.e. they include word categories like `entity.n.01`, which is not directly suitable for human evaluation. Substituting these category labels with surface language is substantially more difficult for our domain than theirs. We also included a human ceiling and sev-

---

[2]In case of interest in reproducing our result, appendix A provides full details on hyper-parameter tuning; the code is available at `https://github.com/arkgithubforyou/story_generation`

eral ablated versions of our final model into the human evaluation. To follow is a list of the systems we evaluated.

- **Human Author**
  Stories directly taken from the `InScript` corpus. Expected to produce an upper bound of the evaluation.

- **Full**
  Our model as is described in section 4.

- **GRU**
  A plain GRU language model trained on `InScript`, intended to be a baseline that has no specific global coherence control. Its generations are seeded with scenario-specific beginnings for some relevance. For example, the seed for the `Going Grocery Shopping` script is '*yesterday i went grocery shopping .*'

- **Neural Checklist**
  The *neural checklist* model as is described in Kiddon et al. (2016). We applied a post-processing similar to the one described in section 4 to clean up the repetitions.

- **Random Event Order**
  A variant of our model with the *agenda generator* ablated. As a substitution, the agendas are now generated by randomly sampling a sequence of events from the set of events corresponding to the respective script. We compare this variant with the `full` model to verify the contribution of the *agenda generator* in implementing global coherence.

For some intuition, see table 1 for sample generations from these systems.

5.2.2 Evaluation Method

Automatic evaluation of text quality, especially its global coherence, is a challenging task (see, e.g. Lapata and Barzilay, 2005; Purdy et al., 2018, for some meaningful attempts though). We also observed poor correlations between a few automatic metrics and the results of human evaluation (see appendix C for more details), and decided that automatic metrics are not suitable for our task. Thus we performed human evaluation through crowdsourcing; it evaluates the following aspects of generated stories.

- **Syntax**
  The syntactical correctness of the sentences.

- **Global Coherence**
  The global coherence of a story with regard to the given script, e.g., GOING GROCERY SHOPPING. We evaluate from three aspects: *Inclusion* (does the story cover the most necessary steps about the topic?), *Relevance* (does the story stay on-topic, and rarely mention anything irrelevant to the topic?), and *Order* (does the story describe the activities relevant to the topic in a plausible order?)

- **Agenda Coverage**
  The correspondence between the generated story and the agenda it was fed with. The participants were asked whether each of the agenda items has been realized in the story.

We ask participants five questions per story: for *Agenda Coverage*, participants were asked to check off the agenda items that were mentioned in the story they saw; for the other four aspects, participants were asked to rate on a 1 to 4 scale. The evaluation experiment was implemented with Lingoturk (Pusse et al., 2016); we hired participants and conducted the experiment on Prolific[3]. See appendix B for more details on conducting the experiment of human evaluation.

5.3 Results

5.3.1 Human Evaluation

Table 2 illustrates the results from human evaluation. The GRU model, a plain language model without coherence modeling, yields the worst performance on all metrics. The output wildly changes between topics and is incoherent globally; the poor coherence probably also negatively affects human judgments on syntactic correctness. The neural checklist saw better performance than plain GRUs, but it failed to include the most necessary steps of the scenario. It seems the model cannot correctly track the progress of the generation, which, as discussed in section 1, we suspect to be a consequence of the limited amount of training data: as its attention-based content-planning cannot make use of the order information and has to learn it from data, the model (and probably also other attention-based models) has a substantially higher demand on training data.

---

[3] `https://prolific.ac/`

GRU
yesterday i went grocery shopping . i did n't know anything all the items in my cart , so that it was ready to pick up up . i got my items off , and found it to the front of the store . i was on narita shopping cart because i had less than twenty of them . i grabbed my cart and went to the cashier . i paid for the items , then i gave the cashier my money and my bag , checked my bags up , and the other items in my hand bag . i am glad i 'm flying for my plane and go through security .

Neural Checklist
yesterday i wanted to go grocery shopping . when i went to the front of the store , i went to the grocery store and drove to the front of the store . i went to the cashier and drove to the front desk .

Random Event Order
yesterday i went grocery shopping . i grabbed a shopping cart and put the items on the list . i put my items in the cart and drove to the store . i drove to the grocery store and went to the grocery store . i made a list of all the items i would need . i put my items on the cart and headed to the store . when i entered the store , i grabbed a shopping cart and walked inside . i put the cart away in the cart .
Agenda: *evoking→ take shop cart→ put conveyor→ get groceries→ go grocery→ move section→ make list→ check off→ put conveyor→ leave→ enter→ take shop cart→ enter→ return shop cart→ story ends*

Full
yesterday i went grocery shopping . i made a list of my list and drove to the grocery store . when i entered the store , i grabbed a shopping cart and pushed the cart down to the meat aisle . i got all my items , and crossed items on my list . i went to the checkout register and paid for my groceries . i put my groceries in my cart and left .
Agenda: *evoking→make list→go to store→enter→take cart→move along sections→take grocery→check list→go to checkout→pay→pack grocery→leave→ story ends*

Human Author
yesterday i went grocery shopping . i took my grocery list with me , along with some reusable shopping bags . my grocery list has all the items i want to buy on it . i selected a shopping cart from in front of the store , and went inside . i put my reusable bags in the cart . i looked at my list and started in the produce section . i put different vegetables and fruits into my cart . next i wheeled my cart to the cereal aisle and took a box of cereal . i went through the store aisle by aisle and selected my groceries . each aisle is organized by types of food and non-food items . one aisle has dried pasta , canned tomatoes , rice , and sauce . i selected a few boxes of pasta and some rice . another aisle carries plastic wrap , trash bags , and aluminum foil . as i went through the store , i kept looking at my list to see what i needed next . when i added each item to my cart , i crossed it off my list . my last stop was the dairy aisle where i got milk and eggs . when i had all the groceries i wanted , i went to the cash register ans stood in line . when it was my turn , i put each item on the conveyor belt and the cashier scanned each one . a bagger put all of the groceries into my reusable bags . i paid , and then the cashier gave me a receipt . i loaded the bags of groceries into the trunk of my car and drove home .

Table 1: Sample generations by different models on GOING GROCERY SHOPPING. The corresponding seeds are displayed in boldface. **Neural Checklist, Full** used the same agenda, which is given in the table.

	Agenda Coverage**	Syntax	Inclusion	Order	Relevance
human author	86%	0.86	0.91	0.93	0.83
full	**71%**	**0.75**	**0.67**	**0.75**	**0.88**
random event order	50%	0.45	0.46	0.14*	0.71
Neural Checklist	20%	0.54	0.34	0.27	0.53
GRU	n/a	0.33	0.24	0.11*	0.22

*: difference between the pair is not statistically significant due to paired T-test on a significant level $\alpha = 0.05$.

**: answers to the agenda coverage questions yield a Fleiss' kappa of 0.34.

Table 2: Results from human evaluation. Highest scores out of automatic systems are displayed in boldface.

Human Author : event *'make a shopping list'* in scenario *'going grocery shopping'*
... next , i used the wipes the store provides at the entrance and wipe off the handle of the shopping cart , and my hands , so i know my hands will stay clean while i choose my food . then ***i took out the shopping list i wrote at home*** and i started . i always start with heavy things ...
Full Model : event *'place fertilizer'* in scenario *'planting a tree'*
... yesterday i planted a tree. first , i decided to buy a small apple tree . i got a shovel and drove to the home . i found a perfect spot in my backyard and dug a hole . ***i put*** the soil in the hole and then watered it . ...

Table 3: Examples where instantiations of agenda items failed to be approved by evaluators. Up: event instantiation that was not explicit enough; down: event that was not instantiated due to an error in the output a from the surface realization module.

The `Full` model was able to significantly outperform all other automatic variants and received positive scores for all criteria. It reflects well the events on the agenda and usually includes the most necessary steps of the scripts in a plausible order, which indicates decent global coherence. It even received a higher *relevance* score than `Human Author`. However, this may result from our model often producing shorter stories than the human originals, see section 5.3.2. Its *agenda coverage* score is lower than that of `Human Author`. We detected two sources of these errors: (1) event instantiations are sometimes not recognized as such by the participants, because they are not explicit enough; this is also the reason for why the agenda coverage score for the original human texts is less than 100%. (2) Errors in the event termination judgments of the surface realization module: when the surface realization module wrongly decided that the *forthcoming event* has been instantiated, it would simply skip the event in the generation. See table 3.

`Random Event Order` witnessed a dramatic performance drop compared to `Full`. Its order score is not significantly different from that of the `GRU` baseline. That means, particularly, our *agenda generator* was crucial for and capable of performing reliable text planning and incorporating global coherence. It retained high relevance score (i.e., it still stays on-topic), as the agendas it use were still about the respective scenarios. However, unexpectedly, the *inclusion* score and *syntax* score also saw a sharp drop. For that we noticed two possible origins. Firstly, it might result from a systematic error of human evaluation – the stories produced by the random model, violating global coherence, are in general messy and would make the assessment cognitively difficult. Thus they are likely to receive lower scores. Secondly, our surface realization is conditioned on a 'previous event / forthcoming event' pair, therefore, for less plausible agendas (e.g., one produced by a random agenda generator), the corresponding pairs would appear less frequently in our small-scale corpus, thus suffering more from data sparsity issues and affect the quality of surface realization.

5.3.2 Qualitative Analysis

Most noticeably, the stories our model generates are less elaborative than the corpus stories. From the samples in table 1, we could see that the story from the `full model` is much shorter than the one taken from the corpus. It turns out that our system often chose not to elaborate on an event: a genuine human would occasionally list what she bought from the grocery store, like vegetables, fruits, pasta, rice; whereas our system would only say *'i got my items'*. The most important reason behind this is that these elaborations are sparse, thus whenever our system sees *'i got my items'* in the history, it will decide that the event `take items` is already instantiated, and move onwards to the next event. Another reason for generating shorter stories is our *agenda generator* cannot correctly reproduce some real-world scenarios where the events 'cycle'. For example, the event chain corresponding to a story about `taking a bus` could occasionally look like *borad* $\rightarrow$ *ride* $\rightarrow$ *exit* $\rightarrow$ *board* $\rightarrow$ *ride* $\rightarrow$ *exit* $\rightarrow$ *board*..., when a passenger simply changes his bus a few times. Future work that incorporates an 'elaboration-level' control and more expressive script knowledge representation might be able to alleviate these issues.

5.3.3 Generalizability Aspects

Due to the stochastic nature of the *agenda generator*, the agendas it produces rarely coincide with the ones in the corpus (less than 0.1%). That means our model can successfully generate new script story lines.

In terms of generalizing to other domains, it is worth noting that events is not the only means of planning a story. Any category of words or symbolic information that could outline a story (conditioned on a specific topic), could take the role of events in our model and allow for the application of our approach. Examples include ingredient usages in a recipe, incidents in a football match, and progresses in a presidential election.

It is well observed that the `InScript` corpus we use contains massive manual annotation effort. However, we note the the event annotations we use is inherently a cluster of utterances that correspond to same script events. Thus it is feasible to substitute the event annotations in our method with predicate-argument structures, which could be acquired by dependency parsing.

6 Conclusion

To incorporate global coherence of story generation on small-scale corpora, we developed a novel, data-driven, hybrid model which exploits a latent intention variable to guide story generation. The model includes a symbolic *agenda generator* that performs text planning and is less demanding on data, and a neural surface realization module that accomplishes surface realization conditioned on the agenda. Our model outperformed various baselines according to the result of a human evaluation experiment which mostly focused on global coherence. The model could be generalized to other domains where words that indicate narration progress are available. Future work will include the exploration of some control over the level of elaboration and developing more expressive script knowledge representation to account for more complicated scripts.

References

James Bergstra and Yoshua Bengio. 2012. Random search for hyper-parameter optimization. *Journal of Machine Learning Research*, 13(Feb):281–305.

Stephan Busemann and Helmut Horacek. 1998. A flexible shallow approach to text generation. *arXiv preprint cs/9812018*.

Kyunghyun Cho, Bart van Merriënboer Caglar Gulcehre, Dzmitry Bahdanau, Fethi Bougares Holger Schwenk, and Yoshua Bengio. 2014. Learning phrase representations using rnn encoder–decoder for statistical machine translation. *arXiv preprint arXiv:1406.1078*.

François Chollet et al. 2015. Keras. `https://keras.io`.

Angela Fan, Mike Lewis, and Yann Dauphin. 2019. Strategies for structuring story generation. *arXiv preprint arXiv:1902.01109*.

Parag Jain, Priyanka Agrawal, Abhijit Mishra, Mohak Sukhwani, Anirban Laha, and Karthik Sankaranarayanan. 2017. Story generation from sequence of independent short descriptions.

Chloé Kiddon, Luke Zettlemoyer, and Yejin Choi. 2016. Globally coherent text generation with neural checklist models. In *Proceedings of the 2016 Conference on Empirical Methods in Natural Language Processing*, pages 329–339.

Diederik P Kingma and Jimmy Ba. 2014. Adam: A method for stochastic optimization. *arXiv preprint arXiv:1412.6980*.

Mirella Lapata and Regina Barzilay. 2005. Automatic evaluation of text coherence: Models and representations. In *IJCAI*, volume 5, pages 1085–1090.

Lara J. Martin, Prithviraj Ammanabrolu, Xinyu Wang, William Hancock, Shruti Singh, Brent Harrison, and Mark O. Riedl. 2018. Event representations for automated story generation with deep neural nets. In *Proceedings of the Thirty-Second AAAI Conference on Artificial Intelligence, Artificial Intelligence (EAAI-18), New Orleans, Louisiana, USA, February 2-7, 2018*, pages 868–875.

James Richard Meehan. 1976. The metanovel: writing stories by computer. Technical report, YALE UNIV NEW HAVEN CONN DEPT OF COMPUTER SCIENCE.

Hongyuan Mei, Mohit Bansal, and Matthew R Walter. 2015. What to talk about and how? selective generation using lstms with coarse-to-fine alignment. *arXiv preprint arXiv:1509.00838*.

Tomas Mikolov, Kai Chen, Greg Corrado, and Jeffrey Dean. 2013. Efficient estimation of word representations in vector space. *arXiv preprint arXiv:1301.3781*.

Ashutosh Modi, Tatjana Anikina, Simon Ostermann, and Manfred Pinkal. 2017a. Inscript: Narrative texts annotated with script information. *arXiv preprint arXiv:1703.05260*.

Ashutosh Modi, Ivan Titov, Vera Demberg, Asad Sayeed, and Manfred Pinkal. 2017b. Modeling semantic expectation: Using script knowledge for referent prediction. *arXiv preprint arXiv:1702.03121*.

Razvan Pascanu, Tomas Mikolov, and Yoshua Bengio. 2013. On the difficulty of training recurrent neural networks. In *International Conference on Machine Learning*, pages 1310–1318.

Nanyun Peng, Marjan Ghazvininejad, Jonathan May, and Kevin Knight. 2018. Towards controllable story generation. In *Proceedings of the First Workshop on Storytelling*, pages 43–49.

Ratish Puduppully, Li Dong, and Mirella Lapata. 2018. Data-to-text generation with content selection and planning. *arXiv preprint arXiv:1809.00582*.

Christopher Purdy, Xinyu Wang, Larry He, and Mark Riedl. 2018. Predicting generated story quality with quantitative measures. In *Fourteenth Artificial Intelligence and Interactive Digital Entertainment Conference*.

Florian Pusse, Asad Sayeed, and Vera Demberg. 2016. Lingoturk: managing crowdsourced tasks for psycholinguistics. In *Proceedings of the 2016 Conference of the North American Chapter of the Association for Computational Linguistics: Demonstrations*, pages 57–61.

Mark O Riedl and Robert Michael Young. 2010. Narrative planning: Balancing plot and character. *Journal of Artificial Intelligence Research*, 39:217–268.

Lifeng Shang, Zhengdong Lu, and Hang Li. 2015. Neural responding machine for short-text conversation. *arXiv preprint arXiv:1503.02364*.

Nitish Srivastava, Geoffrey Hinton, Alex Krizhevsky, Ilya Sutskever, and Ruslan Salakhutdinov. 2014. Dropout: A simple way to prevent neural networks from overfitting. *The Journal of Machine Learning Research*, 15(1):1929–1958.

Ilya Sutskever, Oriol Vinyals, and Quoc V Le. 2014. Sequence to sequence learning with neural networks. In *Advances in neural information processing systems*, pages 3104–3112.

Oriol Vinyals and Quoc Le. 2015. A neural conversational model. *arXiv preprint arXiv:1506.05869*.

Lilian Wanzare, Alessandra Zarcone, Stefan Thater, and Manfred Pinkal. 2017. Inducing script structure from crowdsourced event descriptions via semi-supervised clustering. In *Proceedings of the 2nd Workshop on Linking Models of Lexical, Sentential and Discourse-level Semantics*, pages 1–11.

Tsung-Hsien Wen, Milica Gasic, Dongho Kim, Nikola Mrksic, Pei-Hao Su, David Vandyke, and Steve Young. 2015. Stochastic language generation in dialogue using recurrent neural networks with convolutional sentence reranking. *arXiv preprint arXiv:1508.01755*.

Denis Yarats and Mike Lewis. 2017. Hierarchical text generation and planning for strategic dialogue. *arXiv preprint arXiv:1712.05846*.

Jian Zhang, Xiaofeng Wu, Andy Way, and Qun Liu. 2016. Fast gated neural domain adaptation: Language model as a case study. In *Proceedings of COLING 2016, the 26th International Conference on Computational Linguistics: Technical Papers*, pages 1386–1397.

A   Hyper-parameter Tuning

Hyper-parameters are tuned with a two stage random hyper-parameter search. In both stages we test 60 random hyper-parameter combinations; the 5 best-performing hyper-parameter combinations in the first stage decide the ranges from which the hyper-parameters combinations for the second stage were sampled. Table 4 shows the intervals that the hyper-parameters were sampled from in the first stage. Table 5 shows the hyper-parameters that we finally chose. Each training session takes 3 to 4 hours on a single TITAN X.

B   More Details on Human Evaluation

Four stories per model variant per script (that is, 200 stories in total) were randomly selected for evaluation. Each task included the assessment of five stories (one from each system); participants were compensated with 1.5GBP per task, which corresponds to a payment of approx. 7GBP per hour. For each of the stories, we collected the judgments of about 10 crowd-sourcing participants (about 400 participations in total). All participants were native English speakers. Submissions that left at least one question unanswered or fall beyond 3 standard deviations are excluded from the statistics. As a result, we received 1221 valid evaluation items in total.

C   Automatic Metrics

We attempted a few automatic metrics for evaluating the quality of generated stories proposed in the literature (see Lapata and Barzilay, 2005; Purdy et al., 2018), including `word overlap` (average of word overlap in consecutive sentences), `sentence vector` (average cosine of sentence vectors of consecutive sentences), `coreference rate` (proportion of entities refering to one already mentioned). The results and their correlation with human evaluation are shown in figure 6. Due to their poor correlation with human evaluation results, we decided not to rely on these metrics.

Hyper-parameter	Range	Sampling Criterion
dropout rate	$[0.2, 0.8]$	uniform*
learning rate	$[10^{-5}, 10^{-3}]$	exponential**
gradient norm threshold	$[1.0, 1000.0]$	exponential**
batch size	$[2^3, 2^{10}]$	uniform-p2***
context length	$[5, 100]$	uniform-int****
event embedding size	$[2^6, 2^{10}]$	uniform-p2***
RNN size	$[2^6, 2^{11}]$	uniform-p2***
β: weight on loss term L_a	$[1.0, 2.0]$	uniform*
γ: weight on category-1 cross-entropy	$[1.0, 6.0]$	uniform*

*: sampled from a uniform distribution over the range.

**: sampled from a truncated exponential distribution over the range. i.e., we sampled its logarithm from a uniform distribution.

***: sampled from a uniform distribution over the powers of 2 in the range.

****: sampled from a uniform distribution over all integers in the range.

Table 4: The initial ranges and sampling criteria of the random hyper-parameter search.

event embedding size	learning rate	context length	batch size	maximum gradient norm
512	$1.9e-5$	46	256	3.17
Dropout	GRU size	β	γ	
0.456	1024	1.01	5.46	

Table 5: The final choices of hyper-parameters. β is the weight applied on the output a and γ is weight applied on the loss of the less frequent category in the binary classification.

System	Word Overlap	Sentence Vector	Coreference Rate
human author	0.18(0.020)	0.62(0.019)	0.11(0.015)
full	0.27(0.030)[2]	0.89(0.029)[1]	0.00061(0.00070)
random event order	0.26(0.015)[2]	0.90(0.023)[1]	0.002(0.002)
GRU+Topic	0.35(0.11)	0.74 (0.078)	0.18(0.066)
GRU	0.26(0.018)	0.69(0.0080)	0.23(0.038)
corelation with human evaluation	-0.59	-0.05	-0.55

[1],[2]: differences between pairs are not statistically significant according to pair T-tests.

Table 6: Results from automatic evaluation, and their correlation with overall human evaluation results. Encoding some information about the text though they may, these scores are hardly informative about global coherence.

Guided Neural Language Generation for Automated Storytelling

Prithviraj Ammanabrolu, Ethan Tien, Wesley Cheung,
Zhaochen Luo, William Ma, Lara J. Martin, and Mark O. Riedl
School of Interactive Computing
Georgia Institute of Technology
Atlanta, GA, USA
`{raj.ammanabrolu, etien, wcheung8,`
`zluo, wma61, ljmartin, riedl}@gatech.edu`

Abstract

Neural network based approaches to automated story plot generation attempt to learn how to generate novel plots from a corpus of natural language plot summaries. Prior work has shown that a semantic abstraction of sentences called *events* improves neural plot generation and and allows one to decompose the problem into: (1) the generation of a sequence of events (event-to-event) and (2) the transformation of these events into natural language sentences (event-to-sentence). However, typical neural language generation approaches to event-to-sentence can ignore the event details and produce grammatically-correct but semantically-unrelated sentences. We present an ensemble-based model that generates natural language guided by events. Our method outperforms the baseline sequence-to-sequence model. Additionally, we provide results for a full end-to-end automated story generation system, demonstrating how our model works with existing systems designed for the event-to-event problem.

1 Introduction

Automated story plot generation is the problem of creating a sequence of main plot points for a story in a given domain. Generated plots must remain consistent across the entire story, preserve long-term dependencies, and make use of commonsense and schematic knowledge (Wiseman et al., 2017). Early work focused on symbolic planning and case-based reasoning (Meehan, 1977; Turner and Dyer, 1986; Lebowitz, 1987; Gervás et al., 2005; Porteous and Cavazza, 2009; Riedl and Young, 2010; Ware and Young, 2011; Farrell et al., 2019) at the expense of manual world domain knowledge engineering. Neural-network–based approaches to story and plot generation train a neural language model on a corpus of stories to predict the next character, word, or sentence in a

sequence based on a history of tokens (Jain et al., 2017; Clark et al., 2018; Fan et al., 2018; Martin et al., 2018; Peng et al., 2018; Roemmele, 2018).

The advantage of neural network based approaches is that there is no need for explicit domain modeling beyond providing a corpus of example stories. The primary pitfall of neural language model approaches to story generation is that the space of stories that can be generated is huge, which in turn, implies that in a textual story corpora any given sentence will likely only be seen once. Martin et al. (2018) propose the use of a semantic abstraction called *events*, demonstrating that it aids in reducing the sparsity of the dataset. They define an event to be a unit of a story that creates a world state change; specifically, an event is a tuple containing a subject, verb, direct object, and some additional disambiguation tokens.

The event representation enables the decomposition of the plot generation task into two sub-problems: *event-to-event* and *event-to-sentence*. Event-to-event is broadly the problem of generating the sequence of events that together comprise a plot. A model for addressing this problem is also responsible for maintaining plot coherence and consistency. These events are abstractions and aren't human-readable. Thus the second sub-problem, event-to-sentence, focuses on transforming these events into natural language sentences. This second sub-problem can also be viewed as *guided language generation*, using a generated event as a guide.

Martin et al. (2018) further propose that this latter event-to-sentence problem can be thought of as a translation task—translating from the language of events into natural language. We find, however, that the sequence-to-sequence LSTM networks (Sutskever et al., 2014) that they chose to address the problem frequently ignore the input event and only generate text based on the orig-

Proceedings of the Second Storytelling Workshop, pages 46–55
Florence, Italy, August 1, 2019. ©2019 Association for Computational Linguistics

inal corpus, overwriting the plot-based decisions made during event-to-event. There are two contributing factors. Firstly, event-to-event models tend to produce previously-unseen events, which, when fed into the event-to-sentence model results in unpredictable behavior. The mapping from an unseen event to a sentence is unknown to a basic sequence-to-sequence model. Secondly, sentences are often only seen once in the entire corpus. Despite being converted into events, the sparsity of the data means that each event is still likely seen a very limited number of times.

The contributions of the paper are thus twofold. We present an ensemble-based system for event-to-sentence that allows for guided language generation and demonstrate that this outperforms a baseline sequence-to-sequence approach. Additionally, we present the results of a full end-to-end story generation pipeline as originally proposed by Martin et al. (2018) (Figure 1), showing how all of the sub-systems can be integrated.

2 Related Work

Early storytelling systems were based on symbolic planning (Pérez y Pérez and Sharples, 2001; Riedl and Young, 2010; Meehan, 1977; Lebowitz, 1987; Ware and Young, 2011) and case-based reasoning (Turner and Dyer, 1986; Pérez y Pérez and Sharples, 2001; Gervás et al., 2005). These systems required a high knowledge-engineering overhead in terms of operators or stories transcribed into symbolic form. Consequently, these systems were only capable of generating stories in relatively limited domains.

Machine learning approaches attempt to learn domain information from a corpus of story examples (Swanson and Gordon, 2012; Li et al., 2013). Recent work has looked at using recurrent neural networks (RNNs) for story and plot generation. Roemmele and Gordon (2018) use LSTMs with skip-though vector embeddings (Kiros et al., 2015) to generate stories. Khalifa et al. (2017) train an RNN on a highly specialized corpus, such as work from a single author.

Fan et al. (2018) introduce a form of hierarchical story generation in which a premise is first generated by the model and is then transformed into a passage. This is a form of guided generation wherein a single sentence of guidance is given. Similarly, Yao et al. (2019) decompose story generation into planning out a storyline and then generating a story from it. Our work differs in that we use an event-to-event process that provides guidance to event-to-sentence.

3 Event-to-Event Implementation

In order to create a full improvisational storytelling pipeline, we first needed to implement an event-to-event model such that generated events can be inputted into our event-to-sentence system. Martin et al. (2018) showed that the performance on both event-to-event and event-to-sentence improves when using an abstraction known as an *event* is used instead of natural language sentences.

In our work, events are defined as a 5-tuple of $\langle s, v, p, o, m \rangle$ where v is a verb, s is the subject of the verb, o is the object, p is the corresponding preposition, and m can be a modifier, prepositional object, or indirect object—any of which can be absent. All elements are stemmed and generalized with the exception of the preposition. We follow the same generalization process as Martin et al. (2018), using enumerated named entity recognition tags, VerbNet (Schuler and Kipper-Schuler, 2005) v3.3 to generalize the verbs, and WordNet (Miller, 1995) v3.1 for the nouns.

Our event-to-event system is the policy gradient deep reinforcement learner from Tambwekar et al. (2019). Briefly, the technique starts with a sequence-to-sequence LSTM model trained to perform the event-to-event task. It is trained on a sequence of "eventified" plot summaries. Using the REINFORCE algorithm (Williams, 1992), we backpropagate a reward based on how close the generated event is to a pre-trained goal. Here, we are using genre-appropriate verbs (specifically, VerbNet classes) as goals—verbs that appear often at the end of the stories in our dataset. The reward is the product of the distance of each verb from the goal verb by the normalized frequency of how often the verb occurs before the goal verb in stories. Details of how the reward is calculated are given in Tambwekar et al. (2019).

The final event-to-event network is then placed into the pipeline as the "Event-to-Event" module, seen in Figure 1, and its output is fed into the following event-to-sentence models during testing.

4 Event-to-Sentence

We define event-to-sentence to be the problem of selecting a sequence of words $s_t = s_{t_0}, s_{t_1}, ..., s_{t_k}$

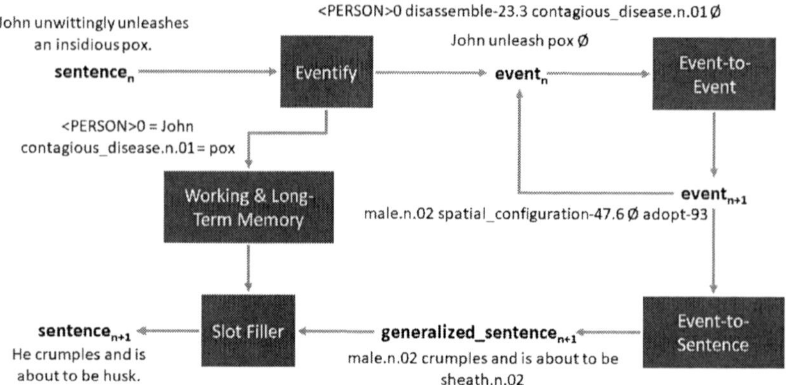

Figure 1: The full automated story generation pipeline illustrating an example where the event-to-event module generates only a single following event.

given the current input event e_t, i.e. the current sentence is generated based on maximizing $Pr(s_t|e_t; \theta)$ where θ refers to the parameters of the generative system. The eventification in Section 3 is a lossy process in which some of the information from the original sentence is dropped. Thus, the task of event-to-sentence involves filling in this missing information. There is also no guarantee that the event-to-event process will produce an event that is part of the event-to-sentence training corpus, simply due to the fact that the space of potential generated events is very large; the correct mapping from the generated event to a natural language sentence would be unknown.

In prior work, Martin et al. (2018) use a sequence-to-sequence LSTM neural network to translate events into sentences. Even with the "split and pruned" sentences that they create—which we also use (see Section 5)—we find that this vanilla sequence-to-sequence technique is not robust to the afore-mentioned challenges. We observe that a sequence-to-sequence network ends up operating as a simple language model and often ignores the input event when generating a sentence. The generated sentence is usually grammatically correct, but retains little of the semantic meaning given by the event.

We thus look for other forms of guided neural language generation, with the goals of preserving the semantic meaning from the event in addition to keeping the generated sentences interesting. We propose four different models—optimized towards these two objectives, and a baseline fifth model that is used as a fallthrough: (1) a retrieve-and-edit model based on Hashimoto et al. (2018);

(2) template filling; (3) sequence-to-sequence with Monte Carlo beam decoding; (4) sequence-to-sequence with a finite state machine decoder; and (5) vanilla sequence-to-sequence. We find that none of these models by themselves can successfully find a balance between the goals of *retaining all of the event tokens* and *generating interesting output*. However, each of the models possess their own strengths and weaknesses—each model essentially being optimized towards a different point on the spectrum between the two goals. We thus combine these models into an ensemble in an attempt to minimize the weaknesses of each individual model and achieve a balance between retaining semantic meaning from the event and generating interesting sentences.

In all of the following experiments, the task is to translate events into "generalized" sentences. A generalized sentence is one in which nouns are replaced by WordNet Synsets.

4.1 Retrieve-and-Edit

The first model is based on the retrieve-and-edit framework for predicting structured outputs (Hashimoto et al., 2018), which we will refer to as *RetEdit*. We first learn a task-specific similarity between event tuples by training an encoder-decoder to map each event onto an embedding that can reconstruct the output sentence; this is our retriever model. Next, we train an editor model which maximizes the likelihood of generating the target sentence given both the input event and a retrieved event-sentence example pair. We used a standard sequence-to-sequence model with attention and copying (Gu et al., 2016) to stand in as our editor architecture. Although this framework was initially applied to the generation of GitHub Python code and Hearthstone cards, we extend this technique to generate sentences from our event tuples. Specifically, we first initialize a new set of word embeddings with GLoVe (Pennington et al., 2014), using random initialization for out-of-vocabulary words. We use our training set to learn weights for the retriever and editor models, set confidence thresholds for the model with the validation set, and evaluate performance using the test set.

In order to generate a sentence from a given input event, there are two key phases: the "retrieve" phase and the "edit" phase. With respect to the input event, we first retrieve the nearest-neighbor event and its corresponding sentence in the training set using the retriever model. Then, passing both the retrieved event-sentence pair and the input event as inputs, we use the editor model to generate a sentence using beam search. Many of the successes produced by the model stem from its ability to retain the complex sentence structures that appear in our training corpus. However, this interaction with the training data can also prove to be a major drawback of the method; target events that are distant in the embedding space from training examples typically result in poor sentence quality.

Since RetEdit relies heavily on having good examples, we set the confidence of the retrieve-and-edit model to be proportional to $1 - retrieval$ $distance$ when generating sentences as a lower retrieve distance implies greater confidence. We also observe that our mapping from event to sentence is not a one-to-one function. There are occasionally multiple sentences that map to a single event, resulting in retrieval distances of 0.In this case, the example sentence is returned without any modifications.

4.2 Sentence Templating

As mentioned earlier, the baseline sequence-to-sequence network operates as a simple language model and can often ignore the input event when generating a sentence. However, we know that our inputs, an event tuple will have known parts of speech.We created a simplified grammar for the

syntax of sentences generated from events:

$$S \rightarrow NP \quad v \quad (NP) \quad (PP)$$
$$NP \rightarrow d \quad n$$
$$PP \rightarrow p \quad NP$$

where d is a determiner that will be added and the rest of the terminal symbols correspond to an argument in the event, with n being s, o, or m, depending on its position in the sentence. The resulting sentence would be $[\_\_ \, s]\{v \, [\_\_ \, o] \, [p \_\_ m]\}$ where blanks indicate where words must be added to make a complete sentence.

First, our algorithm predicts the most likely VerbNet frame based on the contents of the input event (how many and which arguments are filled). VerbNet provides a number of syntactic structures for different verb classes based on how the verb is being used. For example, if the input event contains 2 nouns and a verb without a preposition, we assume that the output sentence takes the form of [NP V NP], but if it has 2 nouns, a verb, *and* a proposition, then it should be [NP V PP].

Second, we apply a Bidirectional LSTM (BiLSTM) language model trained on the generalized sentences in our training corpus. Given a word, we can generate words before and after it, within a particular phrase as given by some of the rules above, and concatenate the generated sentence fragments together. Specifically, we use the AWD-LSTM (Merity et al., 2018) architecture as our language model since it is currently state-of-the-art.

At decode time, we continue to generate words in each phrase until we reach a stopping condition: (1) reaching a maximum length (to prevent run-on sentences); or (2) generating a token that is indicative of an element in the next phrase, for example seeing a verb being generated in a noun phrase. When picking words from the language model, we noticed that the words "the" and "and" were extremely common. To increase the variety of the sentences, we sample from the top k most-likely next words and enforce a number of grammar-related rules in order to keep the coherence of the sentence. For example, we do not allow two determiners nor two nouns to be generated next to each other.

One can expect that many of the results will look structurally similar. However, with this approach, we can guarantee that the provided tokens in the event will appear in the generated sentence. To determine the confidence of the model for each sentence, we sum the loss after each generated token, normalize to sentence length, and subtract from 1 as higher loss translates to lower confidence.

4.3 Monte-Carlo Beam Search

Our third method is an adaptation of *Monte Carlo Beam Search* (Cazenave, 2012) for event-to-sentence. We train a sequence-to-sequence model on pairs of events and generalized sentences. At decoding time, we run Monte Carlo beam search as an alternative search strategy within the decoder network. This method differs from traditional beam search in that it introduces another scoring term that is used to re-weigh all the beams at each timestep.

After top-scoring words are outputted by the model at each time step, playouts are done from each word, or *node*. A node is the final token of the partially-generated sequences on the beam currently and the start of a new playout. During each playout, one word is sampled from a softmax produced at each step over all words in the vocabulary. The decoder network is unrolled until it reaches the "end-of-story" tag. Then, the previously-generated sequence and the sequence generated from the current playout are concatenated together and passed into a scoring function that computes the current playout's score.

The scoring function is a combination of (1) BLEU scores up to 4-grams between the input event and generated sentence, as well as (2) a weighted 1-gram BLEU score between each item in the input event and generated sentence. The weights combining the 1-gram BLEU scores are learned during validation time where the weight for each word in the event that *does not* appear in the final generated sequence gets bumped up. Multiple playouts are done from each word and the score s for the current word is computed as:

$$s_t = \alpha * s_{t-1} + (1 - \alpha) * AVG(playout_t) \quad (1)$$

where α is a constant.

In the end, k of the partial sequences with highest playout scores are kept as the current beam. For the ensemble, this model's confidence score is the final score of the highest-scoring end node.

Monte Carlo beam search excels at creating diverse output. Since the score for each word is based on playouts that sample based on weights at each timestep, it is possible for the output to be different across runs. The Monte Carlo beam decoder has been shown to generate better sentences that are more grammatically-correct than the other techniques in our ensemble, while sticking more to the input than a traditional beam decoder. However, there is no guarantee that all input event tokens will be included in the final output sentence.

4.4 Finite State Machine Constrained Beams

Beam search in its various forms, including Monte Carlo playouts, cannot ensure that the tokens from an input event appear in the outputted sentence. As such, we adapted the algorithm to fit such lexical constraints. Anderson et al. (2016) adapted beam search to fit captions for images, with the lexical constraints coming from sets of image tags. The method they devised, which they named *Constrained Beam Search*, used finite state machines to guide the beam search toward generating the desired tokens. This approach, which we have co-opted for event-to-sentence, attempts to achieve a balance between the flexibility and sentence quality typical of a beam search approach, while also adhering to the context and story encoded in the input events that more direct approaches (e.g. Section 4.2) would achieve.

The algorithm works on a per-event basis, beginning by generating a finite state machine. This finite state machine consists of states that enforce the presence of input tokens in the generated sentence. As an example, assume we have an n-token input event, $\{t_1, t_2, t_3, ..., t_n\}$. The corresponding machine consists of 2^n states. Each state maintains a search beam of size B^s with at most b output sequences, corresponding to the configured beam size s. At each time step, every state (barring the initial state) receives from predecessor states those output sequences whose last generated token matches an input event token. The state then adds to its beam the b most likely output sequences from those received.

In the example, generating token t_1 moves the current state from the initial state to the state corresponding to t_1, t_3 to a state for t_3, and so on. The states t_1 and t_3 then, after generating tokens t_1 and t_3 respectively, transmit said sequences to the state $t_{1,3}$. The states and transitions proceed as such until reaching the final state, wherein they have matched every token in the input event. Completed sequences in the final state contain all input event tokens, thus providing us with the ability to retain the semantic meaning of the event.

As much as the algorithm is based around balancing generating good sentences with satisfying lexical constraints, it does not perform particularly well at either. It is entirely possible, if not at all frequent, for generated sentences to contain all input tokens but lose proper grammar and syntax, or even fail to reach the final state within a fixed time horizon. This is exacerbated by larger tuples of tokens, seen even at just five tokens per tuple. To compensate, we relax our constraint to permit output sequences that have matched at least three out of five tokens from the input event. Still, at least some of the generated sentences will exhibit the problems mentioned above.

4.5 Ensemble

The entire event-to-sentence ensemble is designed as a cascading sequence of the four models above. We use the confidence scores generated by each of the models in order to re-rank the outputs of the individual models. This is done by setting a confidence threshold for each of the models such that if a confidence threshold fails, the next model in the cascade is tried. The thresholds are tuned by measuring the confidence scores generated on the validation set of the corpus. The cascading sequence is defined in the order that the individual models are presented above: (1) retrieve-and-edit, (2) sentence templating, (3) Monte Carlo beam search, (4) finite state constrained beam search, and (5) standard beam search. This structure also saves on computation as it sequentially queries each model, terminating early and returning an output sentence if the confidence threshold for any of the individual models are met.

The event first goes through the retrieve-and-edit framework, which generates a sentence and corresponding confidence score. We observe that this framework performs well when it is able to retrieve a sample from the training set that is relatively close in terms of retrieval distance to the input. Given the sparsity of the dataset, this happens with a relatively low probability, and so we place this model first in the sequence.

The next two models are each optimized towards one of our two main goals. The sentence templating approach retains all of the tokens within the event and so loses none of its semantic meaning, at the expense of generating a more interesting sentence. The Monte-Carlo approach, on the other hand, makes no guarantees regarding retaining the original tokens within the event but is capable of generating a diverse set of sentences. We thus cascade first to the sentence templating model and then the Monte-Carlo approach, implicitly placing greater importance on the goal of retaining the semantic meaning of the event.

The final model queried is the finite state machine constrained beam search. This model has no confidence score; either the model is successful in producing a sentence within the given length with the event tokens or not. In the case that the finite state machine based model is unsuccessful in producing a sentence, the final fallthrough model—the baseline sequence-to-sequence model with standard beam search decoding—is used.

5 Dataset

To aid in the performance of our story generation, we select a single genre: science fiction (sci-fi). We scraped long-running science fiction TV show plot summaries from the fandom wiki service *wikia.com*. This fandom wiki service contains longer and more detailed plot summaries than the dataset used in Tambwekar et al. (2019), both of which are qualities that we believe to be important for the overall story generation process. The corpus contains 2,276 stories in total, each an episode of a TV show. The average story length is 89.23 sentences. There are stories from 11 shows, with an average of 207 stories per show, from shows like *Doctor Who*, *Futurama*, and *The X-Files*. The data was pre-processed to simplify alien names in order to aid named entity recognition.

Then the sentences were split, partially following the "split-and-pruned" methodology of Martin et al. (2018). Sentences were split at S-bars and conjunctions separating S's, and the subject of the sentence was re-inserted in the new sentences. Once the sentences were split, they were "eventified" as described in Section 3. One benefit of having split sentences is that there is a higher chance of having a 1:1 correspondence between sentence and event, instead of a single sentence becoming multiple events. After the data is fully prepared, it is split in a 8:1:1 ratio to create the training, validation, and testing sets respectively.

6 Experiments

We perform two sets of experiments, one set evaluating our models on the event-to-sentence problem by itself, and another set intended to evaluate the full storytelling pipeline.

Each of the models in the event-to-sentence ensemble are trained on the training set in the sci-fi corpus. The exact training details for each of the models are as described above. Note that we present results for the generalized sentences instead of the sentences after slot-filling, as shown in Figure 1, to directly measure the output of the event-to-sentence ensemble. Additionally, all of the models in the ensemble slot-fill the verb automatically—filling a VerbNet class with a verb of appropriate conjugation—except for the sentence templating model which does verb slot-filling during post-processing.

After the models are trained, we pick the cascading thresholds for the ensemble by running the validation set through each of the models and generating confidence scores. This is done by running a grid search through a limited set of thresholds such that the overall BLEU-4 score (Papineni et al., 2002) of the generated sentences in the validation set is maximized. These thresholds are then frozen when running the final set of evaluations on the test set. For the baseline sequence-to-sequence method, we decode our output with a beam size of 5. We report perplexity and BLEU-4 scores, comparing against the gold standard from the test set. Perplexity is a measure of the predictive accuracy of a model and is calculated as:

$$Perplexity = 2^{-\sum_x p(x)\log_2 p(x)} \qquad (2)$$

where x is a token in the text, and

$$p(x) = \frac{count(x)}{\sum_{y \in Y} count(y)} \qquad (3)$$

where Y is the vocabulary. Our BLEU-4 scores are naturally low (where higher is better) because of the creative nature of the task—good sentences may not use any of the ground-truth n-grams.

The second experiment uses event sequences generated by our event-to-event system as summarized in Section 3. Our event-to-event system requires goals in the form of verb classes. For the science fiction data, common endings for stories are VerbNet classes like "escape-51.1", "discover-84", and "get-13.5.1". In this paper, we will use the goal "discover-84". We seed the event-to-event system with events extracted from the first sentences of stories found in the test set. The system then generates a sequence of events until it reaches

Model	Perplexity	BLEU	Length
RetEdit	71.354	0.041	9.27
Templates	203.629	0.0034	5.43
Monte Carlo	71.385	0.0453	7.91
FSM	104.775	0.0125	10.98
Seq2seq	103.176	0.0425	6.59
Ensemble	**70.179**	**0.0481**	9.22

Table 1: Perplexity and BLEU scores along with average sentence lengths, thresholds, and utilization percentages for event-to-sentence models on the test set.

the goal verb. We then present this sequence of events as well as the corresponding generalized sentences generated using our ensemble.

7 Results/Discussion

Model	Thresholds	Test Utilization	Pipeline Utilization
RetEdit	0.8	94.91%	55.71%
Templates	0.8	0.22%	0.91%
Monte Carlo	0.1	4.29%	41.10%
FSM	-	0.15%	0.68%
Seq2seq	-	0.43%	1.60%

Table 2: Thresholds and utilization percentages for the models on the test sets and on the events generated by the event-to-event system.

Our results are presented in the form of three tables. Table 1 shows the perplexity, BLEU-4 scores, and average sentence length for event-to-sentence on the testing set for each of the models, ensemble, and baseline. Note that some of the models, such as the sentence templates, ignore the idea of a gold standard sentence and are thus poorly optimized towards perplexity and BLEU scores. The ensemble, as predicted, still performs better than any of the individual models as it is designed to combine the models such that each of their weaknesses are minimized. The average sentence lengths highlight the differences between the models, with the templates producing the shortest sentences and the finite state machine taking longer to generate sentences due to the constraints it needs to satisfy. Table 2 shows the confidence thresholds after tuning the ensemble. The RetEdit and sentence template models need 80% confidence in their results, or the next model in the cascade is tried. Table 2 also shows how often each model in the ensemble is used generating sentences from the eventified testing corpus and from event-to-event. RedEdit was heavily used on the test set, likely due the train and test sets having a similar distribution of data. On the pipeline examples RetEdit is used much less—events generated by event-to-event may be very different from those in the training set. A majority of the events

Input Event	RetEdit	Templates	Monte Carlo	FSM	Gold Standard
⟨<PRP>, act-114-1-1, to, ∅, event.n.01⟩	<PRP> and <PERSON>0 move to the event.n.01 of the natural_object.n.01.	<PRP> act-114-1-1 to event.n.01.	<PRP> moves to the nearest natural_object.n.01.	physical_entity.n.01 move back to the phenomenon.n.01 of the craft.n.02...	<PRP> move to the event.n.01.
⟨<PERSON>2, send-11.1, through, <PERSON>6, <LOCATION>1⟩	<PERSON>2 sends <PERSON>6 through the <LOCATION>1.	The <PERSON>2 send-11.1 the <PERSON>6 through <LOCATION>1.	<PERSON>2 passes this undercover in the body_part.n.01 and collapses.	∅	In activity.n.01 to avoid <PRP> out.n.01 <PERSON>2 would transport <PERSON>6 through the <LOCATION>1.
⟨<PERSON>0, admire-31.2, ∅, <PERSON>3, ∅⟩	<PERSON>0 believes <PERSON>3.	<PERSON>0 admire-31.2 and <PERSON>3	<PERSON>0 hates <PERSON>3 saying <PRP> s not ready for duration.n.03 .	<PERSON>0 and <PERSON>0 comes in <PRP> content.n.05 for wrongdoing.n.02 and says <PERSON>0 has made on line.n.23 have made trait.n.01.	A pivotal artifact.n.01 in <PRP> act.n.02 is a examination.n.01 divised by <LOCATION>0 to make <PERSON>0 hate <PRP> <PERSON>3.

Table 3: Event-to-sentence examples for each model. ∅ represents an empty parameter; <PRP> is a pronoun.

Input Sentence	Extracted Event	Generated Events (Event-to-Event)	Generated Sentences (Event-to-Sentence; ensemble)
On Tatooine, Jabba the Hutt inspects the drone barge recently delivered to him.	⟨<ORGANIZATION>0, assessment-34.1, ∅, vessel.n.02, ∅⟩	⟨<PERSON>1, settle-36.1.2, ∅, indicator.n.03, indicator.n.03 ⟩; ⟨music.n.01, escape-51.1-1, from, ∅, ∅⟩; ⟨<PRP>, discover-84, to, run-51.3.2, progenitor.n.01⟩	The <ORGANIZATION>0 can not scan the vessel.n.02 of the <VESSEL>0. <PERSON>1 decides to be a little person.n.01 at the structure.n.01. the 'music.n.01 arrives. <PRP> finds a lonely person.n.01 on the upper one of the craft.n.02 which is not an personal_letter.n.01 but does not respond to hails .
Boba Fett has just chased down another bounty, a Rodian art dealer who sold fake works to Gebbu the Hutt.	⟨<PERSON>0, chase-51.6, ∅, bounty.n.04, ∅⟩	⟨<PERSON>0, chase-51.6, to, magnitude.n.01, ∅⟩; ⟨magnitude.n.01, comprehend-87.2, off, craft.n.02, magnitude.n.01⟩; ⟨<PERSON>2, amuse-31.1, off, ∅, ∅⟩; ⟨<PERSON>2, discover-84, off, change_of_integrity.n.01, ∅⟩	<PERSON>0 enters the bounty.n.04 and tells <PRP>. <PERSON>0 attaches the explosive.a.01 to the person.n.01 who is trying to fix the device.n.01 . the magnitude.n.01 doesn't know the craft.n.02 off the craft.n.02. <PERSON>2 is surprised when <PRP> learns that the person.n.01 is actually <PERSON>7 . <PERSON>2 sees the change_of_integrity.n.01 and tells <PRP>.

Table 4: End-to-end pipeline examples on previously-unseen input data.

that fall through RetEdit are caught by our Monte Carlo beam search, irrespective of the fact that RetEdit and sentence templates are most likely to honor the event tokens.

Table 3 presents concrete examples of the generalized sentence outputs of each of the event-to-sentence models and some trends are evident. Retrieve-and-Edit focuses on semantics at the expense of sentence quality. Sentence templates produces output that matches the input event but is very formulaic. Monte Carlo generates entertaining and grammatically-correct sentences, but occasionally loses the semantics of the input event. The finite state machine attempts to achieve a balance between semantics and generating entertaining output, however it sometimes fails to produce an output given the constraints of the state machine itself. We further present the results of an entire working pipeline in Table 4, demonstrating the event-to-sentence's ability to work with an existing plot generator.

8   Conclusions

Although event representations were shown in the past to improve performance on plot generation tasks—allowing for planning toward plot points,

we are faced with the problem of translating these events into syntactically- and semantically-sound sentences that are both interesting and keep the meaning of the original event. We have found that no one model is able to fully solve this task and so we present the combination of four approaches— each of which excel at and struggle with different aspects of the translation—into an ensemble.

RetEdit excels when the input event is drawn from a similar distribution as our training set, but the FSM approach does not depend on the distribution that the input is drawn from. The Sentence Templates generate semantically-sound sentences that are generic in structure, whereas Monte Carlo beam search generates more diverse output but is not guaranteed to retain the meaning of the input event. These models lie at different points on the spectrum between retaining meaning and generating interesting sentences. Future state-of-the-art sentence-filling techniques can also be added to the ensemble to account for the weaknesses of current models. This work completes the end-to-end story generation pipeline previously-conceived by Martin et al. (2018) and serves as a stepping stone for research in sentence expansion or event-to-sentence tasks.

References

Peter Anderson, Basura Fernando, Mark Johnson, and Stephen Gould. 2016. Guided open vocabulary image captioning with constrained beam search. In *Proceedings of the 2017 Conference on Empirical Methods in Natural Language Processing*, page 36945.

Tristan Cazenave. 2012. Monte Carlo Beam Search. *IEEE Transactions on Computational Intelligence and AI in games*, 4(1):68–72.

Elizabeth Clark, Yangfeng Ji, and Noah A. Smith. 2018. Neural Text Generation in Stories Using Entity Representations as Context. In *NAACL-HLT*.

Angela Fan, Mike Lewis, and Yann Dauphin. 2018. Hierarchical Neural Story Generation. In *Proceedings of the 56th Annual Meeting of the Association for Computational Linguistics*, pages 889–898.

R. Farrell, S. G. Ware, and L. J. Baker. 2019. Manipulating narrative salience in interactive stories using indexter's pairwise event salience hypothesis. *IEEE Transactions on Games*, pages 1–1.

Pablo Gervás, Belén Díaz-Agudo, Federico Peinado, and Raquel Hervás. 2005. Story plot generation based on CBR. *Knowledge-Based Systems*, 18(4-5):235–242.

Jiatao Gu, Zhengdong Lu, Hang Li, and Victor O. K. Li. 2016. Incorporating copying mechanism in sequence-to-sequence learning. *Association for Computational Linguistics (ACL)*.

Tatsunori B Hashimoto, Kelvin Guu, Yonatan Oren, and Percy Liang. 2018. A Retrieve-and-Edit Framework for Predicting Structured Outputs. In *32nd Conference on Neural Information Processing Systems (NeurIPS 2018)*, Montréal, Canada.

Parag Jain, Priyanka Agrawal, Abhijit Mishra, Mohak Sukhwani, Anirban Laha, and Karthik Sankaranarayanan. 2017. Story generation from sequence of independent short descriptions. In *SIGKDD Workshop on Machine Learning for Creativity (ML4Creativity)*.

Ahmed Khalifa, Gabriella A. B. Barros, and Julian Togelius. 2017. DeepTingle. In *International Conference on Computational Creativity*, page 8.

Ryan Kiros, Yukun Zhu, Ruslan R Salakhutdinov, Richard Zemel, Raquel Urtasun, Antonio Torralba, and Sanja Fidler. 2015. Skip-thought vectors. In *Advances in neural information processing systems*, pages 3294–3302.

Michael Lebowitz. 1987. Planning Stories. In *Proceedings of the 9th Annual Conference of the Cognitive Science Society*, pages 234–242.

Boyang Li, Stephen Lee-Urban, George Johnston, and Mark O. Riedl. 2013. Story generation with crowdsourced plot graphs. In *Proceedings of the Twenty-Seventh AAAI Conference on Artificial Intelligence*, AAAI'13, pages 598–604. AAAI Press.

Lara J. Martin, Prithviraj Ammanabrolu, Xinyu Wang, William Hancock, Shruti Singh, Brent Harrison, and Mark O. Riedl. 2018. Event Representations for Automated Story Generation with Deep Neural Nets. In *Thirty-Second AAAI Conference on Artificial Intelligence (AAAI-18)*, pages 868–875, New Orleans, Louisiana.

James R. Meehan. 1977. TALE-SPIN, an interactive program that writes stories. *Proceedings of the 5th international joint conference on Artificial intelligence*, 1:91–98.

Stephen Merity, Nitish Shirish Keskar, and Richard Socher. 2018. Regularizing and Optimizing LSTM Language Models. In *6th International Conference on Learning Representations, ICLR 2018*.

George A. Miller. 1995. WordNet: A Lexical Database for English. *Communications of the ACM*, 38(11):39–41.

Kishore Papineni, Salim Roukos, Todd Ward, and Wei-Jing Zhu. 2002. Bleu: a method for automatic evaluation of machine translation. In *Proceedings of the 40th annual meeting on association for computational linguistics*, pages 311–318. Association for Computational Linguistics.

Nanyun Peng, Marjan Ghazvininejad, Jonathan May, and Kevin Knight. 2018. Towards Controllable Story Generation. In *Proceedings of the First Workshop on Storytelling*, pages 43–49, New Orleans, Louisiana. Association for Computational Linguistics.

Jeffrey Pennington, Richard Socher, and Christopher Manning. 2014. Glove: Global vectors for word representation. In *Proceedings of the 2014 conference on empirical methods in natural language processing (EMNLP)*, pages 1532–1543.

Mike Pérez y Pérez and Rafael Sharples. 2001. MEXICA: A computer model of a cognitive account of creative writing. *Journal of Experimental & Theoretical Artificial Intelligence*, 13(2001):119–139.

Julie Porteous and Marc Cavazza. 2009. Controlling narrative generation with planning trajectories: The role of constraints. In *Joint International Conference on Interactive Digital Storytelling*, volume 5915 LNCS, pages 234–245. Springer.

Mark O Riedl and R Michael Young. 2010. Narrative Planning: Balancing Plot and Character. *Journal of Artificial Intelligence Research*, 39:217–267.

Melissa Roemmele. 2018. *Neural Networks for Narrative Continuation*. Ph.D. thesis, University of Southern California.

Melissa Roemmele and Andrew S Gordon. 2018. An Encoder-decoder Approach to Predicting Causal Relations in Stories. In *Proceedings of the First Workshop on Storytelling*, pages 50–59, New Orleans, Louisiana. Association for Computational Linguistics.

Karin Kipper Schuler and Karen Kipper-Schuler. 2005. *VerbNet: A Broad-Coverage, Comprehensive Verb Lexicon*. Ph.D. thesis, University of Pennsylvania.

Ilya Sutskever, Oriol Vinyals, and Quoc V. Le. 2014. Sequence to Sequence Learning with Neural Networks. In *Advances in Neural Information Processing Systems*, pages 3104–3112.

Reid Swanson and Andrew Gordon. 2012. Say Anything: Using textual case-based reasoning to enable open-domain interactive storytelling. *ACM Transactions on Interactive Intelligent Systems*, 2(3):16:1–16:35.

Pradyumna Tambwekar, Murtaza Dhuliawala, Animesh Mehta, Lara J. Martin, Brent Harrison, and Mark O. Riedl. 2019. Controllable Neural Story Plot Generation via Reward Shaping. *arXiv*, page 7.

Scott R Turner and Michael George Dyer. 1986. *Thematic knowledge, episodic memory and analogy in MINSTREL, a story invention system*. University of California, Computer Science Department.

Stephen Ware and R. Michael Young. 2011. Cpocl: A narrative planner supporting conflict. In *Proceedings of the 7th AAAI Conference on Artificial Intelligence and Interactive Digital Entertainment*.

Ronald J. Williams. 1992. Simple Statistical Gradient-Following Algorithms for Connectionist Reinforcement Learning. *Machine Learning*, 8(3):229–256.

Sam Wiseman, Stuart M. Shieber, and Alexander M. Rush. 2017. Challenges in data-to-document generation. In *Proceedings of the 2014 Conference on Empirical Methods in Natural Language Processing (EMNLP)*.

Lili Yao, Nanyun Peng, Ralph Weischedel, Kevin Knight, Dongyan Zhao, and Rui Yan. 2019. Plan-And-Write: Towards Better Automatic Storytelling. In *Proceedings of the Thirty-Third AAAI Conference on Artificial Intelligence (AAAI-19)*.

An Analysis of Emotion Communication Channels in Fan Fiction: Towards Emotional Storytelling

Evgeny Kim and **Roman Klinger**
Institut für Maschinelle Sprachverarbeitung
University of Stuttgart
Pfaffenwaldring 5b, 70569 Stuttgart, Germany
{evgeny.kim,roman.klinger}@ims.uni-stuttgart.de

Abstract

Centrality of emotion for the stories told by humans is underpinned by numerous studies in literature and psychology. The research in automatic storytelling has recently turned towards emotional storytelling, in which characters' emotions play an important role in the plot development (Theune et al., 2004; y Pérez, 2007; Méndez et al., 2016). However, these studies mainly use emotion to generate propositional statements in the form "*A feels affection towards B*" or "*A confronts B*". At the same time, emotional behavior does not boil down to such propositional descriptions, as humans display complex and highly variable patterns in communicating their emotions, both verbally and non-verbally. In this paper, we analyze how emotions are expressed non-verbally in a corpus of fan fiction short stories. Our analysis shows that stories written by humans convey character emotions along various non-verbal channels. We find that some non-verbal channels, such as facial expressions and voice characteristics of the characters, are more strongly associated with *joy*, while gestures and body postures are more likely to occur with *trust*. Based on our analysis, we argue that automatic storytelling systems should take variability of emotion into account when generating descriptions of characters' emotions.

1   Introduction and Motivation

As humans, we make sense of our experiences through stories (McKee, 2003). A key component of any captivating story is a character (Kress, 2005) and a key component of every character is emotion, as "without emotion a character's personal journey is pointless" (Ackerman and Puglisi, 2012, p. 1). Numerous works pinpoint the central role of emotions in storytelling (Hogan, 2015; Johnson-Laird and Oatley, 2016; Ingermanson and Economy, 2009), as well as story com-

prehension and evaluation (Komeda et al., 2005; Van Horn, 1997; Mori et al., 2019).

Emotion analysis and automatic recognition in text is mostly channel-agnostic, *i.e.*, does not consider along which non-verbal communication channels (face, voice, etc.) emotions are expressed. However, we know that the same emotions can be expressed non-verbally in a variety of ways (Barrett, 2017, p. 11), for example, through internal feelings of the character, as shown in Figure 1. We argue that automatic storytelling systems should take this information into account, as versatility of the emotion description is a prerequisite for engaging and believable storytelling (Ackerman and Puglisi, 2012, p. 3).

There is a growing body of literature in the field of natural language generation that uses emotions as a key component for automatic plot construction (Theune et al., 2004; y Pérez, 2007; Méndez et al., 2016) and characterization of virtual agents (Imbert and de Antonio, 2005; Dias and Paiva, 2011). However, these and other studies put an emphasis on emotion *per se* ("*A feels affection towards B*"), or on the social behavior of characters "*A confronts B*") making little or no reference to how characters express emotions, both verbally and non-verbally.

In this paper, we aim at closing this gap by analyzing how characters express their emotions using non-verbal communication signals. Specifi-

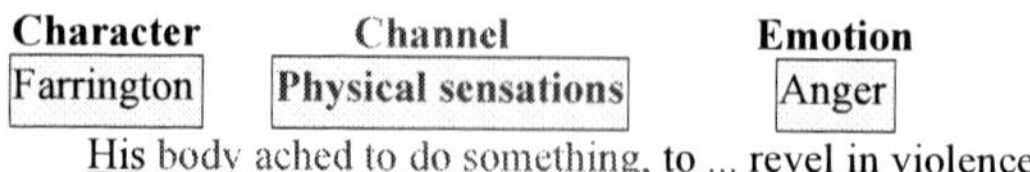

Figure 1: Example of the emotion expressed using non-verbal communication channel. The annotation of *character* and *emotion* are available in the dataset by Kim and Klinger (2019). *Channel* annotation (in blue) is an extension to the original dataset.

Proceedings of the Second Storytelling Workshop, pages 56–64
Florence, Italy, August 1, 2019. ©2019 Association for Computational Linguistics

cally, we analyze how eight emotions (*joy*, *sadness*, *anger*, *fear*, *trust*, *disgust*, *surprise*, and *anticipation*) defined by Plutchik (2001) are expressed along the following channels introduced by van Meel (1995): 1) physical appearance, 2) facial expressions, 3) gaze, looking behavior, 4) arm and hand gesture, 5) movements of body as a whole, 6) characteristics of voice, 7) spatial relations, and 8) physical make-up.

This paper is an extension to our previous study (Kim and Klinger, 2019), in which we presented a corpus of emotion relations between characters in fan fiction short stories. We post-annotate the corpus with non-verbal expressions of emotions and analyze two scenarios of non-verbal emotion expression: when the feeler of an emotion is alone, and when a communication partner, who also plays a role in the development of emotion, is present. In our analysis, we look into the emotions associated with each non-verbal behavior, mapping emotions to non-verbal expressions they frequently occur with.

Our contributions are therefore the following: 1) we propose that natural language generation systems describing emotions should take into account how emotions are expressed non-verbally, 2) we extend the annotations presented in Kim and Klinger (2019) and quantitatively analyze the data, 3) we show that facial expressions, voice, eyes and body movements are the top three channels among which the emotion is expressed, 4) based on the data, we show that some emotions are more likely to be expressed via a certain channel, and this channel is also influenced by the presence or non-presence of a communication partner.

Our corpus is available at https://www.ims. uni-stuttgart.de/data/emotion.

2 Related Work

Emotion analysis has received great attention in natural language processing (Mohammad and Bravo-Marquez, 2017; Mohammad et al., 2018; Klinger et al., 2018; Felbo et al., 2017; Abdul-Mageed and Ungar, 2017; Zhou and Wang, 2018; Gui et al., 2017, *i.a.*). Most existing studies on the topic cast the problem of emotion analysis as a classification task, by classifying documents (*e.g.*, social media posts) into a set of predefined emotion classes. Emotion classes used for the classification are usually based on discrete categories of Ekman (1970) or Plutchik (2001) (*cf.*

Alm et al. (2005), Suttles and Ide (2013), Mohammad (2012)). Fewer studies address emotion recognition using a dimensional emotion representation (*cf.* Buechel and Hahn (2017); Preoţiuc-Pietro et al. (2016)). Such representation is based on the valence-arousal emotion model (Russell, 1980), which can be helpful to account for subjective emotional states that do not fit into discrete categories.

Early attempts to computationally model emotions in literary texts date back to the 1980s and are presented in the works by Anderson and McMaster (1982, 1986), who build a computational model of affect in text tracking how emotions develop in a literary narrative.

More recent studies in the field of digital humanities approach emotion analysis from various angles and for a wide range of goals. Some studies use emotions as feature input for genre classification (Samothrakis and Fasli, 2015; Henny-Krahmer, 2018; Yu, 2008; Kim et al., 2017), story clustering (Reagan et al., 2016), mapping emotions to geographical locations in literature (Heuser et al., 2016), and construction of social networks of characters (Nalisnick and Baird, 2013; Jhavar and Mirza, 2018). Other studies use emotion analysis as a starting point for stylometry (Koolen, 2018), inferring psychological characters' traits (Egloff et al., 2018), and analysis of the causes of emotions in literature (Kim and Klinger, 2018, 2019).

To the best of our knowledge, there is no previous research that addresses the question of how emotions are expressed non-verbally. The only work that we are aware of is a literary study by van Meel (1995), who proposes several non-verbal communication channels for emotions and performs a manual analysis on a set of several books. He finds that voice is the most frequently used category, followed by facial expressions, arm and hand gestures and bodily postures. Van Meel explains the dominancy of voice by the predominant role that speech plays in novels. However, van Meel does not link the non-verbal channels to any specific emotions. In this paper, we extend his analysis by mapping the non-verbal channels to a set of specific emotions felt by the characters.

3 Corpus Creation

We post-annotate our dataset of emotion relations between characters in fan fiction (Kim and

Emotion	Face	Body	Appear.	Look.	Voice	Gesture	Sptrel.	Sensations	No channel	Total
anger	23	20	5	38	51	7	0	4	163	311
anticipation	4	14	0	17	4	2	7	6	267	321
disgust	3	6	1	3	0	0	0	1	149	163
fear	4	28	13	16	8	1	0	25	124	219
joy	76	26	7	12	52	19	5	33	268	498
sadness	3	5	4	4	2	0	3	7	81	109
surprise	10	5	3	13	1	0	0	2	118	152
trust	4	15	1	4	1	21	3	0	144	193
Total	127	119	34	107	119	50	18	78	1314	1966

Table 1: Counts of emotion and expression-channel pairs. *No channel* means that instance contains no reference to how emotion is expressed non-verbally.

Klinger, 2019) with non-verbal communication channels of emotion expressions. The dataset includes complete annotations of 19 fan fiction short stories and of one short story by James Joyce. The emotion relation is characterized by a triple (C_{exp}, e, C_{cause}), in which the character C_{exp} feels the emotion e. The character C_{cause} (to which we refer as a "communication partner") is part of an event which triggers the emotion e. The emotion categorization presented in the dataset follows Plutchik's (2001) classification, namely *joy, sadness, anger, fear, trust, disgust, surprise,* and *anticipation*.

Given an annotation of a character with an emotion, we annotate non-verbal channels of emotion expressions following the classification proposed by van Meel (1995), who defines the following eight categories: 1) physical appearance, 2) facial expressions, 3) gaze, looking behavior, 4) arm and hand gesture, 5) movements of body as a whole, 6) characteristics of voice, 7) spatial relations (references to personal space), and 8) physical make-up. To clarify the category of *physical make-up*, we redefine it under the name of *physical sensations*, *i.e.*, references to one's internal physiological signals perceived by the feeler of the emotion.

The task is exemplified in Figure 1. Labels for emotion (*Anger*) and character (*Farrington*) are given. *Physical sensation* is an example of a channel annotation we use to extend the original dataset.

The annotations were done by three graduate students in our computational linguistics depart-

	a1–a2	a1–a3	a2–a3
Span	31	29	45
Sentence	49	45	59

Table 2: F_1 scores in % for agreement between annotators on a span level. a1, a2, and a3 are different annotators. Span: label of channel and offsets are considered. Sentence: only label of the channel in the sentence is considered.

ment within a one-month period. The annotators were asked to read each datapoint in the dataset and decide if the emotion expressed by the feeler (*character*) has an associated non-verbal channel of expression. If so, the annotators were instructed to mark the corresponding textual span and select a channel label from the list of non-verbal communication channels given above.

The results of inter-annotator agreement (IAA) are presented in Table 2. We measure agreement along two dimensions: 1) span, where we measure how well two people agree on the label of a non-verbal emotion expression, as well as on the exact textual position of this expression, and 2) sentence, where we measure how well two people agree on the label of non-verbal emotion expression in a given sentence (*i.e.*, the exact positions of the channel are not taken into account). The agreement is measured using the F_1 measure, where we assume that annotations by one person are true, and annotations by another person are predicted. As one can see, the agreement scores for spans (*i.e.*, channel label and exact textual po-

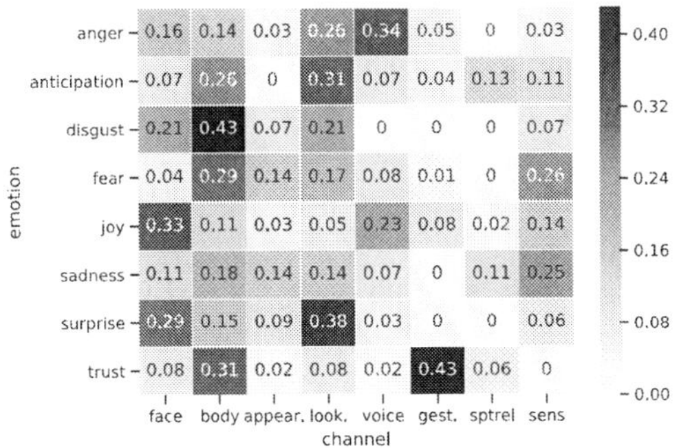

Figure 2: Distribution of non-verbal channels with all emotions. Darker color indicates higher value. Values in the cells are percentage ratios. Each cell is normalized by the row sum of absolute frequencies.

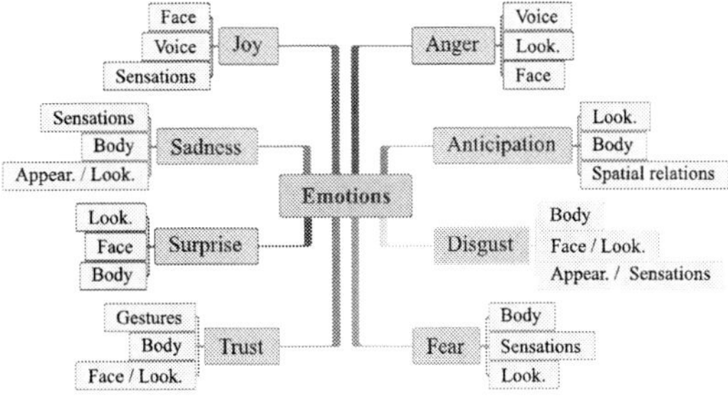

Figure 3: Emotion-channel map. Each branch is an emotion, whose branches are the top three non-verbal channels associated with the emotion.

sitions) are relatively low (lowest 29%, highest 45% F_1 respectively). The IAA scores on a sentence level are higher (lowest agreement is 45%, highest 59% F_1 respectively), as we only consider the label of the non-verbal channel in a sentence without looking into the exact textual positions of the annotations.

4 Analysis

Table 1 summarizes the results of the annotation of non-verbal channels of emotion expressions, Table 3 gives examples of these expressions in the dataset.

In total, there are 652 annotations of non-verbal emotion expressions. By absolute counts, facial expressions (*Face*, 127 occurrences), body movements (*Body*, 119), voice (*Voice*, 199), and looking behavior (*Look.*, 107) have the highest number of annotations. Spatial relations (*Sptrel.*, 78) and physical appearance (*Appear.*, 34) have the lowest number of annotations.

4.1 Emotion-Channel associations

We start our analysis by looking into the emotion-channel associations. Namely, we analyze which non-verbal channels are associated with which emotions. To that end, we plot a heatmap of the emotion–non-verbal-channel matrix. The value of each cell in the heatmap is normalized by the row sum (*i.e.*, total counts of channel annotations) and represents the likelihood of emotion-channel association in the dataset, for each emotion, respectively.

As Figure 2 shows, *anger* is more likely to be expressed with *voice*, while *joy* is more likely to

be expressed with *face*. In contrast to all other emotions, *sadness* is more likely to be experienced internally (*sens.* column in Figure 2) by the feeler, as opposed to being communicated non-verbally. Some channels and emotions show no association, such as *gestures* (*gest.*) and *disgust* or *spatial relations* (*sptrel.*) and *anger*. Given the relatively small size of the dataset, we do not argue that these associations are not possible in principle. For example, *fear* and *spatial relations* have zero association in our analysis, however, it is likely that somebody expresses this emotion by moving away subconsciously (increasing personal space) from the source of danger. At the same time, *fear* is most strongly associated with *body movements* as a whole, which can be difficult to distinguish from spatial relations. However, we believe that these associations still reflect the general trend: emotions that require immediate actions and serve evolutionary survival function, such as anger, disgust, and fear, are more likely to be expressed with actions. For example, anger is an unpleasant emotion that often occurs as a response to an appraisal of a blocked goal (Harmon Jones and Harmon-Jones, 2016), which can be resolved by using voice characteristics (commanding or shouting at someone who prevents you from achieving your goal).

Overall, we observe that *face*, *look.*, *voice*, and *body* channels are predominantly used with all emotions. We visualize the strongest associations of emotions and non-verbal channels in Figure 3. For each emotion, the figure shows the top three (in a descending order) strongly associated non-verbal channels. As one can see, the branches are dominated by *face*, *look.*, *voice*, and *body* channels. The only exception is *trust*, for which the predominant way to express emotions non-

Channel	Emotion	Examples
Facial expressions	anger fear	rolled his eyes smiled nervously
Body movements	anger trust	stormed back out slumped his shoulders
Physical appearance	fear	blushed crimson red
Looking behavior	fear anticipation	averted her eyes pause to look back
Voice	joy fear	purred voice getting smaller and smaller
Arm and hand gestures	trust	opened her arms
Spatial relations	joy trust	leaping into her arms pulled him closer to his chest
Physical sensations	joy fear	tingling all over hear in his throat

Table 3: Textual examples of non-verbal emotion expressions.

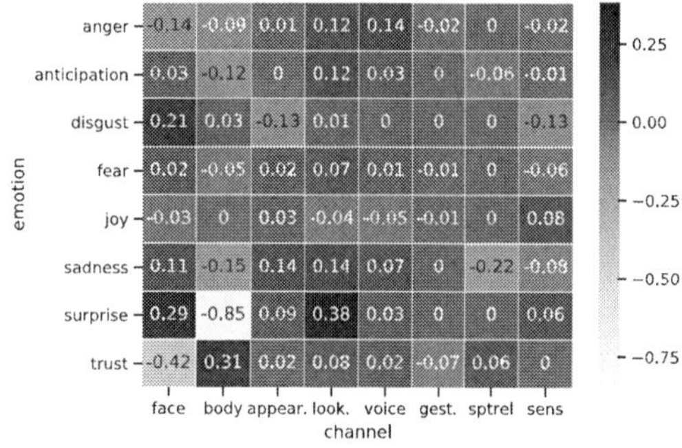

Figure 4: The difference between situations, in which a character feels an emotion and the communication partner is present, and situations in which the communication partner is not present (normalized by row sum). Darker color/higher values indicates that the channel is more likely to be used when there is a communication partner.

verbally is through *gestures*, and *sadness*, which is predominantly felt "internally" (*sensations*).

4.2 Presence of a communication partner

The original dataset contains information whether an emotion of the character is evoked by another character (communication partner). We use this information to understand how the presence of a communication partner affects the choice of a non-verbal channel.

To that end, we plot a heatmap (Figure 4) from the delta values between situations, in which the communication partner is present, and situations in which the communication partner is not present. As it can be seen from Figure 4, *trust* is more strongly associated with *body movements* when a communication partner is present. *Sadness*, which is more likely to associate with inner physical sensations in the feeler, is expressed through the *physical appearance* and *looking behavior* when the communication partner is present. Likewise, *disgust* is more likely to be expressed with *facial expressions*, and *anticipation* is more likely to be expressed with *looking behavior*.

Again, we observe that *body*, *voice*, *face*, and *look.* channels are the predominant non-verbal communication channels for emotion expressions.

4.3 Timeline analysis

To understand if there are patterns in the frequency of use of non-verbal channels in a narrative, we perform an additional analysis.

For this analysis, we split each short story in the dataset in ten equally sized chunks and get frequencies of each non-verbal channel, which are then plotted as time-series with confidence intervals (Figure 5). The averaged values for each channel are plotted as a dark line with circular markers. The lighter area around the main line represents confidence intervals of 95%, which are calculated using bootstrap resampling.

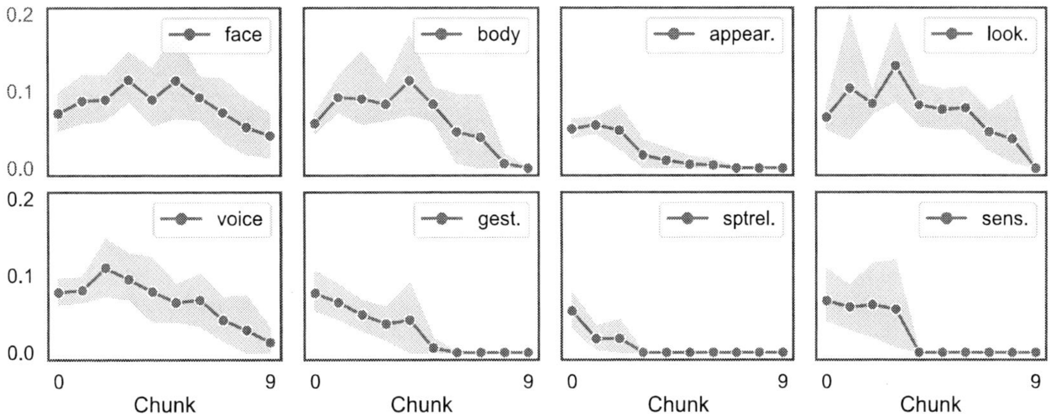

Figure 5: Distribution of non-verbal emotion expressions in the narrative. Markers on the plot lines indicate the text chunk. The plots are given for ten chunks. Light area around the solid line indicates confidence interval of 95%. *y*-axis shows percentage.

We observe the general tendency of all non-verbal channels to vanish towards the end of the story. The only exception is *Facial expressions*, which after peaking in the middle of a story reverts to the mean. Overall, we find no consistent pattern in the use of non-verbal channels from beginning to an end of a story.

5   Discussion and Conclusion

The results of the analysis presented in Section 4 show that emotions are expressed in a variety of ways through different non-verbal channels. However, the preferred communication channel depends on whether a communication partner is present or not. Some channels are used predominantly only when the feeler communicates her emotion to another character, other channels can be used in any situation.

Sadness stands out from other emotions in a sense that it is predominantly not expressed using any external channels of non-verbal communication. In other words, it is more common for the characters in the annotated dataset to go through sadness "alone" and feel it "in the body", rather than show it to the outer world. However, when another character (communication partner) is the reason of sadness experienced by the feeler, he or she will most likely use eyes and overall behavior to show this emotion.

In this paper, we showed that in human-written stories, emotions are not only expressed as propositions in the form of "*A* feels affection towards *B*" or "*A* confronts *B*". As Table 3 shows, of-

ten there is no direct mention of the feelings *A* holds towards *B* ("rolled his eyes", "purred"). It is, therefore, important, that this observation finds its place in automatic storytelling systems. Some attempts have been done in natural language generation towards controllable story generation (Peng et al., 2018; Tambwekar et al., 2018). We propose that emotion expression should be one of the controllable parameters in automatic storytellers. As more and more language generation systems have started using emotion as one of the central components for plot development and characterization of characters, there will be a need for a more versatile and subtle description of emotions, which is realized not only through propositional statements. In the end, no single instance of same emotion is expressed in the same way (Barrett, 2017), and emotion-aware storytelling systems should take this information into account when generating emotional profiles of characters.

6   Future Work

This paper proposes one approach to non-verbal emotion description that relies on a rigid ontology of emotion classes. However, it might be reasonable to make use of unsupervised clustering of non-verbal descriptions to overcome the limitations of using a relatively small number of coarse emotion categories for the description of character emotions. Once clustered, such descriptions could be incorporated in the generated text (*e.g.*, a plot summary) and would elaborate all the simplistic descriptions of character emotions.

Other research directions seems feasible too. For example, the annotations, which we presented in this paper, can be used for building and training a model that automatically recognizes non-verbal channels of emotion expressions. This might, in a multi-task learning setting, improve emotion classification. The data we provide could also be used as a starting point for terminology construction, namely bootstrapping a lexicon of emotion communications with different channels. Finally, our work can serve as a foundation for the development of an automatic storytelling system that takes advantage of such resources.

Acknowledgements

This research has been conducted within the CRETA project (http://www.creta.uni-stuttgart.de/) which is funded by the German Ministry for Education and Research (BMBF) and partially funded by the German Research Council (DFG), projects SEAT (Structured Multi-Domain Emotion Analysis from Text, KL 2869/1-1).

References

Muhammad Abdul-Mageed and Lyle Ungar. 2017. EmoNet: Fine-grained emotion detection with gated recurrent neural networks. In *Proceedings of the 55th Annual Meeting of the Association for Computational Linguistics (Volume 1: Long Papers)*, pages 718–728, Vancouver, Canada. Association for Computational Linguistics.

Angela Ackerman and Becca Puglisi. 2012. *The Emotion Thesaurus: A Writer's Guide to Character Expression*. JADD Publishing.

Cecilia Ovesdotter Alm, Dan Roth, and Richard Sproat. 2005. Emotions from text: Machine learning for text-based emotion prediction. In *Proceedings of the Conference on Human Language Technology and Empirical Methods in Natural Language Processing*, HLT '05, pages 579–586, Stroudsburg, PA, USA. Association for Computational Linguistics.

Clifford W. Anderson and George E. McMaster. 1982. Computer assisted modeling of affective tone in written documents. *Computers and the Humanities*, 16(1):1–9.

Clifford W. Anderson and George E. McMaster. 1986. Modeling emotional tone in stories using tension levels and categorical states. *Computers and the Humanities*, 20(1):3–9.

Lisa Feldman Barrett. 2017. *How emotions are made: The secret life of the brain*. Houghton Mifflin Harcourt.

Sven Buechel and Udo Hahn. 2017. Emobank: Studying the impact of annotation perspective and representation format on dimensional emotion analysis. In *Proceedings of the 15th Conference of the European Chapter of the Association for Computational Linguistics: Volume 2, Short Papers*, pages 578–585, Valencia, Spain. Association for Computational Linguistics.

João Dias and Ana Paiva. 2011. Agents with emotional intelligence for storytelling. In *Affective Computing and Intelligent Interaction*, pages 77–86, Berlin, Heidelberg. Springer Berlin Heidelberg.

Mattia Egloff, Antonio Lieto, and Davide Picca. 2018. An ontological model for inferring psychological profiles and narrative roles of characters. In *Digital Humanities 2018: Conference Abstracts*, Mexico City, Mexico.

Paul Ekman. 1970. Universal facial expressions of emotion. *California Mental Health Research Digest*, 8(4):151–158.

Bjarke Felbo, Alan Mislove, Anders Søgaard, Iyad Rahwan, and Sune Lehmann. 2017. Using millions of emoji occurrences to learn any-domain representations for detecting sentiment, emotion and sarcasm. In *Proceedings of the 2017 Conference on Empirical Methods in Natural Language Processing*, pages 1615–1625, Copenhagen, Denmark. Association for Computational Linguistics.

Lin Gui, Jiannan Hu, Yulan He, Ruifeng Xu, Qin Lu, and Jiachen Du. 2017. A question answering approach for emotion cause extraction. In *Proceedings of the 2017 Conference on Empirical Methods in Natural Language Processing*, pages 1593–1602, Copenhagen, Denmark. Association for Computational Linguistics.

Eddie Harmon Jones and Cindy Harmon-Jones. 2016. Anger. In Michael Lewis, Jeannette M. Haviland-Jones, and Lisa Feldman Barrett, editors, *Handbook of Emotions*, chapter 44, pages 774–792. Guilford Publications, New York.

Ulrike Edith Gerda Henny-Krahmer. 2018. Exploration of sentiments and genre in spanish american novels. In *Digital Humanities 2018: Conference Abstracts*, Mexico, Mexico.

Ryan Heuser, Franco Moretti, and Erik Steiner. 2016. The Emotions of London. Technical report, Stanford University. Pamphlets of the Stanford Literary Lab.

Patrick Colm Hogan. 2015. *What Literature Teaches Us about Emotion*, pages 273–290. Oxford University Press, USA.

Ricardo Imbert and Angélica de Antonio. 2005. An emotional architecture for virtual characters. In *Virtual Storytelling. Using Virtual Reality Technologies for Storytelling*, pages 63–72, Berlin, Heidelberg. Springer Berlin Heidelberg.

Randy Ingermanson and Peter Economy. 2009. *Writing fiction for dummies*. John Wiley & Sons.

Harshita Jhavar and Paramita Mirza. 2018. EMOFIEL: Mapping emotions of relationships in a story. In *Companion Proceedings of the The Web Conference 2018*, WWW '18, pages 243–246, Republic and Canton of Geneva, Switzerland. International World Wide Web Conferences Steering Committee.

Philip N. Johnson-Laird and Keith Oatley. 2016. Emotions in Music, Literature, and Film. In Michael Lewis, Jeannette M. Haviland-Jones, and Lisa Feldman Barrett, editors, *Handbook of Emotions*, chapter 4, pages 82–97. Guilford Publications, New York.

Evgeny Kim and Roman Klinger. 2018. Who feels what and why? Annotation of a literature corpus with semantic roles of emotions. In *Proceedings of the 27th International Conference on Computational Linguistics*, pages 1345–1359, Santa Fe, New Mexico, USA. Association for Computational Linguistics.

Evgeny Kim and Roman Klinger. 2019. Frowning Frodo, Wincing Leia, and a Seriously Great Friendship: Learning to Classify Emotional Relationships of Fictional Characters. In *Proceedings of the Annual Conference of the North American Chapter of the Association for Computational Linguistics*, Minneapolis, USA. Association for Computational Linguistics. Accepted.

Evgeny Kim, Sebastian Padó, and Roman Klinger. 2017. Investigating the relationship between literary genres and emotional plot development. In *Proceedings of the Joint SIGHUM Workshop on Computational Linguistics for Cultural Heritage, Social Sciences, Humanities and Literature*, pages 17–26, Vancouver, Canada. Association for Computational Linguistics.

Roman Klinger, Orphée de Clercq, Saif M. Mohammad, and Alexandra Balahur. 2018. IEST: WASSA-2018 implicit emotions shared task. In *Proceedings of the 9th Workshop on Computational Approaches to Subjectivity, Sentiment and Social Media Analysis*, Brussels, Belgium. Association for Computational Linguistics.

Hidetsugu Komeda, Yoshiaki Nihei, and Takashi Kusumi. 2005. Roles of reader's feelings in understanding narratives: forefeel, empathy, and a sense of strangeness. *Shinrigaku kenkyu: The Japanese Journal of Psychology*, 75(6):479–486.

Corina Koolen. 2018. Women's books versus books by women. In *Digital Humanities 2018: Conference Abstracts*, Mexico City, Mexico.

Nancy Kress. 2005. *Characters, Emotion & Viewpoint: Techniques and Exercises for Crafting Dynamic Characters and Effective Viewpoints*. Writer's Digest Books.

Robert McKee. 2003. Storytelling that moves people. A conversation with screenwriting coach Robert Mckee. *Harvard business review*, 81(6):51—5, 136.

Jacques M. van Meel. 1995. Representing emotions in literature and paintings: A comparative analysis. *Poetics*, 23(1):159 – 176. Emotions and Cultural Products.

Gonzalo Méndez, Pablo Gervás, and Carlos León. 2016. On the use of character affinities for story plot generation. In *Knowledge, Information and Creativity Support Systems*, pages 211–225, Cham. Springer International Publishing.

Saif M. Mohammad. 2012. From once upon a time to happily ever after: Tracking emotions in mail and books. *Decision Support Systems*, 53(4):730–741.

Saif M. Mohammad and Felipe Bravo-Marquez. 2017. WASSA-2017 shared task on emotion intensity. In *Proceedings of the 8th Workshop on Computational Approaches to Subjectivity, Sentiment and Social Media Analysis*, pages 34–49, Copenhagen, Denmark. Association for Computational Linguistics.

Saif M. Mohammad, Felipe Bravo-Marquez, Mohammad Salameh, and Svetlana Kiritchenko. 2018. SemEval-2018 task 1: Affect in tweets. In *Proceedings of The 12th International Workshop on Semantic Evaluation*, pages 1–17, New Orleans, Louisiana. Association for Computational Linguistics.

Yusuke Mori, Hiroaki Yamane, Yoshitaka Ushiku, and Tatsuya Harada. 2019. How narratives move your mind: A corpus of shared-character stories for connecting emotional flow and interestingness. *Information Processing & Management*.

Eric T. Nalisnick and Henry S. Baird. 2013. Extracting sentiment networks from shakespeare's plays. In *2013 12th International Conference on Document Analysis and Recognition*, pages 758–762.

Nanyun Peng, Marjan Ghazvininejad, Jonathan May, and Kevin Knight. 2018. Towards controllable story generation. In *Proceedings of the First Workshop on Storytelling*, pages 43–49, New Orleans, Louisiana. Association for Computational Linguistics.

Rafael Pérez y Pérez. 2007. Employing emotions to drive plot generation in a computer-based storyteller. *Cognitive Systems Research*, 8(2):89–109.

Robert Plutchik. 2001. The nature of emotions. *American Scientist*, 89(4):344–350.

Daniel Preoţiuc-Pietro, H. Andrew Schwartz, Gregory Park, Johannes Eichstaedt, Margaret Kern, Lyle Ungar, and Elisabeth Shulman. 2016. Modelling valence and arousal in facebook posts. In *Proceedings of the 7th Workshop on Computational Approaches to Subjectivity, Sentiment and Social Media Analysis*, pages 9–15, San Diego, California. Association for Computational Linguistics.

Andrew J. Reagan, Lewis Mitchell, Dilan Kiley, Christopher M. Danforth, and Peter Sheridan Dodds. 2016. The emotional arcs of stories are dominated by six basic shapes. *EPJ Data Science*, 5(1):31.

James A. Russell. 1980. A circumplex model of affect. *Journal of Personality and Social Psychology*, 39:1161–1178.

Spyridon Samothrakis and Maria Fasli. 2015. Emotional sentence annotation helps predict fiction genre. *PloS one*, 10(11):e0141922.

Jared Suttles and Nancy Ide. 2013. Distant supervision for emotion classification with discrete binary values. In *Computational Linguistics and Intelligent Text Processing*, pages 121–136, Berlin, Heidelberg. Springer Berlin Heidelberg.

Pradyumna Tambwekar, Murtaza Dhuliawala, Animesh Mehta, Lara J. Martin, Brent Harrison, and Mark O. Riedl. 2018. Controllable neural story generation via reinforcement learning. *arXiv preprint arXiv:1809.10736*.

Mariët Theune, Sander Rensen, Rieks op den Akker, Dirk Heylen, and Anton Nijholt. 2004. Emotional characters for automatic plot creation. In *International Conference on Technologies for Interactive Digital Storytelling and Entertainment*, pages 95–100. Springer.

Leigh Van Horn. 1997. The characters within us: Readers connect with characters to create meaning and understanding. *Journal of Adolescent & Adult Literacy*, 40(5):342–347.

Bei Yu. 2008. An evaluation of text classification methods for literary study. *Literary and Linguistic Computing*, 23(3):327–343.

Xianda Zhou and William Yang Wang. 2018. MojiTalk: Generating emotional responses at scale. In *Proceedings of the 56th Annual Meeting of the Association for Computational Linguistics (Volume 1: Long Papers)*, pages 1128–1137, Melbourne, Australia. Association for Computational Linguistics.

Narrative Generation in the Wild: Methods from NaNoGenMo

Judith van Stegeren
Human Media Interaction
University of Twente
Enschede, The Netherlands
`j.e.vanstegeren@utwente.nl`

Mariët Theune
Human Media Interaction
University of Twente
Enschede, The Netherlands
`m.theune@utwente.nl`

Abstract

In text generation, generating long stories is still a challenge. Coherence tends to decrease rapidly as the output length increases. Especially for generated stories, coherence of the narrative is an important quality aspect of the output text. In this paper we examine how narrative coherence is attained in the submissions of NaNoGenMo 2018, an online text generation event where participants are challenged to generate a 50,000 word novel. We list the main approaches that were used to generate coherent narratives and link them to scientific literature. Finally, we give recommendations on when to use which approach.

1 Introduction

Coherence is generally considered to be a property of a good story. For a story to be coherent, "all the parts of the story must be structured so that the entire sequence of events is interrelated in a meaningful way" (Shapiro and Hudson, 1991), p.960. For generated stories, in particular those generated using neural models, coherence tends to decrease rapidly as the output length increases. For this reason, generating long stories is still a challenge (Kiddon et al., 2016).

To gain more insight in how generation of long stories is done 'in the wild', we review a collection of story generation projects that were created as part of the online challenge NaNoGenMo.

NaNoGenMo, or National Novel Generation Month[1], is a yearly online event that challenges participants to create a novel using text generation. Participants have one month (November) to develop a text generator and use it to procedurally generate the text of their novel. GitHub is used to register for the event and share participants' progress throughout the month. To qualify as a NaNoGenMo winner, participants have to publish their code and share a generated text of at least 50,000 words.

Since NaNoGenMo takes place online, we can use it to study practical approaches to text generation and story generation. Participants do not necessarily use state-of-the-art techniques from story generation research. Instead, the NaNoGenMo entries offer us a look into practical novel generation methods used in a (mostly) non-academic context. NaNoGenMo provides an accessible repository of story generation projects (including both code and output) that is incomparable to any academic generation challenge in terms of diversity and scale. What makes NaNoGenMo extra interesting is that it focuses on the generation of texts with a much longer length than addressed in most scientific research.

We analysed the work of participants from NaNoGenMo 2018[2], see Section 3. We start with categorising the projects by their output type, focusing on projects that generate text with a novel-like structure. We then list the main methods for text generation used by participants in Section 4, since text generation methods influence the coherence of the output text. In Section 5, we discuss projects that generate text with a coherent narrative structure. We list the different approaches that were used to achieve this narrative structure, and link them to scientific literature. Finally, we provide some recommendations on when to use which approach.

2 Related work

2.1 NaNoGenMo

NaNoGenMo was invented in 2013 by Darius Kazemi. His inspiration was NaNoWriMo, or National Novel Writing Month, another online event

---

[1] `https://www.github.com/nanogenmo`

[2] `https://github.com/NaNoGenMo/2018`

Proceedings of the Second Storytelling Workshop, pages 65–74
Florence, Italy, August 1, 2019. ©2019 Association for Computational Linguistics

in November where participants are challenged to write a 50,000 word novel.

The first attempt to create a survey of text generation methods used by NaNoGenMo participants was a blog post[3] in Russian. The author discussed projects of NaNoGenMo 2013-2015, and categorised them by generation technique, such as Markov chains, recycling existing works of fiction, simulation, high-level plot generation, and neural networks. Inspired by this blog post, the NaNoGenMo community conducted their own survey[4] of methods (2016) and programming languages (2014–2017) as part of the event.

There is some cross-pollination between the NaNoGenMo community and academia. Participants sometimes refer to research articles, either for their own projects or to help other participants. Additionally, NaNoGenMo has been mentioned in scientific literature in fields that have a close connection to the goal of the event: procedural generation for games (Karth, 2018), story generation (Montfort, 2014; Horswill, 2016) and computational creativity (McGovern and Scott, 2016; Cook and Colton, 2018; Compton et al., 2015).

Cook and Colton (2018) discuss the NaNoGenMo community in detail in their paper on online communities in computational creativity. Although they review some of the projects from NaNoGenMo 2016, the focus of their article was not the methods or quality of the projects, but rather the community of NaNoGenMo itself. Montfort (2014) developed a novel generator called World Clock, as entry for NaNoGenMo 2013. Interestingly, most of the researchers citing NaNoGenMo have participated themselves in the past.

2.2 Story generation

Story generation is the procedural creation of stories. Mostafazadeh et al. (2016) define a *story* or *narrative* as "anything which is told in the form of a causally (logically) linked set of events involving some shared characters." Yao et al. (2019) split story generation into two distinct tasks: on the one hand generating the sequence of events, and on the other hand generating the surface text, i.e. the actual text that makes up the story. This is reminiscent of the classic NLG pipeline (see, e.g., (Reiter and Dale, 1997), in which planning stages precede surface realisation. Story generation is sometimes limited to the first aspect, generating the underlying sequence of events, or *fabula*, with generation of the surface text of the story out of scope (Martin et al., 2018; Porteous and Cavazza, 2009; Lebowitz, 1987). Some story generation systems focus on generating the surface text, given a fabula as input. For example, Storybook (Callaway and Lester, 2002), the Narrator (Theune et al., 2007) and Curveship (Montfort, 2009) all generate story text from an underlying fabula. Other research focused on aspects of the *telling* of the story, for example stylistic variation (Montfort, 2007), affective language (Strong et al., 2007) and personality (Lukin et al., 2014; Walker et al., 2011).

2.3 Narrative coherence

The generation of long stories, such as the 50,000 word novels of NaNoGenMo, places strong demands on coherence: the set of events in the story need to be linked, and preferably also fit into some overarching dramatic structure.

One way of achieving coherence in generated stories is by imposing a specific structure on the output text. Researchers have investigated the structure inherent in existing stories to find out how humans do this. Propp's model of the structure of Russian folktales has been used in various story generation systems (Gervás, 2013). Alternative narrative structures that have been used to guide story generation are Booker's seven basic plots (Hall et al., 2017), the Hero's journey or Monomyth (García-Ortega et al., 2016) and the Fool's journey from tarot cards (Sullivan et al., 2018).

In neural text generation, it is less easy to impose a narrative structure on the generated texts – unless the task is split into two steps, like in the work of Yao et al. (2019). An alternative way improve the global coherence in texts generated with recurring neural networks was proposed by Holtzman et al. (2018), who used a set of discriminators to encode various aspects of proper writing.

Another way of achieving coherence is through emergent narrative (Aylett, 1999). This is a type of narrative (at the fabula level) that emerges from simulating simple behaviours that, when interacting, create a complex whole. The simulation gives rise to a sequence of causally linked events which give coherence to the story. The coherence in emergent narrative tends to be mostly local in nature:

---

[3] https://habr.com/en/post/313862/

[4] The programming language surveys can be found by searching for issues labeled 'admin' in the GitHub repositories for those respective years.

although the events are linked through their immediate causes and consequences, it is difficult to impose a global dramatic arc on them. Examples of generation systems that use the emergent narrative approach are FearNot! (Aylett et al., 2005), the Virtual Storyteller (Swartjes and Theune, 2008) and the simulation framework from Talk of the Town (Ryan et al., 2016).

Simulation-based narratives are particularly suitable for game-based story generation, since games often already have a world-state, characters, objects and a set of rules that describe valid changes to the game state. The rule system of role-playing game Dungeons & Dragons is the most well-known of its kind. Various story and quest generation systems (Martens, 2015; Tapscott et al., 2018; Kybartas and Verbrugge, 2014) have been built upon this and other related rule systems.

3 Data

NaNoGenMo uses GitHub's built-in issue tracker to keep track of all user submissions. Every issue corresponds to one NaNoGenMo project. In the issue thread, participants can post comments, interact with other users, share their development process and publish previews of the generated novels.

We downloaded all issues from the NaNoGenMo 2018 repository as JSON data using the GitHub API. We took issues into account that were opened between the start of NaNoGenMo 2018 and March 2019, that were labels as 'completed' and not labeled as 'admin'. The label 'completed' means that both the generator code and a 50,000 word output are publicly available. All 61 issues[5] were manually reviewed by the first author, by looking at the programming code, the output, the tools and used datasets. For practical reasons, we ignored projects in other languages than English.

NaNoGenMo uses a loose definition of 'novel': any text of more than 50,000 words qualifies as an acceptable output. There are no rules dictating the format, style, grammaticality, subject or content of the text. As a result, the outputs vary greatly from one another. See Figure 1 for a categorisation of NaNoGenMo projects according to their output type. Most projects generate a novel-like text, with a form that resembles sentences, paragraphs and chapters. One participant (project 72) created a

---

[5]Throughout this paper we will reference each project by its issue number on GitHub. The details of each project can be found on the corresponding issue page on GitHub, i.e. https://github.com/NaNoGenMo/2018/issues/{issuenumber}.

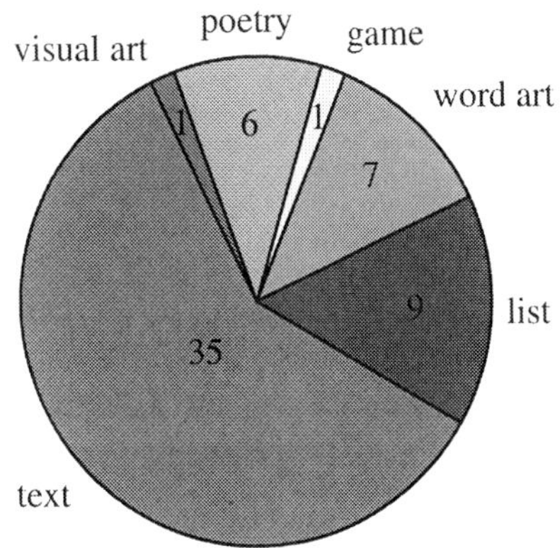

Figure 1: Output type of completed NaNoGenMo 2018 projects.

Language	Projects
Python	19
Javascript	8
Lua	3
Bash	3
C	2
Samovar	1
Ruby	1
Perl	1
PHP	1
ML	1
Julia	1
Java	1

Figure 2: Programming languages used in NaNoGenMo projects that generate novel-like text. Projects that use more than one programming language are counted multiple times.

generator for an Interactive Fiction game. Other projects generated word art, e.g. repetitions of one word, ASCII art or text without meaning, poems, graphs or lists. In the rest of this paper, we will limit our discussion to the 35 projects that generate novel-like text.

For an overview of the programming languages used in the projects, see Figure 2. Some projects used multiple languages. The availability of good NLP and NLG resources in a particular language has probably contributed to people choosing those languages. Consequently, the choice for a particular programming language may have influenced the chosen text generation and narrative generation approach, and vice versa. Both Python and Javascript,

the two most popular programming languages with
NaNoGenMo participants, have accessible libraries
for text processing and text generation. Participants
that programmed in Python mainly used Markovify,
SpaCy and NLTK; Javascript projects used mostly
Tracery (Compton et al., 2015), a Javascript library
for text generation with context-free grammars.
The developers of Tracery specifically mention the
NaNoGenMo community as the target audience
for Tracery, which could explain the wide adoption
of Tracery within the NaNoGenMo community, as
well as the large number of projects in Javascript,
a programming language that is not typically used
for text generation or text processing.

In addition to NLP libraries and tools, most participants use externally sourced text data. Public domain books from Project Gutenberg[6] and The Internet Archive[7] were very popular with NaNoGenMo
participants, as was Darius Kazemi's Corpora[8]
repository, which is a collection of word lists organized by subject, such as games, medicine and religion. Some participants created their own corpus
from online resources, such as subtitles, marathon
reports, horror stories and reports of personal experiences with psycho-active drugs.

4 Text generation methods

The 35 novel generation projects of NaNoGenMo
2018 use a variety of text generation methods to
create the surface text of their novel. In this section,
we provide a survey of the various approaches we
have seen.

4.1 Templating

More than 10 projects use some form of *templating*.
Libraries like Tracery offer a fast way to implement
this in Javascript and Python. Most text templates
were hard-coded in the generator, which is time-
consuming and requires manual effort. An alternative approach used in some projects (projects
64, 101 and 104) was to create templates automatically, e.g. by running all sentences from a corpus
through a part-of-speech (POS) tagger and creating
sentence templates from the POS-tags.

The popularity of templating is not surprising,
as templates offer a strong form of control over the
surface text. However, using templates does not
guarantee a good quality output. If templates are

filled with randomly chosen phrases, as was done
in some projects, the quality of the generated text
may be worse than that of a text generated with
Markov chains (discussed next).

4.2 Markov chains

At least 8 projects used *Markov chains* for text
generation. Markov chains are statistical language
models, which can be created fully automatically
from corpora. They can be used for text generation
by choosing a start token and using the probabilities in the model to choose the next token. Using
Markov chains is an accessible approach to text
generation, as it does not require coding the content of the output. Markovify[9], a Python library
for working with Markov chains, was used by the
majority of users that used Markov chains for generation. We believe that Markovify has contributed
to the popularity of the Markov chain approach
under NaNoGenMo participants.

Not your average ultra (project 89) creatively
mixes the outputs of two Markov chains. One
Markov chain was trained on a collection of
marathon reports, the other on a dataset of reports
of personal experiences with psychoactive drugs.
As the generator produced more text, the influence
of the second Markov chain on the generator grew
stronger, which resulted in output in the form of a
race journal that becomes progressively delirious
over time.

Although the outputs from a Markov chain are
often less coherent than those produced by templates, the advantage of Markov chains is that they
often yield surprising or interesting results. For
participants that value creativity over coherence,
Markov chains are a suitable technique for text generation. As we will see in Section 5, the lack of
coherence is not always a problem.

4.3 Remixing

Remixing external sources, such as text from existing novels, was also a popular approach with participants. More than half of the projects use some
form of remixing to create their output. One example of remixing is creating a new text by taking
a source text and substituting words from the text
according to specific rules. A hilarious example
of this is *Textillating* (project 96), where Dickens'
Great Expectations is 'improved' by increasing the
number of exclamation marks and substituting each

---

[6]www.gutenberg.org
[7]www.archive.org
[8]https://github.com/dariusk/corpora

[9]https://github.com/jsvine/markovify

adjective in the text with its most extreme synonym.

Some participants collected external sources and composed their novel by cutting-and-pasting sentences from these. For example, *Doctor, doctor!* (project 86) used the corpus of Yahoo! health questions and answers to generate a dialogue between a doctor and a patient. Another participant scraped sentences from GoogleBooks about a set of topic words, and created an original text by cutting-and-pasting snippets from Google Books preview files. In some cases, remixing was paired with statistical modeling. The author of *Angela's claustrum* (project 28) transformed an old NaNoWriMo novel draft into an outline and remixed this into a new novel by using a stochastic model of Gutenberg texts.

With this category of methods, either the output text is very similar to the source text (and similarly coherent), or the output is completely new but loses some coherence in the process, often because developers chose to introduce random words into existing sentences in their word substitution.

4.4 Machine Translation

There were various generators that used *machine translation* techniques for creating a novel. Project 22 created a new text by mapping every sentence of Northanger Abbey by Jane Austen to a sentence written by Sir Arthur Conan Doyle, using sentence embeddings.

Project 61 used machine translation to transform the text of one of L. Frank Baum's Oz books. All dialogue from the book was translated to the "language" of The Muppets' Swedish Chef, and all other text was translated to Valleyspeak.[10]

One participant (project 33) used a public domain movie as the basis for their novel. They turned the movie into a collection of screenshots and fed this to Microsoft Cognitive services to generate captions for the screenshots. The captions were then transformed into novel text. This can be seen as a form of machine translation. Instead of translating between different languages, this project translates between different modalities (video to image, image to text).

Machine translation within NaNoGenMo can be seen as a form of remixing, and the drawbacks are indeed very similar. Either the output text shows a strong resemblance to the original text, or it is

more creative but ends up incoherent.

4.5 Deep learning

Finally, there were three projects that used deep learning to create their novel. Two projects, project 73 and project 76, used Torch[11] to create an LSTM architecture trained on an external dataset. Project 73 trained the LSTM on a crowdsourced collection[12] of Dungeons & Dragons character biographies, and project 76 used user-written horror stories scraped from CreepyPasta[13]. Both projects have output that is neither coherent nor grammatical. However, the LSTM does manage to convey the typical style of RPG biographies and horror stories. Finally, project 99 used machine learning to see whether a neural network trained on the text of Moby Dick could succesfully reconstruct the original text, by predicting the sequence of sentences.

5 Methods for narrative coherence

NaNoGenMo output is at least 50,000 words, or roughly 75 pages of text. This is a much greater length than is usually produced by story generation systems. In computational creativity and creative NLG, typical outputs range from tweets (140-280 characters) to stories of one or two pages, with exceptions such as Curveship (Montfort, 2009), UNIVERSE (Lebowitz, 1987) and World clock (Montfort, 2014).

To see how NaNoGenMo participants generate coherent novel-length narratives, the first author performed an informal analysis of the outputs of the 35 text generation projects, specifically focusing on coherence and the presence of narrative structure. Out of the 61 projects of NaNoGenMo, only 14 projects had a narrative structure, that is, they exhibited coherence as discussed in Section 2.3. Below we give an overview of the approaches used to achieve this. We can categorise the approaches for generating this narrative as follows.

5.1 High-level specification

Some projects achieve coherence by hard-coding a narrative structure in their input. *The League of Extraordinarily Dull Gentlemen* (project 6) defines that narrative structure in a specification written in Samovar, a PROLOG-like domain-specific language for world-modeling using propositions. The

---

[10]Valleyspeak is an American social dialect that originates from the San Fernando Valley in Southern California.

[11]http://torch.ch/
[12]https://github.com/janelleshane/DnD_bios
[13]https://www.creepypasta.com/

specification is a high-level description of the story, with its representation level a mix of a fabula and surface text: it is not just a sequence of events, but also includes dialogue and narrative exposition. The surface text for its output was generated by running the specification through Samovar's assertion-retraction engine[14], taking the resulting sequence of events and realising those into sentences with a Python script. This approach is similar to that of other story generation systems that use logic programming to generate stories or fabulas, such as (Martens, 2015), (Robertson and Young, 2015) and (García-Ortega et al., 2016).

Hard-coding a narrative arc in a specification can be seen as high-level templating. It also has similar advantages as templating: because the author specifies the narrative arc by hand, they have tight control over the surface text, which results in an output that looks like it was written by a human. However, this approach places an authorial burden on the developer of the generator. The story of project 6 of 50,000 words was generated in 930 lines of Samovar. We expect that the effort of writing this specification could be further reduced with code generation. Another disadvantage is that one story specification defines exactly one surface text. The surface text of project 6 includes little variation. The book consists of scenes where multiple characters perform the same action in sequence. Repeating patterns are clearly visible in the output text, making for a dull read – hence the title of the project. However, the output of project 6 sets itself apart from other generated novels by having grammatical surface text and maintaining a clear traditional narrative arc throughout the entire story with a beginning, an incident, a climax and a problem resolution.

For authors that want to generate a story out of a high-level story description, using a domain specific language like Samovar might be a suitable solution. The code for this NaNoGenMo project is very readable and could serve as an introduction to this approach. As this approach requires the user to write part of the story, it is less suitable for projects where the author also wants the generator to create the contents of the fabula, or requires a lower cost in terms of writing the code and specification.

---

[14]https://catseye.tc/article/Languages.md#samovar

5.2 Hard-coded narrative elements

Instead of hard-coding the narrative structure of the entire story in the generator, it can be hard-coded only in specific places. An example of this approach from outside NaNoGenMo is described in Reed (2012), where the author used a grammar to generate 'satellite sentences' that can be inserted in a larger human-authored narrative for an interactive fiction game. Satellite sentences are sentences that "moderate pacing and reestablish context within dialogue scenes" (Reed, 2012), such as "She coughed", "The clock was ticking" and "It was getting late".

There were a few NaNoGenMo projects where the generated text itself had no structure at all, but where the developer still created a narrative by providing a hard-coded section at the beginning and/or ending of the book. Having a fixed beginning and ending can tie otherwise incoherent pieces of generated text together, as it gives readers a context in which they can interpret the generated text. Even text generation techniques that normally do not lead to coherent output, such as Markov chains and random generation, can still be 'saved' by using this technique.

An example is *Not your average ultra* (project 89), which succesfully frames the (in)coherence of Markov chains by naming the specific setting of the novel at the beginning and end: an ultramarathon.

Similarly, *The Defeat at Procyon V* (project 83) contains 50,000 words of dialogue between a science fiction Fleet Commander and their Super Admiral. The lines of dialogue are randomly generated from a grammar of science fiction technobabble, occasionally interspersed with exposition sentences, similar to the satellite sentences from Reed (2012). Because the beginning and ending of the novel are fixed, the reader has a context in which to interpret the conversation: the conversation is about the various weapons and technologies that were deployed in the defense of Procyon V.

With this approach, the problem of generating a coherent narrative is transformed into writing narrative elements that frame the generated text in such a way that the reader perceives a narrative in the entire text. It particularly useful in instances where developers prefer straight-forward text generation techniques over narrative generation techniques, and for developers that want to write as few lines of code as possible.

5.3 Simulation

There were various projects (projects 11, 18, 39, 60 and 100) that used simulation as the basis for their narrative. The projects with simulation-based narratives had two things in common.

Firstly, most projects used rule systems that are similar to those of well-known role-playing games. For example, *The Longest Corridor* (project 18) uses a combat system that closely resembles that of Dungeons & Dragons. The project generates stories about a mythical corridor filled with monsters and treasure. For each chapter of the novel, the system generates a hero who has to fight their way through the corridor. If the hero is defeated by the inhabitants, the hero's remains will stay in the corridor for later heroes to find. If the hero reaches the end of the corridor and finds the treasure, they install themselves as the new master of the corridor, waiting for new adventurers to come and challenge them. This continuity, where characters of previous chapters (old world state) can interact with characters from current chapters (current world state), is what moves this project from a straight-forward simulation into the realm of narrative. Similarly, *Of Ork, Fae, Elf and Goblin* (project 39) generates a fabula of a group of creatures that fight each other with procedurally generated weapons in different rooms.

Another roleplaying-game inspired project is *High Fantasy with Language Generator* (project 60). Instead of having one global text-level simulation that tracks the world state and governs the entire narrative, it uses multiple low-level simulations that each govern one type of event. The project follows a group of adventurers on their quest. During their travels, the characters encounter monsters, visit local taverns and play dice games with strangers. For each of these scenes, the generator uses a separate simulation.

A second property of simulation-based novels is that they often have a journal-like format. The world state of the simulation gives rise to the surface text of the story. Since the world state is updated with each clock tick, it is intuitive to let the novel's sections (chapters, paragraphs) correspond to one clock tick. Consequently, simulation-based narratives are particularly suitable for generating journals or logbooks, in which each section corresponds to one unit of time. *The Pilgramage* (project 11) is an example of a project that follows a journal format.

A weakness of some of the simulation-based projects in NaNoGenMo is that they generate events that are not linked to each other. An example is *Wheel of Fortune* (project 100), which simulates characters who slowly grow old and die, all the while experiencing events that are generated from randomly drawn tarot cards. The resulting sequence of events looks like a fabula. However, the events are not related to each other and do not influence each other: the characters' actions happen completely in a vacuum. This does invite the reader to imagine their own narrative, but this requires a lot of effort on part of the reader. Still, symbolism from tarot cards can be used successfully to shape a narrative when combined with other methods, such as high-level specification of narrative structure (see Section 5.1). A story generator from outside NaNoGenMo that also used the tropes from tarot was developed by Sullivan et al. (2018). However, Sullivan et al. (2018) used the tarot cards to generate movie-like story synopses, with a plot structure based on Booker's seven basic plots and screenwriting principles.

5.4 Evoking a narrative

Some of the project outputs *evoke* a narrative, even though there is no narrative structure explicitly present in the text. This can even be the case for output texts that are not grammatical. Incoherent texts that still have a recognizable novel form force the reader to guess the meaning of the author. This subjective interpretation might still evoke a narrative in the reader.

As Veale (2016) notes in his paper on poetry generation, form can be more important than content. Veale calls this effect 'charity of interpretation': if humans see a text in a well-known form (or *container*), they are disposed to attribute more meaning to the text than it actually has. We saw two distinct ways of achieving this.

If the text of the novel is limited to a specific subject, readers will try to fill in the gaps in the structure with their own knowledge and expectations. An example of a project that limits its topic to instill a sense of coherence is *Doctor, doctor!* (project 86). The output text has the form of a dialogue, consisting of randomly chosen questions and answers from a dataset of Yahoo! questions from the health domain. The questions and answers have no logical connection whatsoever, but the vocabulary and writing style will be recognizable to readers who are familiar with medical discussions on the internet. Even though the answers of the doctor make no sense in the context of the respective questions, readers will infer that this novel is about a dialogue between a doctor and their hypochondriac patient.

Another technique for evoking a narrative is by connecting unrelated random elements with each other to improve the perceived coherence. *Out of Nowhere* (project 57) simulates an interaction between its characters by connecting interactions at the word level, which we explain below. Out of Nowhere produces the script for a play, based on lines of English text from public-domain phrase books. The characters represent different nationalities, and their dialogue lines are based on the text of phrase books for their respective languages. The character dialogue is generated by choosing lines from each character's phrase book. Most dialogue lines are chosen randomly, but the generator increases the coherence of the output with a few tricks. Both the location and the interactions are influenced by the words that occur in previous lines. For example, if the previous line contains the word 'waiter', the generator will include a restaurant or cafe in the scene. Similarly, if one of the previous lines contains a question mark and an interrogative word ("what", "who", etc.), the generator will assign a higher probability to lines that would constitute a logical answer. For example, if previous lines contain the phrase "Where is ...?" the generator favors sentences like "In Timbuktu" or "At my house". This is a similar approach as is used in Reed (2012), where the text generator takes different types of context into account, such as dialogue progression, location and time of day. The difference is that Reed tagged his text with locations for the satellite sentences, whereas the generator of project 6 generates all sentences and their connections on the fly. The result of project 57 is a script that has similar quality as the generators that use the simulation approach, even though there is no underlying world state for this play. All the coherence comes from word-level choices.

Besides limiting the topic of a text, using the right style can increase the perceived coherence of a text as well. If a reader recognizes a particular style from a particular type of narrative, the reader might infer meaning where there is none. A project that adapts this idea in an original way is *Velvet black skies* (project 65), which uses statistical modeling to find the most cliche sentences in a corpus of science fiction writing. The developers defined cliches as "n-grams that occur in the texts of more than 30 authors." The generator creates a new text from these cliches by clustering them by topic and by remixing them into a chapter for each topic. Readers of science fiction classics will immediately recognize the particular style of vintage science fiction.

The above techniques ask something extra of the reader during the interpretation of the text. As such, they are suitable for situations where the writer wants to highlight the subjective experience of the reader in ascribing meaning to a text. Additionally, these techniques could be used for collaborative creation in text generation (authoring aids), i.e. applications where a computer generates a first draft of a story and the human finishes it. In the latter case, the human author can take the concepts created by the generator and polish them before publication.

6 Conclusion

We discussed the most prevalent text generation methods from NaNoGenMo 2018 and their respective advantages and disadvantages. We discussed four different approaches that were used to achieve coherence (or the semblance of it) in novel-length texts, highlighting some of the most creative projects.

If there is already a high-level story arc thought out for the surface text, using a high-level specification to define this story arc is a good approach. Hard-coding the high-level narrative arc in a specification can reduce the authorial burden of manually writing the full text significantly. However, the approach is not suitable for projects where the generator should generate the fabula in addition to the surface text.

If the generator is also in charge of generating the events that underlie the surface text, simulation-based approaches are a good choice. It has been applied in various story generation systems already, most notably for the game domain, because of the overlap in functionality between simulations for narratives and rule systems for games. A weakness of simulation approaches is that, if the generated events are not interrelated, the sequence of events generated by a simulation lacks narrative coherence.

However, even text generation methods that do

not create coherent text can be turned into a narrative, either by hardcoding narrative elements, such as a contextualising beginning or ending, or by evoking a narrative by exploiting readers' charity of interpretation.

In this paper we could only give a high-level overview of the different approaches, and briefly discuss a few example projects. Those who want to see more examples and study the different approaches in detail can refer to the NaNoGenMo repository on GitHub. We have made the data for our analysis in this paper available online.[15]

7 Acknowledgments

This research is supported by the Netherlands Organisation for Scientific Research (NWO) via the DATA2GAME project (project number 055.16.114). We would like to thank the reviewers for their useful remarks.

References

Ruth Aylett. 1999. Narrative in virtual environments-towards emergent narrative. In *Proceedings of the AAAI fall symposium on narrative intelligence*, pages 83–86.

Ruth S Aylett, Sandy Louchart, Joao Dias, Ana Paiva, and Marco Vala. 2005. Fearnot!–an experiment in emergent narrative. In *International Workshop on Intelligent Virtual Agents*, pages 305–316. Springer.

Charles B Callaway and James C Lester. 2002. Narrative prose generation. *Artificial Intelligence*, 139(2):213–252.

Kate Compton, Ben Kybartas, and Michael Mateas. 2015. Tracery: an author-focused generative text tool. In *International Conference on Interactive Digital Storytelling*, pages 154–161. Springer.

Michael Cook and Simon Colton. 2018. Neighbouring communities: Interaction, lessons and opportunities. In *International Conference on Computational Creativity*.

Rubén H García-Ortega, Pablo García-Sánchez, Juan J Merelo, Aránzazu San-Ginés, and Ángel Fernández-Cabezas. 2016. The story of their lives: Massive procedural generation of heroes' journeys using evolved agent-based models and logical reasoning. In *European Conference on the Applications of Evolutionary Computation*, pages 604–619. Springer.

Pablo Gervás. 2013. Propp's morphology of the folk tale as a grammar for generation. In *Proceedings of the 2013 Workshop on Computational Models of Narrative*, volume 32. Schloss Dagstuhl-Leibniz-Zentrum für Informatik.

Jason Andrew Hall, Benjamin Williams, and Christopher J Headleand. 2017. Artificial folklore for simulated religions. In *2017 International Conference on Cyberworlds (CW)*, pages 229–232. IEEE.

Ari Holtzman, Jan Buys, Maxwell Forbes, Antoine Bosselut, David Golub, and Yejin Choi. 2018. Learning to write with cooperative discriminators. In *Proceedings of the 56th Annual Meeting of the Association for Computational Linguistics (Volume 1: Long Papers)*, pages 1638–1649, Melbourne, Australia. Association for Computational Linguistics.

Ian D Horswill. 2016. Dear leader's happy story time: A party game based on automated story generation. In *Twelfth Artificial Intelligence and Interactive Digital Entertainment Conference*.

Isaac Karth. 2018. Preliminary poetics of procedural generation in games. *Proc. Digital Games Research Association*.

Chloé Kiddon, Luke Zettlemoyer, and Yejin Choi. 2016. Globally coherent text generation with neural checklist models. In *Proceedings of the 2016 Conference on Empirical Methods in Natural Language Processing*, pages 329–339.

Ben Kybartas and Clark Verbrugge. 2014. Analysis of ReGEN as a graph-rewriting system for quest generation. *IEEE Transactions on Computational Intelligence and AI in Games*, 6(2):228–242.

Michael Lebowitz. 1987. Planning stories. In *Proceedings of the 9th annual conference of the cognitive science society*, pages 234–242.

Stephanie M. Lukin, James O. Ryan, and Marilyn A. Walker. 2014. Automating direct speech variations in stories and games. In *Tenth Artificial Intelligence and Interactive Digital Entertainment Conference*.

Chris Martens. 2015. Ceptre: A language for modeling generative interactive systems. In *Eleventh Artificial Intelligence and Interactive Digital Entertainment Conference*.

Lara J Martin, Prithviraj Ammanabrolu, Xinyu Wang, William Hancock, Shruti Singh, Brent Harrison, and Mark O Riedl. 2018. Event representations for automated story generation with deep neural nets. In *Thirty-Second AAAI Conference on Artificial Intelligence*.

Jeffrey D McGovern and Gavin Scott. 2016. Eloquentrobot: A tool for automatic poetry generation. In *Proceedings of the Seventh ACM Conference on Bioinformatics, Computational Biology, and Health Informatics*.

Nick Montfort. 2007. *Generating narrative variation in interactive fiction*. Ph.D. thesis, University of Pennsylvania.

---

[15]`https://github.com/jd7h/narrative-gen-nanogenmo18`

Nick Montfort. 2009. Curveship: An interactive fiction system for interactive narrating. In *Proceedings of the Workshop on Computational Approaches to Linguistic Creativity*, pages 55–62, Boulder, Colorado. Association for Computational Linguistics.

Nick Montfort. 2014. New novel machines: Nanowatt and World clock. Trope Tank Technical Report TROPE-13–03, July 2014.

Nasrin Mostafazadeh, Nathanael Chambers, Xiaodong He, Devi Parikh, Dhruv Batra, Lucy Vanderwende, Pushmeet Kohli, and James Allen. 2016. A corpus and cloze evaluation for deeper understanding of commonsense stories. In *Proceedings of the 2016 Conference of the North American Chapter of the Association for Computational Linguistics: Human Language Technologies*, pages 839–849, San Diego, California. Association for Computational Linguistics.

Julie Porteous and Marc Cavazza. 2009. Controlling narrative generation with planning trajectories: the role of constraints. In *Joint International Conference on Interactive Digital Storytelling*, pages 234–245. Springer.

Aaron A Reed. 2012. Sharing authoring with algorithms: Procedural generation of satellite sentences in text-based interactive stories. In *Proceedings of The third workshop on Procedural Content Generation in Games*. ACM.

Ehud Reiter and Robert Dale. 1997. Building applied natural language generation systems. *Natural Language Engineering*, 3(1):57–87.

Justus Robertson and R Michael Young. 2015. Automated gameplay generation from declarative world representations. In *Eleventh Artificial Intelligence and Interactive Digital Entertainment Conference*.

James Ryan, Michael Mateas, and Noah Wardrip-Fruin. 2016. Characters who speak their minds: Dialogue generation in talk of the town. In *Twelfth Artificial Intelligence and Interactive Digital Entertainment Conference*.

Lauren R. Shapiro and Judith A. Hudson. 1991. Tell me a make-believe story: Coherence and cohesion in young children's picture-elicited narratives. *Developmental Psychology*, 27(6):960–974.

Christina R. Strong, Manish Mehta, Kinshuk Mishra, Alistair Jones, and Ashwin Ram. 2007. Emotionally driven natural language generation for personality rich characters in interactive games. In *Proceedings of the Third Artificial Intelligence and Interactive Digital Entertainment (AIIDE)*, pages 98–100.

Anne Sullivan, Mirjam Palosaari Eladhari, and Michael Cook. 2018. Tarot-based narrative generation. In *Proceedings of the 13th International Conference on the Foundations of Digital Games*, page 54. ACM.

Ivo Swartjes and Mariët Theune. 2008. The virtual storyteller: Story generation by simulation. In *Proceedings of the 20th Belgian-Netherlands Conference on Artificial Intelligence (BNAIC)*, pages 257–264.

Alan Tapscott, Carlos León, and Pablo Gervás. 2018. Generating stories using role-playing games and simulated human-like conversations. In *Proceedings of the 3rd Workshop on Computational Creativity in Natural Language Generation (CC-NLG 2018)*, pages 34–42.

Mariet Theune, Nanda Slabbers, and Feikje Hielkema. 2007. The Narrator: NLG for digital storytelling. In *Proceedings of the Eleventh European Workshop on Natural Language Generation*, pages 109–112, Saarbrücken, Germany.

Tony Veale. 2016. The shape of tweets to come: Automating language play in social networks. *Multiple Perspectives on Language Play*, 1:73–92.

Marilyn A. Walker, Ricky Grant, Jennifer Sawyer, Grace I. Lin, Noah Wardrip-Fruin, and Michael Buell. 2011. Perceived or not perceived: Film character models for expressive NLG. In *International Conference on Interactive Digital Storytelling*, pages 109–121. Springer.

Lili Yao, Nanyun Peng, Weischedel Ralph, Kevin Knight, Dongyan Zhao, and Rui Yan. 2019. Plan-and-write: Towards better automatic storytelling. In *Thirty-Third AAAI Conference on Artificial Intelligence (AAAI-19)*.

Lexical concreteness in narrative

Michael Flor
Educational Testing Service
Princeton
NJ 08541, USA
mflor@ets.org

Swapna Somasundaran
Educational Testing Service
Princeton
NJ 08541, USA
ssomasundaran@ets.org

Abstract

This study explores the relation between lexical concreteness and narrative text quality. We present a methodology to quantitatively measure lexical concreteness of a text. We apply it to a corpus of student stories, scored according to writing evaluation rubrics. Lexical concreteness is weakly-to-moderately related to story quality, depending on story-type. The relation is mostly borne by adjectives and nouns, but also found for adverbs and verbs.

1 Introduction

The influential writing-style guide, *The Elements of Style* (1999), (a.k.a. *Strunk and White*), recommends writers to '*prefer the specific to the general, the definite to the vague, the concrete to the abstract.*' This involves two related but distinct notions, two different senses of the word 'concrete' - *tangible* and *specific*. Tangibility, or the *concreteness/abstractness continuum* relates to objects and properties that afford sensorial perception - tangible things that can be seen, heard, smelled and touched. The *specificity* notion relates to the amount and level of detail that is conveyed in a story, to what extent things are presented in specific rather than general terms. The two notions go hand in hand, since to provide specific details the writer often has to mention more concrete objects and attributes and use less abstract terms. There are exceptions. Emotions and states of mind are usually not concrete (i.e. tangible) entities, though they are often specific. Numerical quantities (e.g. *6 million dollars, 30% of the population*) are quite specific but not quite sensorially concrete. Still, the importance of both concreteness and specificity for good writing is frequently mentioned in writer guides (Hacker and Sommers, 2014), in advice to college students (Maguire, 2012) and in recommendations for business writers (Matson, 2017).

College writing labs often suggest that students can improve their writing by including more concrete details in their essays.[1] Concreteness is also noted as an important aspect of writing literacy for K-12 education. The Common Core State Standards[2] (a federally recommended standard in the USA) specifies the following capability for students in Grade 6: "*Develop the topic with relevant facts, definitions, **concrete** details, quotations, or other information and examples.*" Despite its purported importance, few studies have measured lexical concreteness in stories, and no studies explored a quantitative relation between concreteness and story quality.

This work explores lexical concreteness in narrative essays. We use a quantitative measure, utilizing per-word concreteness ratings. We investigate whether better stories are more concrete and whether the story type (e.g. hypothetical situation versus personal narratives) influences the concreteness trends. We also perform a fine-grained analysis by parts-of-speech (nouns, verbs, adjectives and adverbs) to explore how their concreteness varies with story quality.

2 Related Work

The literature on using lexical concreteness for analysis of writing is rather limited.[3] Louis and Nenkova (2013) used imageability of words as a feature to model quality of science-journalism writing. For reading, concrete language was found to be more comprehensible and memorable than abstract language (Sadoski et al., 2000, 1993). Concreteness has also been related to reader engagement, promoting interest for expository materials (Sadoski, 2001).

---

[1] For example, see Purdue University and Roane State
[2] corestandards.org
[3] For recent research on specificity, see (Lugini and Litman, 2017; Li and Nenkova, 2015; Louis and Nenkova, 2011)

Proceedings of the Second Storytelling Workshop, pages 75–80
Florence, Italy, August 1, 2019. ©2019 Association for Computational Linguistics

Researchers have also looked at developmental aspects of mastery in producing expository and narrative texts. Proportion of abstract nouns in language production increases with age and schooling, although it is more pronounced in expository than in narrative writing (Ravid, 2005). Berman and Nir-Sagiv (2007) have found that the proportion of very concrete nouns tends to decrease from childhood to adulthood, whereas the proportion of abstract nouns tends to increase, in both expository and narrative texts. Sun and Nippold (2012) conducted a study in which students ages 11-17 were asked to write a personal story. The essays were examined for the use of abstract nouns (e.g., *accomplishment, loneliness*) and metacognitive verbs (e.g., *assume, discover*). The use of both types of words significantly increases with age. Goth et al. (2010) analyzed fables created by sixth graders (age 12) and found that boys use more concrete terms than girls.

How are concrete and abstract words identified and measured is an important methodological point. Goth et al. (2010) used the Coh-Metrix tool (Graesser et al., 2004), which measured individual word concreteness *"using the hypernym depth values retrieved from the WordNet lexical taxonomy, and averaged across noun and verb categories."* Berman and Nir-Sagiv (2007) rated <u>nouns</u> manually, using a four-level ordinal ranking. The most concrete (level 1) included objects and specific people; level 2 - categorial nouns, roles and locations (*teacher, city, people*). Higher abstractions were: level 3 - rare nouns (e.g., *rival, cult*), and abstract but common terms such as *fight, war*; level 4: low frequency abstract nouns (e.g. *relationship, existence*). Sun and Nippold (2012) used a dichotomous distinction (abstract/non-abstract) while manually rating all <u>nouns</u> in their data set. Abstract nouns were defined as intangible entities, inner states and emotions.

In psycholinguistic research, the notion of word concreteness became prominent due to the dual-coding theory of word representation (Pavio, 2013, 1971). Experimental studies often utilize the MRC database (Coltheart, 1981), which provides lexical concreteness ratings norms for 4,292 words. Such ratings were obtained experimentally, averaging across ratings provided by multiple participants in rating studies. Recently, Brysbaert et al. (2013) provided concreteness norms for 40,000 English lemmas. This new

Prompt	Count essays	Text Type
A Fork in the Road	47	Fictional
At First Glance	69	Fictional
Finding Your Way Home	2	Fictional
Message in a Bottle	31	Fictional
Movie Sequel	12	Fictional
Pitch Session	6	Fictional
Special Object	37	Fictional
The Antique Trunk	8	Fictional
The Quest	6	Fictional
Different Country	47	Hypothetical
Electricity-Free	32	Hypothetical
Living Art	3	Hypothetical
Trading Places	22	Hypothetical
Weirdest Day Ever!	78	Hypothetical
You are the Teacher	121	Hypothetical
Travel	75	Personal
Memorable School Day	153	Personal
Proudest Moment	191	Personal
Totals	171	Fictional
	303	Hypothetical
	466	Personal

Table 1: Essay counts for 18 prompts and their text-type classifications.

database opens the possibility for wide-coverage automated analysis of texts for estimating concreteness/abstractness. We utilize this resource for analyzing stories produced by students, and investigate the relation between concreteness and quality of narrative.

3 Data

We used a corpus of narrative essays[4] provided by Somasundaran et al. (2018). The corpus consists of 940 narrative essays written by school students from grade levels 7-12. Each essay was written in response to one of 18 story-telling prompts. The total size of the corpus is 310K words, and average essay length is 330 words.

The writing prompts were classified according to the type of story they are calling for, using the three-fold schema from Longobardi et al. (2013) - Fictional, Hypothetical and Personal. Table 1 presents the prompt titles, story types and essay counts. Example prompts are shown in the appendix.

---

[4]i.e. stories, not expository or persuasive writing

3.1 Essay scores

All essays were manually scored by experienced research assistants (Somasundaran et al., 2018), using a rubric that was created by education experts and teachers, and presented by Smarter Balanced assessment consortium, an assessment aligned to U.S. State Standards for grades K-12 (Smarter Balanced, 2014b,a).

The essays were scored along three traits (dimensions): Organization, Development and Conventions. *Organization* is concerned with event coherence, whether the story has a coherent start and ending, and whether there is a plot to hold all the pieces of the story together. It is scored on a scale of 0-4 integer points. *Development* evaluates whether the story provides vivid descriptions, and whether there is character development. It is also scored on a scale of 0-4 integer points, with 4 being the highest score. The *Conventions* dimension evaluates language proficiency, and is concerned with aspects of grammar, mechanics, and punctuation. Scores are on a scale of 0-3 integer points (3 is the highest score).

Somasundaran et al. (2018) computed Narrative and Total composite scores for each essay. The Narrative score (range 0-8) is the sum of Organization and Development scores. Total score (range 0-11) is the sum of Organization, Development and Conventions. Not surprisingly, the Organization, Development, Narrative and Total scores are highly intercorrelated (0.88 and higher, see Table 3 in Somasundaran et al. (2018)). For the present study, we used the Narrative scores, focusing on essay narrative quality and de-emphasizing grammar and mechanics.

POS	Count	Missing values
nouns	64,374	2,113 (3.3%)
verbs	66,718	753 (1.1%)
adjectives	19,090	658 (3.45%)
adverbs	19,399	212 (1.1%)
all content words	169,581	3,736 (2.2%)

Table 2: Content word counts by part-of-speech, with counts and proportion of tokens that did not have concreteness scores, for 940 essays.

3.2 Concreteness scores

We focus on concreteness of only the content words in the essays and ignore all function words. Each essay in the data set was POS-tagged with the Apache OpenNLP [5] tagger, and further analysis filtered in only nouns, verbs, adjective and adverbs. Those content words were checked against the database of concreteness scores (Brysbaert et al., 2013). The database provides real-valued ratings in the 1-5 range, from very abstract (score 1) to very concrete (score 5.0). For words that were not matched in the database, we checked if the lemma or an inflectional variant of the word was present in the database (using an in-house morphological toolkit). The database does not include names, but the essays often include names of persons and places. For our scoring, any names (identified by POS-tags *NNP* or *NNPS*), that were not found in the database, were assigned a uniform concreteness score of 4.0.

Concreteness scores were accumulated for each essay as described above. Average and median concreteness score was computed for each essay, separately for each of the categories (nouns, verbs, adjective and adverbs), and also jointly for all content-words. The total numbers of content words are given in Table 2. The concreteness-ratings coverage for our data is 97.8%.

4 Results

Pearson correlations of essay scores with per-essay levels of concreteness are presented in Table 3. Overall, the correlation of average-concreteness with essay score is r=0.222, which is considered a weak correlation (Evans, 1996). Breakdown by parts of speech shows that adjectives have the highest correlation of concreteness with score (0.297), followed by that for nouns (0.251), and adverbs (0.231). The correlation is weakest for verbs, only 0.122. Results for median-concreteness per essay show a similar pattern, though nouns now overtake adjectives.

	Average C.	Median C.
nouns	0.251	0.284
verbs	0.122	0.113
adjectives	0.297	0.242
adverbs	0.231	0.132
all content words	0.222	0.188

Table 3: Pearson correlations of essay narrative scores with per-essay levels of concreteness, for 940 essays. All correlations are significant, $p < .001$. C.=concreteness score

---

[5] `http://opennlp.apache.org`

(A) Prompt	N	Nouns	Verbs	Adjectives	Adverbs	All CW
Travel	75	0.400**	-0.017	0.401**	0.268*	0.371**
At First Glance	69	0.404**	0.006	0.326**	0.286*	0.240†
Memorable School Day	153	0.080	0.040	0.212**	0.239**	0.089
Proudest Moment	191	0.207**	0.072	0.118	0.060	0.137
Weirdest Day Ever	78	0.125	0.326**	0.355**	0.330**	0.322**
You are the Teacher	121	0.218*	0.102	0.298**	0.131	0.071
(B) Story type						
Fictional	171	0.465**	0.164†	0.417**	0.384**	0.413**
Hypothetical	303	0.263**	0.222**	0.287**	0.143*	0.217**
Personal	466	0.199**	0.045	0.237**	0.209**	0.138**

Table 4: Pearson correlations of essay narrative scores with per-essay average levels of concreteness; (A) for prompts that have above 60 essays, (B) for all essays, grouped by story-type. Significance of correlation **: $p < 0.01$, *: $p < .03$, † : $p < .05$. CW=content words.

Next, we present the correlations of concreteness levels with essay scores for each of the six prompts that have more than 50 essays (Table 4A). For two of the prompts, *Travel* and *At First Glance*, average concreteness of nouns is moderately correlated with essay narrative score ($r = 0.4$). For four prompts, adjectives show weak correlation with essay scores (from 0.21 to 0.35), while for the *Travel* prompt, average concreteness of adjectives is moderately correlated with essay narrative score ($r=0.4$). For four prompts, the average concreteness of adverbs is weakly correlated with essay score (0.24 to 0.33). For verbs, only one prompt, *Weirdest Day Ever*, shows some correlation of concreteness with essay score (0.33).

Next, we grouped essays by three types of story that their prompts were classified into. This move allows to use data from all essays. Results are presented in Table 4B. The *Fictional* story type has the highest correlation of concreteness and essay score ($r=0.413$), and it also has the highest correlation for nouns, for adjectives and for adverbs (as compared to other story types). Stories of the *Hypothetical* type show weak (yet significant) correlation of concreteness with scores, for nouns, verbs, adjectives and overall. Interestingly, the *Personal* story type shows the least relation of concreteness to scores, 0.138 overall; the adjectives there have correlation of 0.237, adverbs 0.209, and the nouns barely reach 0.2.

The results above suggest that the relation of concreteness to essay score varies for different story types. We checked whether the essays from three story types differ in concreteness or quality. An analysis of variance of narrative scores for three groups, F(2,937)=1.427, p=0.241, reveals that they did not differ in the average quality of stories. We also compared the average per-essay concreteness for the three groups. Mean concreteness for *Fiction* essays is 2.91, for *Hypothetical* essays it is 2.99, and 2.90 for *Personal*. An analysis of variance, F(2,937)=19.774, p<0.0001, shows that average concreteness is not equal in those groups. Post hoc comparisons (Tukey HSD test) indicated that only the *Hypothetical* group differed significantly from the two other groups. Those results indicate that the different strength of correlation between lexical concreteness and essay score that we observe in the three groups is not due to between-group differences in either narrative scores or lexical concreteness.

5 Conclusions

We presented a novel methodology for computing per-text lexical concreteness scores. For student-written stories, lexical concreteness is weakly to moderately positively correlated with narrative quality. Better essays score higher on lexical concreteness and use relatively less abstract words. While those results support the old adage 'prefer the concrete to the abstract', we also found that this relation varies for different story-types. It is prominent for *Fictional* stories, less pronounced for *Hypothetical* stories, and rather weak for *Personal* stories. Nouns and adjectives carry this relation most prominently, but it is also found for adverbs and verbs. This study lays the groundwork towards automatic assessment of lexical concreteness. In future work we will extend its application for text evaluation and feedback to writers.

References

Ruth A. Berman and Bracha Nir-Sagiv. 2007. Comparing narrative and expository text construction across adolescence: A developmental paradox. *Discourse processes*, 43(2):79–120.

Marc Brysbaert, Amy Beth Warriner, and Victor Kuperman. 2013. Concreteness ratings for 40 thousand generally known English word lemmas. *Behavior Research Methods*, 46:904–911.

Max Coltheart. 1981. The MRC psycholinguistic database. *Journal of Experimental Psychology*, 33:497–505.

James D. Evans. 1996. *Straightforward Statistics for the Behavioral Sciences*. Brooks/Cole Pub. Co., Pacific Grove, CA, USA.

Julius Goth, Alok Baikadi, Eun Ha, Jonathan Rowe, Bradford Mott, and James Lester. 2010. Exploring individual differences in student writing with a narrative composition support environment. In *Proceedings of the NAACL HLT 2010 Workshop on Computational Linguistics and Writing: Writing processes and authoring aids*, pages 56–64. Association for Computational Linguistics.

Arthur Graesser, Danielle McNamara, and Max Louwerse. 2004. Coh-Metrix: Analysis of text on cohesion and language. *Behavior Research Methods Instruments and Computers*, 36(2):193–202.

Diana Hacker and Nancy Sommers. 2014. *The Bedford Handbook*, 9 edition. Bedford/St. Martins, Boston, MA, USA.

William Strunk Jr. and Edward A. Tenney. 1999. *The Elements of Style*, 4 edition. Pearson, Harlow, UK.

Junyi Jessy Li and Ani Nenkova. 2015. Fast and Accurate Prediction of Sentence Specificity. In *Proceedings of the Twenty-Ninth AAAI Conference on Artificial Intelligence*, pages 2381–2387. Association for the Advancement of Artificial Intelligence.

Emiddia Longobardi, Pietro Spataro, Maria-Luisa Renna, and Clelia Rossi-Arnaud. 2013. Comparing fictional, personal, and hypothetical narratives in primary school: Story grammar and mental state language. *European Journal of Psychology of Education*, 29:257–275.

Annie Louis and Ani Nenkova. 2011. Automatic identification of general and specific sentences by leveraging discourse annotations. In *Proceedings of 5th International Joint Conference on Natural Language Processing*, pages 605–613, Chiang Mai, Thailand. Asian Federation of Natural Language Processing.

Annie Louis and Ani Nenkova. 2013. What makes writing great? First experiments on article quality prediction in the science journalism domain. *Transactions of the Association for Computational Linguistics*, 1:341–352.

Luca Lugini and Diane Litman. 2017. Predicting specificity in classroom discussion. In *Proceedings of the 12th Workshop on Innovative Use of NLP for Building Educational Applications*, pages 52–61, Copenhagen, Denmark. Association for Computational Linguistics.

John Maguire. 2012. The Secret to Good Writing: It's About Objects, Not Ideas. *The Atlantic*.

Owen Matson. 2017. Why Concrete Language is Essential to Engaging Content.

Allan Pavio. 1971. *Imagery and verbal processes*. Holt, Rinehart & Winston, Oxford, England.

Allan Pavio. 2013. Dual Coding Theory, Word Abstractness, and Emotion: A Critical Review of Kousta et al. (2011). *Journal of Experimental Psychology: General*, 142(1):282–287.

Dorit Ravid. 2005. Emergence of linguistic complexity in later language development: Evidence from expository text construction. In *Perspectives on language and language development*, pages 337–355. Springer.

Mark Sadoski. 2001. Resolving the effects of concreteness on interest, comprehension, and learning important ideas from text. *Educational Psychology Review*, 13(3):263–281.

Mark Sadoski, Ernest T. Goetz, and Joyce B. Fritz. 1993. Impact of concreteness on comprehensibility, interest, and memory for text: Implications for dual coding theory and text design. *Journal of Educational Psychology*, 85(2):291–304.

Mark Sadoski, Ernest T. Goetz, and Maximo Rodriguez. 2000. Engaging Texts: Effects of Concreteness on Comprehensibility, Interest, and Recall in Four Text Types. *Journal of Educational Psychology*, 92(1):85–95.

Smarter Balanced. 2014a. English Language Arts/Literacy Item Specifications - Narrative.

Smarter Balanced. 2014b. Scoring Guide For Grades 3, 6, and 11, English/Language Arts Performance Task full-write baseline sets.

Swapna Somasundaran, Michael Flor, Martin Chodorow, Hillary Molloy, Binod Gyawali, and Laura McCulla. 2018. Towards evaluating narrative quality in student writing. *Transactions of the Association for Computational Linguistics*, 6:91–106.

Lei Sun and Marilyn A. Nippold. 2012. Narrative writing in children and adolescents: Examining the literate lexicon. *Language, speech, and hearing services in schools*, 43(1):2–13.

A Appendix

Example prompts for three types of text styles:

Personal Experience: "Proudest Moment" - *There are moments in everyones lives when they feel pride and accomplishment after completing a challenging task. Write a story about your proudest moment.*

Hypothetical Situation: "You are the Teacher" - *Pretend that one morning you wake up and find out that you've become your teacher for a day! What happened? What do you do? Do you learn anything? Write a story about what happens. Use your imagination!*

Fictional Story: "Message in a Bottle" - *Throughout the years, many have placed messages in sealed bottles and dropped the bottles into the ocean where they eventually washed up on foreign shores. Occasionally the finder has even contacted the sender. Write a story about finding your own message in a bottle.*

A Simple Approach to Classify Fictional and Non-Fictional Genres

Mohammed Rameez Qureshi
IISER Bhopal
mohr@iiserb.ac.in

Sidharth Ranjan
IIT Delhi
sidharth.ranjan03@gmail.com

Rajakrishnan P. Rajkumar
IISER Bhopal
rajak@iiserb.ac.in

Kushal Shah
IISER Bhopal
kushals@iiserb.ac.in

Abstract

In this work, we deploy a logistic regression classifier to ascertain whether a given document belongs to the fiction or non-fiction genre. For genre identification, previous work had proposed three classes of features, *viz.*, low-level (character-level and token counts), high-level (lexical and syntactic information) and derived features (type-token ratio, average word length or average sentence length). Using the Recursive feature elimination with cross-validation (RFECV) algorithm, we perform feature selection experiments on an exhaustive set of nineteen features (belonging to all the classes mentioned above) extracted from Brown corpus text. As a result, two simple features *viz.*, the ratio of the number of adverbs to adjectives and the number of adjectives to pronouns turn out to be the most significant. Subsequently, our classification experiments aimed towards genre identification of documents from the Brown and Baby BNC corpora demonstrate that the performance of a classifier containing just the two aforementioned features is at par with that of a classifier containing the exhaustive feature set.

1 Introduction

Texts written in any human language can be classified in various ways, one of them being fiction and non-fiction genres. These categories/genres can either refer to the actual content of the write-up or the writing style used, and in this paper, we use the latter meaning. We associate *fiction* writings with literary perspectives, i.e., an imaginative form of writing which has its own purpose of communication, whereas *non-fiction* writings are written in a matter-of-fact manner, but the contents may or may not refer to real life incidents (Lee, 2001). The distinction between imaginative and informative prose is very important and can have several practical applications. For example, one could use a software to identify news articles, which are expected to be written in a matter-of-fact manner, but tend to use an imaginative writing style to unfairly influence the reader. Another application for such a software could be for publishing houses which can use it to automatically filter out article/novel submissions that do not meet certain expected aspects of fiction writing style.

The standard approach in solving such text classification problems is to identify a large enough set of relevant features and feed it into a machine learning algorithm. In the genre identification literature, three types of linguistic features have been discussed *i.e.*, *high-level, low-level* and *derived features* (Karlgren and Cutting, 1994; Kessler et al., 1997; Douglas, 1992; Biber, 1995). High-level features include lexical and syntactic information whereas low-level features involve character-level and various types of token count information. The *lexical* features deal with word frequency statistics such as frequency of content words, function words or specific counts of each pronoun, etc. Similarly, the *syntactic* features incorporate statistics of parts of speech, i.e., noun, verb, adjectives, adverbs and grammatical functions such as active and passives voices or affective markers such as modal auxiliary verbs. The *character-level* features involve punctuation usage, word count, word length, sentence length. And, lastly, the *derived* features involve ratio metrics such as type-token ratio, average word length or average sentence length based information. Majorly, all the previous work involved a combination of different features to represent a particular nature of the document and developing a model that classify different genres, sentiments or opinions.

Notably, researchers have adopted the frequentist approach (Sichel, 1975; Zipf, 1932, 1945) and used lexical richness (Tweedie and Baayen, 1998) as a prominent cue for genre classification (Bur-

81

Proceedings of the Second Storytelling Workshop, pages 81–89
Florence, Italy, August 1, 2019. ©2019 Association for Computational Linguistics

rows, 1992; Stamatatos et al., 2000, 1999). These studies vouch that coming out with statistical distribution from word frequencies would be the *de-facto-arbiter* for document classification. In this regard, Stamatatos and colleagues have shown that most frequent words in the training corpus as well as in the entire English language are one of the good features for detecting the genre type (Stamatatos et al., 2000). With respect to syntactic and semantics properties of the text, previous studies have used various parts of speech counts in terms of number of *types* and *tokens* (Rittman et al., 2004; Rittman, 2007; Rittman and Wacholder, 2008; Cao and Fang, 2009). Researchers have tried to investigate the efficacy of counts vs. ratio features and their impact on the classification model performance. In general, a large number of features often tend to overfit the machine learning model performance. Hence, concerning the derived ratio features, Kessler et al. (1997) argues in his genre identification study that ratio features tend to eliminate over-fitting as well as high computational cost during training.

Although these earlier approaches have made very good progress in text classification, and are very powerful from an algorithmic perspective, they do not provide many insights into the linguistic and cognitive aspects of these fiction and non-fiction genres. The main objective of our work is to be able to extract the features that are most relevant to this particular classification problem and can help us in understanding the underlying linguistic properties of these genres. We begin by extracting nineteen linguistically motivated features belonging to various types (described at the outset) from the Brown corpus and then perform feature selection experiments using Recursive feature elimination with cross-validation (RFECV) algorithm (Guyon et al., 2002). Interestingly, we find that a classifier containing just two simple ratio features *viz.*, the ratio of the number of adverbs to adjectives and number of adjectives to pronouns perform as well as a classifier containing an exhaustive set of features from prior work described above [96.31% and 100% classification accuracy for Brown (Francis and Kučera, 1989) and British National corpus (BNC Baby, 2005), respectively]. This is perhaps the best accuracy reported in the literature so far to the best of our knowledge. Essentially, we find that texts from the fiction genre tend to have a higher ratio of adverb to adjectives,

Genre	Subgenre	No. of words	No. of files
Non-fiction	Government	70117	30
	News	100554	44
	Learned	181888	80
	Hobbies	82345	36
	Reviews	40704	17
Fiction	Science Fiction	14470	6
	Fiction	68488	29
	Romance	70022	29
	Adventure	69342	29
	Mystery	57169	24

Table 1: Brown corpus subgenre details

and texts from the non-fiction genre tend to have a higher ratio of adjectives to pronouns. We discuss the implications of this finding for style guides for non-fiction writing (Zinsser, 2006) as well as standard advice proffered to creative writers (King, 2001).

In Section 2, we share details about our linguistic features design, data set and experimental methodology. Section 3 presents the experiments conducted as a part of our study and discusses their critical findings. Finally, Section 4 summarizes the conclusions of the study and discusses the implications of our findings.

2 Data and Methods

For our experiments, we use the Brown Corpus (Francis and Kučera, 1989), one of the earliest collections of annotated texts of present-day American English and available free of cost with the NLTK toolkit (Loper and Bird, 2002). The nature of the distribution of texts in the Brown corpus helps us to conduct our studies conveniently. The Brown corpus consists of 500 text samples with different genres distributed among 15 categories/genres, which are further divided into two major classes, namely, *Informative prose* and *Imaginative prose*. As per our proposed definition in this study, we associate informative prose with the non-fictional genre and imaginative prose as a fictional one. We conduct a binary classification task to separate text samples into these two genres (i.e., fiction and non-fiction) with our proposed linguistic features. Out of the 15 genres, we excluded the 5 genres of *humour, editorial, lore, religion* and *letters* from our dataset as it is difficult to accurately associate them with either fiction and non-fiction genres. Finally, the fictional category consists of 5 subcategories, namely: *fiction, mystery, romance, adventure, and science fiction*. Similarly, the non-fiction category includes 5 subcategories namely: *news, hobbies, government, reviews, and learned.* This leads us to use 324 samples out of 500 articles in the Brown corpus; out of which 207 samples fall under fiction category and 117 under non-fiction. Despite having less number of samples, the total word count of all texts in the non-fiction category/genre (479,708 words) is higher than that of fiction (284,429 words), and the total number of sentences in the non-fiction category/genre (21,333) is also higher than that of fiction (18,151). Hence, we chose to divide the data by sub-categories rather than having a number of samples or number of words as the base for distribution. Table 1 provides more details regarding the documents in these genres.

To further our understanding of the model's classification performance for Brown corpus and investigate its applicability to British English, we use the British National Corpus (BNC Baby, 2005). This approach helps us to examine model prediction more robustly. Baby BNC consists of four categories, namely, fiction, newspaper, spoken and academic. Due to the clear demarcation between these categories, we use only fiction documents (25 samples) labeled as fiction and academic documents (30 samples) as non-fiction for our experiments. Finally, we apply our algorithm on the articles in the news category (97 samples) to check whether they fall under fiction or non-fiction genre.

Keeping in mind the binary nature of our classification task, we use logistic regression (LR) as our numerical method (McCullagh and Nelder, 1989). Among many classification algorithms, the result of LR is among the most informative ones. By informative, we mean that it not only gives a measure of the *relevance* of a feature (coefficient value) but also the *nature* of its association with the outcome (negative or positive). It models the binary dependent variable using a linear combination of one or more predictor values (features) with the help of following equations where ϕ is the estimated response probability:

$$g(\phi) = log(\phi/(1 - \phi)) \tag{1}$$

$$\phi = P(x) = \frac{1}{1 + e^{-(x_i\beta_i+\beta_0)}} \tag{2}$$

where, x_i is the feature vector for text i, β_i is the estimated weight vector, and β_0 is intercept of the linear regression equation.

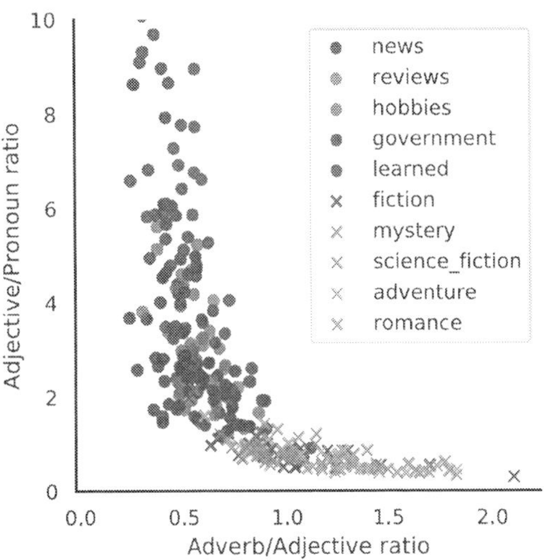

Figure 1: Scatter plot of Brown corpus samples of different subgenres. Fiction samples are marked with 'x' whereas non-fiction samples are marked with 'o' with Y-axis limit set up to 10.

3 Experiments and Results

This section describes our experiments aimed to classify texts into the fictional and non-fictional genres using machine learning. The next subsection describes various linguistic features we deploy in detail and the use of feature selection to identify the most useful features. Subsequently, Section 3.2 provides the results of our classification experiments.

3.1 Linguistic Features and Feature Selection

We compute different low-level and high-level features as discussed in Section 1 and after that take their ratios as the relative representative metric for the classification task. Table 2 depicts the features used in this work. Some of the ratio features such as average token/type (punctuation) ratio, hyphen exclamation ratio, etc., have been explored in earlier work (Kessler et al., 1997). For calculating high-level ratio features, we use tags from two kind of POS tagsets, *i.e*, gold standard tags provided as part of the Brown Corpus (87 tags) and automatic tags (based on the 36-tag Penn Treebank tagset) predicted by Stanford tagger[1] (Toutanova et al., 2003). Grammatical categories like noun, verb, and adjective are inferred from the POS tags using the schema given in Ta-

---

[1] https://nlp.stanford.edu/software/tagger.shtml

83

Type	Features
Low-level normalized	**Average Sentence Length** **Average Word Length** Standard Deviation of Sentence Length Standard Deviation of Word Length
Low-level ratio	Average token/type Standard Deviation of token/type Average token/type (punctuation) Standard Deviation of token/type (punctuation) **Hyphen/Quote** Hyphen/Exclamation Quote/Question
High-level ratio	Adverb/Noun Adverb/Pronoun Adjective/Verb Noun/Verb Verb/Pronoun **Adverb/Adjective** **<u>Adjective/Pronoun</u>** **Noun/Pronoun**

Table 2: Derived linguistic features (Features selected after RFECV on: Brown tagset-bold; Penn tagset-underlined)

Category	POS tag	Tagset
Adjective	JJ, JJR, JJS	
Adverb	RB, RBR, RBS. WRB	
Noun	NN, NNS, NNP, NNPS	Penn
Verb	VB, VBD, VBG, VBN,VBP, VBZ	Treebank
Pronoun	PRP, WP	
Adjective	JJ, JJR, JJS, JJT	
Adverb	RB, RBR, WRB, RBT, RN, RP, NR	
Noun	NN, NNS, NN$, NNS$, NP, NP$, NPS, NPS$	Brown
Verb	VB, VBD, VBG, VBN, VBP, VBZ	
Pronoun	PN, PN$, PP$, PP$, PPL, PPLS PPO, PPS, PPSS, PRP, PRP$, WP$, WPO, WPS	

Table 3: Rules to ascertain grammatical categories from POS tags

ble 3. We consider both personal pronouns and *wh*-pronouns as part of the pronoun category.

We use the recursive feature elimination with cross-validation (RFECV) method to eliminate non-significant features. Recursive feature elimination (Guyon et al., 2002) follows the greedy search algorithm to select the best performing features. It forms models iteratively with different combinations of features and removes the worst performing features at each step, thus giving the set of best performing set of features. The motivation behind these experiments is not only to get a good accuracy score but also to decipher the importance of these features and to understand their impact on writing. After applying RFECV on the automatically tagged Brown Corpus, we get all features as the optimum set of features. We attribute this result to the POS-tagging errors introduced by the Stanford tagger. So we apply our feature selection method to features extracted from the Brown Corpus with gold standard tags. Here, 13 out of 19 features are marked as non-

significant, and we obtain six most significant features (shown in bold in Table 2). Subsequently, we extract these six features from the automatically tagged Brown Corpus, and feature selection on this set revealed only two of these features as being the most significant (underlined in Table 2). The two most notable features which emerge from our second feature selection experiment are *adverb/adjective ratio* and *adjective/pronoun ratio*. The *Noun/pronoun* ratio feature gets eliminated in the process. Figure 1 illustrates how both these ratios provide distinct clusters of data points belonging to the fiction and non-fiction genres (and even their subgenres). Thus, the Brown corpus tagset encoding finer distinctions in grammatical categories (compared to the Penn Treebank tagset), does help in isolating a set of six significant ratio features. These features are useful for identifying the final two POS-ratios based on automatic tags.

3.2 Classification Experiments

As described in the previous section, we apply logistic regression to individual files of two data-sets (Brown Corpus and Baby British National Corpus) after extracting various low-level features and features encoding ratios of POS tags based on automatic tags emitted by the Stanford tagger (see Table 2). We use a logistic regression classifier with ten-fold cross-validation and L1 regularization for training to carry out our analyses and report the *accuracy* achieved over the total number of files in our test sets. We use the Scikit-learn[2] (Pedregosa et al., 2011) library for our classification experiments. The individual performance by non-significant features has not been reported in our study. We report results for three data sets after tagging them using the Stanford POS-tagger:

1. Brown Corpus with a 60%-40% train-test split (194 training files; 130 test files).

2. Brown Corpus with Baby BNC combined with a 60%-40% train-test split (227 training files; 152 test files).

3. Testing on Baby BNC with Training on Brown Corpus (324 training files; 55 test files).

We calculate testing accuracy for the first two datasets for ten different combinations of training and testing sets, and report the mean accuracy with

---

[2] https://scikit-learn.org/stable/

S.No.	Data	Feature Sets	Testing Accuracy %	F1 score (non-fiction)	F1 score (fiction)	Baseline Accuracy %	Accuracy Gain %
(a)	Brown Corpus with 60 % - 40 % Train - Test data	All Low level features	94.15 ± 1.82	0.9540 ± 0.0141	0.9194 ± 0.0269	63.77 ± 2.00	83.85
		19 Features	96.92 ± 1.26	0.9760 ± 0.0095	0.9569 ± 0.0186		91.50
		6 Features	96.08 ± 1.51	0.9692 ± 0.0122	0.9457 ± 0.0206		89.18
		2 Features	96.31 ± 0.49	0.9711 ± 0.0038	0.9486 ± 0.0081		89.82
(b)	Brown Corpus and Baby BNC combined with 60 % - 40 % Train - Test data	All Low level features	95.39 ± 1.72	0.9634 ± 0.0138	0.9371 ± 0.0257	63.13 ± 3.13	87.50
		19 Features	96.73 ± 1.73	0.9736 ± 0.0143	0.9565 ± 0.0233		91.13
		6 Features	97.21 ± 1.42	0.9777 ± 0.0117	0.9624 ± 0.0196		92.43
		2 Features	97.13 ± 1.04	0.9769 ± 0.0087	0.9617 ± 0.0138		92.22
(c)	Training on Brown Corpus & Testing on Baby BNC	All Low level features	92.73	0.9286	0.9259	54.54	84.01
		19 Features	52.73	0.2353	0.6579		-3.98
		6 Features	100	1	1		100
		2 Features	100	1	1		100

Table 4: Classification accuracy for Brown Corpus and Baby BNC with different feature sets (most frequent class *i.e.*, *non-fiction* baseline results reported).

standard deviation for the same as well as for the most frequent baseline accuracy. While for the third dataset, only one training and testing set possible exists, and therefore, we report the testing accuracy and the most frequent class baseline accuracy accordingly. The most frequent class baseline is the percentage accuracy obtained if a model labels all the data points as the most frequent class in the data (*non-fiction* in our study). Table 4 illustrates our results. Here, we also use another performance metric known as *accuracy gain* which is considered more rigorous and interpretable measure as compared to the standard measure of accuracy. The accuracy gain percentage is calculated as:

$$\text{Accuracy Gain \%} = \frac{(acc - baseline)}{(100 - baseline)} \times 100 \quad (3)$$

where '*acc*' is the reported mean accuracy of model, whereas '*baseline*' is the mean of most frequent class baseline.

We begin with the Brown Corpus and take 117 sample texts of non-fiction and 207 of fiction categories. Our training set consists of 60% of the total sample size whereas testing set comprises of remaining 40% of samples. We have four combinations of the set of features (refer Row 1 of Table 4). It can be noted that two features model performed better than the model corresponding to the six features and low-level ratio features and is performing as good as 19 features model. To make the model more robust, we follow the same approach for the combination of Brown corpus and Baby BNC with 147 sample texts of non-fiction and 232 sample texts of fiction categories. Baby BNC has been included to check the impact of British English on the performance of the model. One may observe that the model performed even

better when exposed to Baby BNC. Similar observations can be made about the accuracy of the two features model (refer Row 2 of Table 4). In our final experiment, we use the Brown corpus for training and the Baby BNC for testing with the available set of features. In this case, the features obtained after feature selection on the exhaustive set of features results in 100% classification accuracy (Row 3 of Table 4). This result also signifies the universal applicability of the ratio features and high-level POS ratios are not something which is affected by bias due to the language variety (*i.e.*, British vs. American English). However, the low performance of the 19 features model (53% classification accuracy) shows how they are prone to overfitting.

The two most significant features, *adverb/adjective* ratio and *adjective/pronoun* ratio have regression coefficients 2.73 and -2.90 respectively. Thus, fiction documents tend to have higher values for the ratio of number adverbs to adjectives and a lower value for the ratio of the number of adjectives to pronouns. It is worth noting that the high accuracy scores of more than 95% we obtained by using 19 features in the case of the first two datasets are in the vicinity of the accuracy score given by only these two features. Also, the fact that the F1 scores are close to the accuracy values signifies the fact that the results obtained are robust in nature.

Finally, in order to check the dominant tendencies in the behaviour of classifiers containing different feature sets, we examine the predictions of various classifiers using a separate test set consisting of 97 news documents in the Baby BNC corpus. We also studied model predictions using different training sets. Initially, we use the same data sets mentioned in the last two rows of Ta-

Training data	19 features	6 features	2 features
Brown (324 training files)	100	92.78	89.69
Brown (w/o news category) (280 training files)	100	92.78	90.72
Brown + Baby BNC (379 training files)	1.03	92.78	90.72
Brown + Baby BNC (w/ news category) (476 training files)	65.98	97.94	93.81

Table 5: Percentage of documents classified as non-fiction in a test set of 97 Baby BNC news documents

ble 4. Apart from this, to check the bias of the model, we create a new test set after removing the news category from the *non-fiction* class of brown corpus. Similarly, in the combined Brown+Baby BNC corpus, we later include news samples from Baby BNC to measure the improvement in the model's predictions. The results are shown in Table 5. It can be observed that most of the samples are classified as non-fiction, as expected. Also, removing news articles from the Brown corpus non-fiction category does not impact the results indicating the unbiased behavior of the model. However, an important conclusion one can draw from Table 5 results is that both the two features as well as the six features model are pretty stable as compared to their 19-feature counterpart. Even the introduction of news samples from Baby BNC in the training data does not seem to help the predictions of 19 features model. This shows the vulnerability of more complex models to a slight change in the training data.

4 Discussion and Conclusion

In this paper, we have identified two important features that can be very helpful in classifying fiction and non-fiction genres with high accuracy. Fiction articles, *i.e.*, those which are written with an imaginative flavor, tend to have a higher adverb/adjective ratio of POS tags, whereas non-fiction articles, i.e., those which are written in a matter of fact manner, tend to have a higher adjective/pronoun ratio. This not only helps in classification using machine learning but also provides useful linguistic insights. A glance at the percentages of each of these grammatical categories computed over the total number of words in the dataset (Figure 2) reveals several aspects of the genres themselves. In both corpora, the trends are

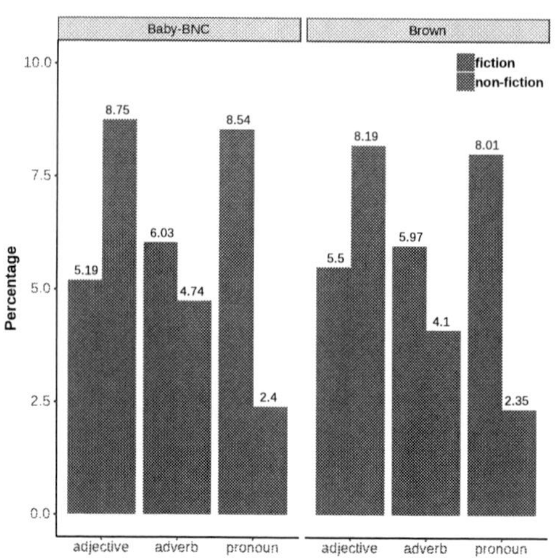

Figure 2: Adjectives, adverbs and pronouns as a percentage of the total number of words

roughly the same. In fiction, both adjectives and adverbs have a roughly similar proportion, while non-fiction displays almost double the number of adjectives compared to adverbs. Also, the percentage of pronouns vary sharply across the two genres in both our datasets as compared to adjectives and adverbs. Figure 3 presents a much more nuanced picture of personal pronouns in the Brown corpus. Fiction displays the greater percentage of third person masculine and feminine pronouns as well as the first person singular pronoun compared to non-fiction, while both genres have comparable percentages of first-person plural *we* and *us*. Moreover, differences in modification strategies using adverbs vs. *wh*-pronouns requires further exploration. Even the usage of punctuation marks differ across genres (Figure 4).

It is worth noting that many guides to writing both fiction (King, 2001) as well as non-fiction (Zinsser, 2006) advise writers to avoid the overuse of both adverbs and adjectives. In a statistical study of classic works of English literature, Blatt (2017) also points to adverb-usage patterns in the works of renowned authors. Nobel prize winning writer Toni Morrison's oft-cited dispreference for adverbs is analyzed quantitatively to show that on an average she used 76 adverbs per 10,000 words (compared to 80 by Hemingway; much higher numbers for the likes of Steinbeck, Rushdie, Salinger, and Wharton). The cited work discusses Morrison's point about eliminating prose like *She says softly* by virtue of the fact that the preceding scene would be described such that

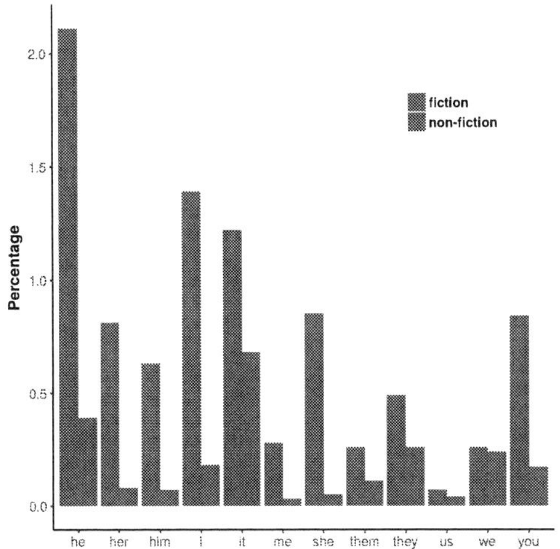

Figure 3: Brown corpus pronouns as a percentage of the total number of words

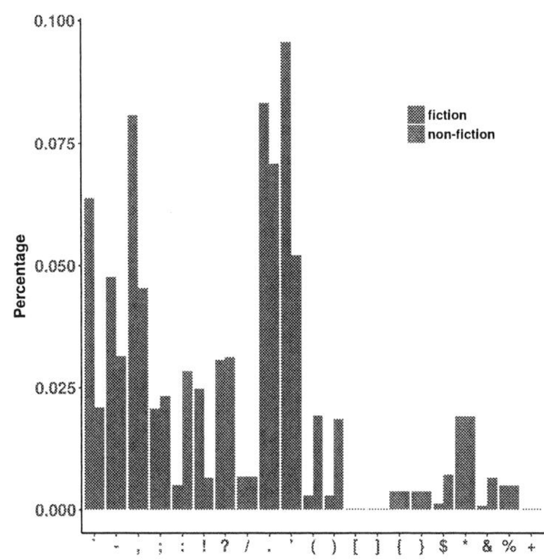

Figure 4: Brown corpus punctuation as a percentage of the number of words

the emotion in the speech is conveyed to the reader without the explicit use of the adverb *softly*. In fact, Sword (2016) advocates the strategy of using expressive verbs encoding the meaning of adverbs as well, as exemplified below (adverbs in bold and paraphrase verbs italicized):

1. She walked **painfully** (*dragged*) toward the car.

2. She walked **happily** (*sauntered*) toward the car.

3. She walked **drunkenly** (*stumbled*) toward the car.

4. She walked **absent-mindedly** (*meandered*) toward the car.

A long line of research undeniably argues that *adjective* and *adverbs* are strong indicators of affective language and serve as an important feature in text classification tasks viz., automatic genre identification (Rittman et al., 2004; Rittman, 2007; Rittman and Wacholder, 2008; Cao and Fang, 2009).In this regard, Rittman and Wacholder (2008) propound that both these grammatical classes have sentimental connotations and capture human personality along with their expression of judgments. For our classifer, rather than the number of adjectives, it is the relative balance of adjectives and adverbs that determine the identity of a particular genre. A large-scale study needs to validate whether this conclusion can be generalized to the English language as a whole. Thus, prescriptions for both technical as well as creative writing should be based on systematic studies involving large-scale comparisons of fictional texts with other non-fiction genres. In

particular, the paranoia about elements of modification like adjectives and adverbs seem unjustified as many other mechanisms of nominal and verbal modification like prepositional phrases and subordinate clauses exist in language.[3]

Since our classification is based on the ratios of these POS tags taken across the whole document, it is difficult to identify a few sentences which can demonstrate the role of our features (adverb/adjective and adjective/pronoun ratio) convincingly. Qualitatively, the importance of adjectives can be comprehended with the help of an excerpt taken from the sample file of Brown corpus (*fileid cp09*; adjectives in bold):

" *Out of the church and into his* **big** *car, it tooling over the road with him driving and the headlights sweeping the pike ahead and after he hit college, his expansiveness, the* **quaint** *little pine board tourist courts, cabins really, with a* **cute naked** *light bulb in the ceiling (unfrosted and naked as a streetlight, like the one on the corner where you used to play when you were a kid, where you watched the bats swooping in after the bugs, watching in between your bouts at hopscotch), a room* **complete** *with moths pinging the light and the few* **casual** *cockroaches cruising the walls, an insect Highway Patrol with feelers waving.*"

---

[3]We are indebted to Mark Liberman's blog post for this idea: https://tinyurl.com/y59jbr64

After removing adjectives (identified using Brown corpus tags), we get:

" Out of the church and into his car, it tooling over the road with him driving and the headlights sweeping the pike ahead and after he hit college, his expansiveness, the little pine board tourist courts, cabins really, with a light bulb in the ceiling (unfrosted and naked as a streetlight, like the one on the corner where you used to play when you were a kid, where you watched the bats swooping in after the bugs, watching in between your bouts at hopscotch), a room with moths pinging the light and the few cockroaches cruising the walls, an insect Highway Patrol with feelers waving."

Although the text with adjectives removed still belongs to the fiction genre, we can clearly see the role that these words can play in enhancing the imaginative quotient of the text. However, counter-intuitively, Figure 2 shows that texts in the non-fiction genre tend to have a higher percentage of adjectives as compared to texts in the fiction genre, but the latter have a higher percentage of adverbs. Hence, this example reiterates the point that the role played by our salient features (adverb/adjective and adjective/pronoun ratios) in classifying fiction and non-fiction genres is difficult to appreciate with only a few lines of text. An interesting question could be to find out the minimum length of a text required for accurate classification into fiction and non-fiction genres and also more significant features in this regard, which we will take up in the future. We also intend to carry out this study on a much larger dataset in the future in order to verify the efficacy of our features.

References

Douglas Biber. 1995. *Dimensions of register variation: A cross-linguistic comparison.* Cambridge University Press.

Benjamin Blatt. 2017. *Nabokov's Favourite Word is Mauve: The Literary Quirks and Oddities of Our Most-loved Authors.* Simon & Schuster.

BNC Baby. 2005. *British National Corpus, Baby edition.* Distributed by Oxford University Computing Services on behalf of the BNC Consortium.

John F Burrows. 1992. Not unles you ask nicely: The interpretative nexus between analysis and information. *Literary and Linguistic Computing,* 7(2):91–109.

Jing Cao and Alex C Fang. 2009. Investigating variations in adjective use across different text categories. *Advances in Computational Linguistics, Journal of Research In Computing Science Vol,* 41:207–216.

Douglas Douglas. 1992. The multi-dimensional approach to linguistic analyses of genre variation: An overview of methodology and findings. *Computers and the Humanities,* 26(5-6):331–345.

W.N. Francis and H. Kučera. 1989. *Manual of Information to Accompany a Standard Corpus of Present-day Edited American English, for Use with Digital Computers.* Brown University, Department of Linguistics.

Isabelle Guyon, Jason Weston, Stephen Barnhill, and Vladimir Vapnik. 2002. Gene selection for cancer classification using support vector machines. *Machine Learning,* 46(1):389–422.

Jussi Karlgren and Douglass Cutting. 1994. Recognizing text genres with simple metrics using discriminant analysis. In *Proceedings of the 15th conference on Computational linguistics-Volume 2,* pages 1071–1075. Association for Computational Linguistics.

Brett Kessler, Geoffrey Numberg, and Hinrich Schtze. 1997. Automatic detection of text genre. *Proceedings of the 35th annual meeting on Association for Computational Linguistics -.*

S. King. 2001. *On Writing: A Memoir of the Craft.* Hodder & Stoughton.

David YW Lee. 2001. Genres, registers, text types, domain, and styles: Clarifying the concepts and navigating a path through the bnc jungle. *Language Learning & Technology,* 5(3):37–72.

Edward Loper and Steven Bird. 2002. Nltk: The natural language toolkit. In *Proceedings of the ACL-02 Workshop on Effective Tools and Methodologies for Teaching Natural Language Processing and Computational Linguistics - Volume 1,* ETMTNLP '02, pages 63–70, Stroudsburg, PA, USA. Association for Computational Linguistics.

Peter McCullagh and John A. Nelder. 1989. *Generalized linear models,* volume 37. CRC press, London, New York.

F. Pedregosa, G. Varoquaux, A. Gramfort, V. Michel, B. Thirion, O. Grisel, M. Blondel, P. Prettenhofer, R. Weiss, V. Dubourg, J. Vanderplas, A. Passos, D. Cournapeau, M. Brucher, M. Perrot, and E. Duchesnay. 2011. Scikit-learn: Machine learning in Python. *Journal of Machine Learning Research,* 12:2825–2830.

R.J. Rittman. 2007. *Automatic Discrimination of Genres: The Role of Adjectives and Adverbs as Suggested by Linguistics and Psychology*. Rutgers The State University of New Jersey - New Brunswick.

Robert Rittman and Nina Wacholder. 2008. Adjectives and adverbs as indicators of affective language for automatic genre detection. In *AISB 2008 Convention Communication, Interaction and Social Intelligence*, volume 1, page 65.

Robert Rittman, Nina Wacholder, Paul Kantor, Kwong Bor Ng, Tomek Strzalkowski, and Ying Sun. 2004. Adjectives as indicators of subjectivity in documents. *Proceedings of the American Society for Information Science and Technology*, 41(1):349–359.

Herbert S Sichel. 1975. On a distribution law for word frequencies. *Journal of the American Statistical Association*, 70(351a):542–547.

E. Stamatatos, N. Fakotakis, and G. Kokkinakis. 1999. Automatic authorship attribution. In *Proceedings of the Ninth Conference on European Chapter of the Association for Computational Linguistics*, EACL '99, pages 158–164, Stroudsburg, PA, USA. Association for Computational Linguistics.

Efstathios Stamatatos, Nikos Fakotakis, and George Kokkinakis. 2000. Text genre detection using common word frequencies. In *Proceedings of the 18th conference on Computational linguistics-Volume 2*, pages 808–814. Association for Computational Linguistics.

Helen Sword. 2016. *The Writer's Diet: A Guide to Fit Prose*. Chicago Guides to Writing, Editing, and Publishing. University of Chicago Press.

Kristina Toutanova, Dan Klein, Christopher D Manning, and Yoram Singer. 2003. Feature-rich part-of-speech tagging with a cyclic dependency network. In *Proceedings of the 2003 conference of the North American chapter of the association for computational linguistics on human language technology-volume 1*, pages 173–180. Association for computational Linguistics.

Fiona J Tweedie and R Harald Baayen. 1998. How variable may a constant be? measures of lexical richness in perspective. *Computers and the Humanities*, 32(5):323–352.

W. Zinsser. 2006. *On Writing Well: The Classic Guide to Writing Nonfiction*. HarperCollins.

George Kingsley Zipf. 1932. Selected studies of the principle of relative frequency in language. *Cambridge, Massachusetts: Harvard University Press*.

George Kingsley Zipf. 1945. The meaning-frequency relationship of words. *The Journal of General Psychology*, 33(2):251–256.

Detecting Everyday Scenarios in Narrative Texts

Lilian D. A. Wanzare[1] **Michael Roth**[2] **Manfred Pinkal**[1]
Universität des Saarlandes[1] Universität Stuttgart[2]
{wanzare,pinkal}coli.uni-saarland.de   rothml@ims.uni-stuttgart.de

Abstract

Script knowledge consists of detailed information on everyday activities. Such information is often taken for granted in text and needs to be inferred by readers. Therefore, script knowledge is a central component to language comprehension. Previous work on representing scripts is mostly based on extensive manual work or limited to scenarios that can be found with sufficient redundancy in large corpora. We introduce the task of *scenario detection*, in which we identify references to scripts. In this task, we address a wide range of different scripts (200 scenarios) and we attempt to identify all references to them in a collection of narrative texts. We present a first benchmark data set and a baseline model that tackles scenario detection using techniques from topic segmentation and text classification.

1 Introduction

According to Grice's (1975) theory of pragmatics, people tend to omit basic information when participating in a conversation (or writing a story) under the assumption that left out details are already known or can be inferred from commonsense knowledge by the hearer (or reader). Consider the following text fragment about `eating in a restaurant` from an online blog post:

Example 1.1 *(. . .) we drove to Sham Shui Po and looked for a place to eat. (. . .) [O]ne of the restaurants was fully seated [so we] chose another. We had 4 dishes—Cow tripe stir fried with shallots, ginger and chili. 1000-year-old-egg with watercress and omelet. Then another kind of tripe and egg—all crispy on the top and soft on the inside. Finally calamari stir fried with rock salt and chili. Washed down with beers and tea at the end. (. . .)*

The text in Example 1.1 obviously talks about a restaurant visit, but it omits many events that are involved while `eating in a restaurant`,

such as *finding a table*, *sitting down*, *ordering food* etc., as well as participants such as *the waiter, the menu,the bill*. A human reader of the story will naturally assume that all these ingredients have their place in the reported event, based on their common-sense knowledge, although the text leaves them completely implicit. For text understanding machines that lack appropriate common-sense knowledge, the implicitness however poses a non-trivial challenge.

Writing and understanding of narrative texts makes particular use of a specific kind of common-sense knowledge, referred to as *script knowledge* (Schank and Abelson, 1977). Script knowledge is about prototypical everyday activity, called *scenarios*. Given a specific scenario, the associated script knowledge enables us to infer omitted events that happen before and after an explicitly mentioned event, as well as its associated participants. In other words, this knowledge can help us obtain more complete text representations, as required for many language comprehension tasks.

There has been some work on script parsing (Ostermann et al., 2017, 2018c), i.e., associating texts with script structure given a specific scenario. Unfortunately, only limited previous work exists on determining which scenarios are referred to in a text or text segment (see Section 2). To the best of our knowledge, this is the first dataset of narrative texts which have annotations at sentence level according to the scripts they instantiate.

In this paper, we describe first steps towards the automatic detection and labeling of scenario-specific text segments. Our contributions are as follows:

- We define the task of scenario detection and introduce a benchmark dataset of annotated narrative texts, with segments labeled according to the scripts they in-

Proceedings of the Second Storytelling Workshop, pages 90–106
Florence, Italy, August 1, 2019. ©2019 Association for Computational Linguistics

stantiate (Section 3). To the best of our knowledge, this is the first dataset of its kind. The corpus is publicly available for scientific research purposes at this `http://www.sfb1102.uni-saarland.de/?page_id=2582`.

- As a benchmark model for scenario detection, we present a two-stage model that combines established methods from topic segmentation and text classification (Section 4).

- Finally, we show that the proposed model achieves promising results but also reveals some of the difficulties underlying the task of scenario detection (Section 5).

2   Motivation and Background

A major line of research has focused on identifying specific events across documents, for example, as part of the Topic Detection and Tracking (TDT) initiative (Allan et al., 1998; Allan, 2012). The main subject of the TDT intiative are instances of world events such as *Cuban Riots in Panama*. In contrast, everyday scenarios and associated sequences of event types, as dealt with in this paper, have so far only been the subject of individual research efforts focusing either on acquiring script knowledge, constructing story corpora, or script-related downstream tasks. Below we describe significant previous work in these areas in more detail.

Script knowledge. Scripts are descriptions of prototypical everyday activities such as `eating in a restaurant` or `riding a bus` (Schank and Abelson, 1977). Different lines of research attempt to acquire script knowledge. Early researchers attempted to handcraft script knowledge (Mueller, 1999; Gordon, 2001). Another line of research focuses on the collection of scenario-specific script knowledge in form of event sequence descriptions (ESDs) via crowdsourcing, (Singh et al., 2002; Gupta and Kochenderfer, 2004; Li et al., 2012; Raisig et al., 2009; Regneri et al., 2010; Wanzare et al., 2016)). ESDs are sequences of short sentences, in bullet style, describing how a given scenario is typically realized. The top part of Table 1 summarizes various script knowledge-bases (ESDs). While datasets like OMICS seem large, they focus only on mundane indoor scenarios (e.g. `open door, switch off lights`). A third line of research tries to leverage existing large text corpora to induce script-like knowledge

about the topics represented in these corpora. For instance, Chambers and Jurafsky (2008, 2009); Pichotta and Mooney (2014) leverage newswire texts, Manshadi et al. (2008); Gordon (2010); Rudinger et al. (2015); Tandon et al. (2014, 2017) leverage web articles while Ryu et al. (2010); Abend et al. (2015); Chu et al. (2017) leverage organized procedural knowledge (e.g. from eHow.com, wikiHow.com).

The top part of Table 1 summarizes various script knowledge-bases. Our work lies in between both lines of research and may help to connect them: we take an extended set of specific scenarios as a starting point and attempt to identify instances of those scenarios in a large-scale collection of narrative texts.

Textual resources. Previous work created script-related resources by crowdsourcing stories that instantiate script knowledge of specific scenarios. For example, Modi et al. (2016) and Ostermann et al. (2018a, 2019) asked crowd-workers to write stories that include mundane aspects of scripts "as if explaining to a child". The collected datasets, *InScript* and *MCScript*, are useful as training instances of narrative texts that refer to scripts. However, the texts are kind of unnatural and atypical because of their explicitness and the requirement to workers to tell a story that is related to one single scenario only. Gordon and Swanson (2009) employed statistical text classification in order to collect narrative texts about personal stories. The *Spinn3r*[1] dataset (Burton et al., 2009) contains about 1.5 Million stories. *Spinn3r* has been used to extract script information (Rahimtoroghi et al., 2016, see below). In this paper, we use the Spinn3r personal stories corpus as a source for our data collection and annotation. The bottom part of Table 1 summarizes various script-related resources. The large datasets come with no scenarios labels while the crowdsourced datasets only have scenario labels at story level. Our work provides a more fine grained scenario labeling at sentence level.

Script-related tasks. Several tasks have been proposed that require or test computational models of script knowledge. For example, Kasch and Oates (2010) and Rahimtoroghi et al. (2016) propose and evaluate a method that automatically creates event schemas, extracted from scenario-specific texts. Ostermann et al. (2017) attempt to iden-

---

[1] http://www.icwsm.org/data/

Scenario ESD collections	Scenarios	#ESDs
SMILE (Regneri et al., 2010)	22	386
Cooking (Regneri, 2013)	53	2500
OMICS (Singh et al., 2002)	175	9044
Raisig et al. (2009)	30	450
Li et al. (2012)	9	500
DeScript (Wanzare et al., 2016)	40	4000

Story Corpora	Scenarios	#stories	Classes	Segs.
Modi et al. (2016)	10	1000	✓	✗
Ostermann et al. (2019)	200	4000	✓	✗
Rahimtoroghi et al. (2016)	2	660	✓	✗
Mostafazadeh et al. (2016)	✗	~50000	✗	✗
Gordon and Swanson (2009)	✗	~1.5M	✗	✗
This work	200	504	✓	✓

Table 1: Top part shows scenario collections and number of associated event sequence descriptions (ESDs). Bottom part lists story corpora together with the number of stories and different scenarios covered. The last two columns indicate whether the stories are classified and segmented, respectively.

tify and label mentions of events from specific scenarios in corresponding texts. Finally, Ostermann et al. (2018b) present an end-to-end evaluation framework that assesses the performance of machine comprehension models using script knowledge. Scenario detection is a prerequisite for tackling such tasks, because the application of script knowledge requires awareness of the scenario a text segment is about.

3 Task and Data

We define scenario detection as the task of identifying segments of a text that are about a specific scenario and classifying these segments accordingly. For the purpose of this task, we view a segment as a consecutive part of text that consists of one or more sentences. Each segment can be assigned none, one, or multiple labels.

Scenario labels. As a set of target labels, we collected scenarios from all scenario lists available in the literature (see Table 1). During revision, we discarded scenarios that are too vague and general (e.g. `childhood`) or atomic (e.g. `switch on/off lights`), admitting only reasonably structured activities. Based on a sample annotation of Spinn3r stories, we further added 58 new scenarios, e.g. `attending a court hearing`, `going skiing`, to increase cover-

age. We deliberately included narrowly related scenarios that stand in the relation of specialisation (e.g. `going shopping` and `shopping for clothes`, or in a subscript relation (`flying in an airplane` and `checking in at the airport`). These cases are challenging to annotators because segments may refer to different scenarios at the same time.

Although our scenario list is incomplete, it is representative for the structural problems that can occur during annotation. We have scenarios that have varying degrees of complexity and cover a wide range of everyday activities. The complete list of scenarios[2] is provided in Appendix B.

Dataset. As a benchmark dataset, we annotated 504 texts from the Spinn3r corpus. To make sure that our dataset contains a sufficient number of relevant sentences, i.e., sentences that refer to scenarios from our collection, we selected texts that have a high affinity to at least one of these scenarios. We approximate this affinity using a logistic regression model fitted to texts from MCScript, based on LDA topics (Blei et al., 2003) as features to represent a document.

3.1 Annotation

We follow standard methodology for natural language annotation (Pustejovsky and Stubbs, 2012). Each text is independently annotated by two annotators, student assistants, who use an agreed upon set of guidelines that is built iteratively together with the annotators. For each text, the students had to identify segments referring to a scenario from the scenario list, and assign scenario labels. If a segment refers to more than one script, they were allowed to assign multiple labels. We worked with a total of four student assistants and used the Webanno[3] annotation tool (de Castilho et al., 2016).

The annotators labeled 504 documents, consisting of 10,754 sentences. On average, the annotated documents were 35.74 sentences long. A scenario label could be either one of our 200 scenarios or *None* to capture sentences that do not refer to any of our scenarios.

Guidelines. We developed a set of more detailed guidelines for handling different issues related to

---

[2] The scenario collection was jointly extended together with the authors of MCScript (Ostermann et al., 2018a, 2019). The same set was used in building MCScript 2.0 (Ostermann et al., 2019)

[3] https://webanno.github.io/webanno/

Annotators	2	3	4
1	0.57 (*0.65*)	0.63 (***0.72***)	**0.64** (*0.70*)
2		0.62 (*0.71*)	0.61 (*0.70*)
3			0.62 (*0.71*)

Table 2: Kappa (*and raw*) agreement between pairs of annotators on sentence-level scenario labels

Annotators	2	3	4
1	**78.8**	70.6	*59.3*
2		66.0	64.2
3			67.0

Table 3: Relative agreement on segment spans between annotated segments that overlap by at least one token and are assigned the same scenario label

the segmentation and classification, which is detailed in Appendix A. A major challenge when annotating segments is deciding when to count a sentence as referring to a particular scenario. For the task addressed here, we consider a segment only if it explicitly realizes aspects of script knowledge that go beyond an evoking expression (i.e., more than one event and participant need to be explicitly realized). Example 3.1 below shows a text segment with minimal scenario information for `going grocery shopping` with two events mentioned. In Example 3.2, only the evoking expression is mentioned, hence this example is not annotated.

Example 3.1 ✓`going grocery shopping`
...*We also **stopped at a small shop** near the hotel to **get some sandwiches** for dinner...*

Example 3.2 ✗`paying for gas`
... *A customer was heading for the store to **pay for gas** or whatever,...*

3.2 Statistics

Agreement. To measure agreement, we looked at sentence-wise label assignments for each double-annotated text. We counted agreement if the same scenario label is assigned to a sentence by both annotators. As an indication of chance-corrected agreement, we computed Kappa scores (Cohen, 1960). A kappa of 1 means that both annotators provided identical (sets of) scenario labels for each sentence. When calculating raw agreements, we counted agreement if there was at least one same scenario label assigned by both annotators. Table 2 shows the Kappa and raw (*in italics*) agreements for each pair of annotators. On average, the Kappa score was *0.61* ranging from 0.57 to 0.64. The average raw agreement score was *0.70* ranging from 0.65 to 0.72. The Kappa value indicates relatively consistent annotations across annotators even though the task was challenging.

We used fuzzy matching to calculate agreement in span between segments that overlap by at least one token. Table 3 shows pairwise % agreement scores between annotators. On average, the annotators achieve 67% agreement on segment spans. This shows considerable segment overlap when both annotators agreed that a particular scenario is referenced.

Analysis. Figure 1 shows to what extent the annotators agreed in the scenario labels. The *None* cases accounted for 32% of the sentences. Our scenario list is by far not complete. Although we selected stories with high affinity to our scenarios, other scenarios (not in our scenario list) may still occur in the stories. Sentences referring to other scenarios were annotated as *None* cases. The *None* label was also used to label sentences that described topics related to but not directly part of the script being referenced. For instance, sentences not part of the narration, but of a different discourse mode (e.g. argumentation, report) or sentences where no specific script events are mentioned[4]. About 20% of the sentences had *Single* annotations where only one annotator indicated that there was a scenario reference. 47% of the sentences were assigned some scenario label(s) by both annotators (*Identical, At least one, Different*). Less than 10% of the sentences had *Different* scenario labels for the case where both annotators assigned scenario labels to a sentence. This occurred frequently with scenarios that are closely related (e.g. `going to the shopping center, going shopping`) or scenarios in a sub-scenario relation (e.g. `flying in a plane, checking in at the airport`) that share script events and participants. In about 7% of the sentences, both annotators agreed on *At least one* scenario label. The remaining 30% of the sentences were assigned *Identical* (sets of) scenario labels by both annotators.

---

[4]See examples in Appendix A.

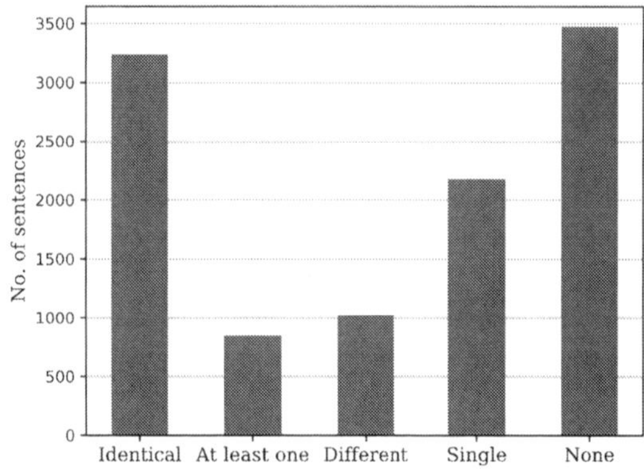

Figure 1: Absolute counts on sentence-level annotations that involve the same (*Identical*), overlapping (*At least one*) or disagreed (*Different*) labels; also shown are the number of sentences that received a label by only one annotator (*Single*) or no label at all (*None*).

3.3 Adjudication and Gold Standard

The annotation task is challenging, and so are gold standard creation and adjudication. We combined *automatic merging* and *manual adjudication* (by the main author of the paper) as two steps of gold-standard creation, to minimize manual post-processing of the dataset.

We automatically merged annotated segments that are identical or overlapping and have the same scenario label, thus maximizing segment length. Consider the two annotations shown in Example 3.3. One annotator labeled the whole text as `growing vegetables`, the other one identified the two bold-face sequences as `growing vegetables` instances, and left the middle part out. The result of the merger is the maximal `growing vegetables` chain, i.e., the full text. Taking the maximal chain ensures that all relevant information is included, although the annotators may not have agreed on what is script-relevant.

Example 3.3 `growing vegetables`
The tomato seedlings Mitch planted in the compost box have done really well and we noticed flowers on them today . Hopefully we will get a good *It has rained and rained here for the past month so that is doing the garden heaps of good . We bought some organic herbs seedlings recently and now have some thyme , parsley , oregano and mint growing in the garden .**We also planted some lettuce and a grape vine . We harvested our first crop of sweet potatoes a week or so ago** (...)*

The adjudication guidelines were deliberately designed in a way that the adjudicator could not easily

Scenario	# docs	# sents.	# segs.
eat in a restaurant	21	387	22
go on vacation	16	325	17
go shopping	34	276	35
take care of children	15	190	19
review movies	8	184	8
...			
taking a bath	3	34	6
borrow book from library	3	33	3
mow the lawn	3	33	3
drive a car	9	32	11
change a baby diaper	3	32	3
...			
replace a garbage bag	1	3	2
unclog the toilet	1	3	1
wash a cut	1	3	1
apply band aid	2	2	2
change batteries in alarm	1	2	1

Table 4: Distribution of scenario labels over documents (docs), sentences (sents) and segments (segs); the top and bottom parts show the ten most and least frequent labels, respectively. The middle part shows scenario labels that appear at an average frequency.

overrule the double-annotations. The segmentation could not be changed, and only the labels provided by the annotators were available for labeling. Since segment overlap is handled automatically, manual adjudication must only care about label disagreement: the two main cases are (1) a segment has been labeled by only one annotator and (2) a segment has been assigned different labels by its two annotators. In case (1), the adjudicator had to take a binary decision to accept the labeled segment, or to discard it. In case (2), the adjudicator had three options: to decide for one of the labels or to accept both of them.

Gold standard. The annotation process resulted in 2070 single segment annotations. 69% of the single segment annotations were automatically merged to create gold segments. The remaining segments were adjudicated, and relevant segments were added to the gold standard. Our final dataset consists of 7152 sentences (contained in 895 segments) with gold scenario labels. From the 7152 gold sentences, 1038 (15%) sentences have more than one scenario label. 181 scenarios (out of 200) occur as gold labels in our dataset, 179 of which are referred to in at least 2 sentences. Table 4 shows

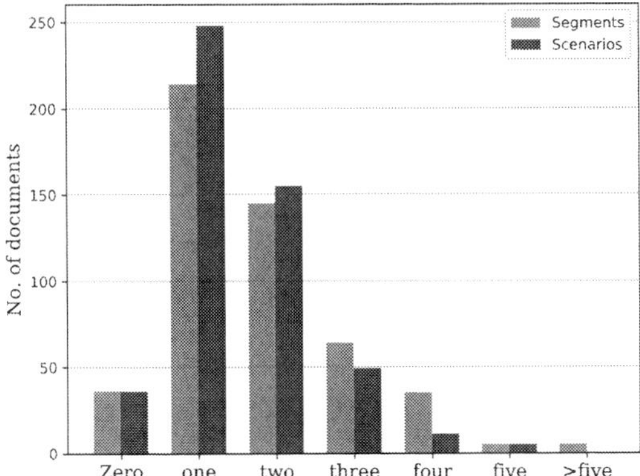
Figure 2: Segment and scenario distribution per text

example scenarios[5] and the distribution of scenario labels: the number of documents that refer to the given scenario, the number of gold sentences and segments referring to the given scenario, and the average segment length (in sentences) per scenario. 16 scenarios are referred to in more than 100 gold sentences, 105 scenarios in at least 20 gold sentences, 60 scenarios in less than 20 gold sentences. Figure 2 shows the distribution of segments and scenario references per text in the gold standard. On average, there are 1.8 segments per text and 44% of the texts refer to at least two scenarios.

4 Benchmark model

Texts typically consist of different passages that refer to different scenarios. When human hearers or readers come across an expression that evokes a particular script, they try to map verbs or clauses in the subsequent text to script events, until they face lexical material that is clearly unrelated to the script and may evoke a different scenario. Scenario identification, scenario segmentation, and script parsing are subtasks of story comprehension, which ideally work in close mutual interaction. In this section, we present a model for scenario identification, which is much simpler in several respects: we propose a two-step model consisting of a segmentation and a classification component. For segmentation, we assume that a change in scenario focus can be modeled by a shift in lexical cohesion. We identify segments that might be related to specific scripts or scenarios via topic segmentation, assuming that scenarios can be approximated as distributions over topics. After segmentation, a supervised classifier component is used to predict the scenario label(s)

for each of the found segment. Our results show that the script segmentation problem can be solved in principle, and we propose our model as a benchmark model for future work.

Segmentation. The first component of our benchmark model reimplements a state-of-art unsupervised method for topic segmentation, called TopicTiling (Riedl and Biemann, 2012). TopicTiling (TT) uses latent topics inferred by a Latent Derichlet Allocation (LDA, Blei et al. (2003)) model to identify segments (i.e., sets of consecutive sentences) referring to similar topics.[6] The TT segmenter outputs topic boundaries between sentences where there are topic shifts. Boundaries are computed based on coherence scores. Coherence scores close to 1 indicate significant topic similarity while values close to 0 indicate minimal topic similarity. A window parameter is used to determine the block size i.e. the number of sentences to the left and right that should be considered when calculating coherence scores. To discover segment boundaries, all local minima in the coherence scores are identified using a depth score (Hearst, 1994). A threshold $\mu - \sigma/x$ is used to estimate the number of segments, where μ is the mean and σ is the standard deviation of the depth scores, and x is a weight parameter for setting the threshold.[7] Segment boundaries are placed at positions greater than the threshold.

Classification. We view the scenario classification subtask as a supervised multi-label classification problem. Specifically, we implement a multi-layer perceptron classifier in Keras (Chollet et al., 2015) with multiple layers: an input layer with 100 neurons and ReLU activation, followed by an intermediate layer with dropout (0.2), and finally an output layer with sigmoid activations. We optimize a cross-entropy loss using adam. Because multiple labels can be assigned to one segment, we train several one-vs-all classifiers, resulting in one classifier per scenario.

We also experimented with different features and feature combinations to represent text segments: term frequencies weighted by inverted document frequency (*tf.idf*, Salton and McGill (1986))[8] and topic features derived from LDA (see above), and

---

[6]We used the Gensim (Rehurek and Sojka, 2010) implementation of LDA.

[7]We experimentally set x to 0.1 using our held out development set.

[8]We use SciKit learn (Pedregosa et al., 2011) to build *tf.idf* representations

we tried to work with word embeddings. We found the performance with *tf.idf* features to be the best.

5 Experiments

The experiments and results presented in this section are based on our annotated dataset for scenario detection described in section 3.

5.1 Experimental setting

Preprocessing and model details. We represent each input to our model as a sequence of lemmatized content words, in particular nouns and verbs (including verb particles). This is achieved by preprocessing each text using Stanford CoreNLP (Chen and Manning, 2014).

Segmentation. Since the segmentation model is unsupervised, we can use all data from both MCScript and the Spinn3r personal stories corpora to build the LDA model. As input to the TopicTiling segmentor, each sentence is represented by a vector in which each component represents the (weight of a) topic from the LDA model (i.e. the value of the ith component is the normalized weight of the words in the sentence whose most relevant topic is the ith topic). For the segmentation model, we tune the number of topics (200) and the window size (2) based on an artificial development dataset, created by merging segments from multiple documents from MCScript.

Classification. We train the scenario classification model on the scenario labels provided in MCScript (one per text). For training and hyperparameter selection, we split MCScript dataset (see Section 2) into a training and development set, as indicated in Table 5. We additionally make use of 18 documents from our scenario detection data (Section 3) to tune a classification threshold. The remaining 486 documents are held out exclusively for testing (see Table 5). Since we train separate classifiers for each scenario (one-vs-all classifiers), we get a probability distribution of how likely a sentence refers to a scenario. We use entropy to measure the degree of scenario content in the sentences. Sentences with entropy values higher than the threshold are considered as not referencing any scenario (*None* cases), while sentences with lower entropy values reference some scenario.

Baselines. We experiment with three informed baselines: As a lower bound for the classification task, we compare our model against the baseline

Dataset	# train	# dev	# test
MCScript	3492	408	-
Spinn3r (gold)	-	18	486

Table 5: Datasets (number of documents) used in the experiments

Model	Precision	Recall	F_1-score
sent_maj	0.08	0.05	0.06
sent_*tf.idf*	0.24	0.28	0.26
random_*tf.idf*	0.32	0.45	0.37
TT_*tf.idf* (F_1)	0.36	**0.54**	**0.43**
TT_*tf.idf* (Gold)	0.54	0.54	0.54

Table 6: Results for the scenario detection task

sent_maj, which assigns the majority label to all sentences. To assess the utility of segmentation, we compare against two baselines that use our proposed classifier but not the segmentation component: the baseline *sent_tf.idf* treats each sentence as a separate segment and *random_tf.idf* splits each document into random segments.

Evaluation. We evaluate scenario detection performance at the sentence level using micro-average precision, recall and F_1-score. We consider the top 1 predicted scenario for sentences with only one gold label (including the *None* label), and top n scenarios for sentences with n gold labels. For sentences with multiple scenario labels, we take into account partial matches and count each label proportionally. Assuming the gold labels are `washing ones hair` and `taking a bath`, and the classifier predicts `taking a bath` and `getting ready for bed`. `Taking a bath` is correctly predicted and accounts for 0.5 true positive (TP) while `washing ones hair` is incorrectly missed, thus accounts for 0.5 false negative (FN). `Getting ready for bed` is incorrectly predicted and accounts for 1 false positive (FP).

We additionally provide separate results of the segmentation component based on standard segmentation evaluation metrics.

5.2 Results

We present the micro-averaged results for scenario detection in Table 6. The *sent_maj* baseline achieves a F_1-score of only 6%, as the majority class forms only a small part of the dataset (4.7%). Our TT model with *tf.idf* features surpasses both

True label	Predicted label	# sents.	PMI
go_vacation	visit_sights	92	3.96
eat_restaurant	food_back	67	4.26
work_garden	grow_vegetables	57	4.45
attend_wedding	prepare_wedding	48	4.12
eat_restaurant	dinner_reservation	39	4.26
throw_party	go_party	36	4.09
shop_online	order_ on_phone	35	3.73
work_garden	planting a tree	33	4.81
shop_clothes	check_store_open	33	0.00
play_video_games	learn_board_game	32	0.00

Table 7: Top 10 misclassified scenario pairs (number of misclassified sentences (# sents.)) by our approach TT_tf.idf in relation to the PMI scores for each pair.

Scenario	# sents.	P	R	F_1
go to the dentist	47	0.90	0.96	0.93
have a barbecue	43	0.92	0.88	0.90
go to the sauna	28	0.80	0.89	0.84
make soup	60	0.81	0.87	0.84
bake a cake	69	0.71	0.97	0.82
go skiing	42	0.78	0.83	0.80
attend a court hearing	66	0.71	0.92	0.80
clean the floor	6	1.00	0.67	0.80
take a taxi	27	0.74	0.85	0.79
attend a church service	60	0.70	0.92	0.79

Table 8: Top 10 scenario-wise Precision (P), Recall (R) and F_1-score (F_1) results using our approach TT_tf.idf and the number of gold sentences (# sents.) for each scenario.

baselines that perform segmentation only naively (26% F_1) or randomly (37% F_1). This result shows that scenario detection works best when using predicted segments that are informative and topically consistent.

We estimated an upper bound for the classifier by taking into account the predicted segments from the segmentation step, but during evaluation, only considered those sentences with gold scenario labels (TT_tf.idf (Gold)), while ignoring the sentences with *None* label. We see an improvement in precision (54%), showing that the classifier correctly predicts the right scenario label for sentences with gold labels while also including other sentences that may be in topic but not directly referencing a given scenario.

To estimate the performance of the TT segmentor individually, we run TT on an artificial development set, created by merging segments from different scenarios from MCScript. We evaluate the performance of TT by using two standard topic segmentation evaluation metrics, P_k (Beeferman et al., 1999) and WindowDiff (WD, Pevzner and Hearst (2002)). Both metrics express the probability of segmentation error, thus lower values indicate better performance. We compute the average performance over several runs. TT attains P_k of 0.28 and WD of 0.28. The low segmentation errors suggest that TT segmentor does a good job in predicting the scenario boundaries.

5.3 Discussion

Even for a purpose-built model, scenario detection is a difficult task. This is partly to be expected as the task requires the assignment of one (or more) of 200 possible scenario labels, some of which are hard to distinguish. Many errors are due to misclassifications between scenarios that share script events as well as participants and that are usually mentioned in the same text: for example, `sending food back in a restaurant` requires and involves participants from `eating in a restaurant`. Table 7 shows the 10 most frequent misclassifications by our best model *TT_tf.idf* (F_1). These errors account for 16% of all incorrect label assignments (200 *by* 200 matrix). The 100 most frequent misclassifications account for 63% of all incorrect label assignments. In a quantitative analysis, we calculated the commonalities between scenarios in terms of the pointwise mutual information (PMI) between scenario labels in the associated stories. We calculated PMI using Equation (1). The probability of a scenario is given by the document frequency of the scenario divided by the number of documents.

$$PMI(S_1, S_2) = log \left(\frac{P(S_1 \wedge S_2)}{P(S_1) \cdot P(S_2)} \right) \quad (1)$$

Scenarios that tend to co-occur in texts have higher PMI scored. We observe that the scenario-wise recall and F_1-scores of our classifier are negatively correlated with PMI scores (Pearson correlation of -0.33 and -0.17, respectively). These correlations confirm a greater difficulty in distinguishing between scenarios that are highly related to other scenarios.

On the positive side, we observe that scenario-wise precision and F_1-score are positively correlated with the number of gold sentences annotated with the respective scenario label (Pearson correlation of 0.50 and 0.20, respectively). As one would

order pizza	laundry	gardening	barbecue
pizza	clothes	tree	invite
order	dryer	plant	guest
delivery	laundry	hole	grill
decide	washer	water	friend
place	wash	grow	everyone
deliver	dry	garden	beer
tip	white	dig	barbecue
phone	detergent	dirt	food
number	start	seed	serve
minute	washing	soil	season

Table 9: Example top 10 scenario-words

expect, our approach seems to perform better on scenarios that appear at higher frequency. Table 8 shows the 10 scenarios for which our approach achieves the best results.

Scenario approximation using topics. We performed an analyses to qualitatively examine in how far topic distributions, as used in our segmentation model, actually approximate scenarios. For this analysis, we computed a LDA topic model using only the MCScript dataset. We created *scenario-topics* by looking at all the prevalent topics in documents from a given scenario. Table 9 shows the top 10 words for each scenario extracted from the *scenario-topics*. As can be seen, the topics capture some of the most relevant words for different scenarios.

6 Summary

In this paper we introduced the task of scenario detection and curated a benchmark dataset for automatic scenario segmentation and identification. We proposed a benchmark model that automatically segments and identifies text fragments referring to a given scenario. While our model achieves promising first results, it also revealed some of the difficulties in detecting script references. Script detection is an important first step for large-scale data driven script induction for tasks that require the application of script knowledge. We are hopeful that our data and model will form a useful basis for future work.

Acknowledgments

This research was funded by the German Research Foundation (DFG) as part of SFB 1102 Information Density and Linguistic Encoding.

References

Omri Abend, Shay B Cohen, and Mark Steedman. 2015. Lexical event ordering with an edge-factored model. In *Proceedings of the 2015 Conference of the North American Chapter of the Association for Computational Linguistics: Human Language Technologies*, pages 1161–1171.

James Allan. 2012. *Topic detection and tracking: event-based information organization*, volume 12. Springer Science & Business Media.

James Allan, Jaime G Carbonell, George Doddington, Jonathan Yamron, and Yiming Yang. 1998. Topic detection and tracking pilot study final report.

Doug Beeferman, Adam Berger, and John Lafferty. 1999. Statistical models for text segmentation. *Machine learning*, 34(1-3):177–210.

David M. Blei, Andrew Y. Ng, and Michael I. Jordan. 2003. Latent dirichlet allocation. *Journal of machine Learning research*, 3(Jan):993–1022.

Kevin Burton, Akshay Java, and Ian Soboroff. 2009. The ICWSM 2009 Spinn3r Dataset. In *Third Annual Conference on Weblogs and Social Media (ICWSM 2009)*, San Jose, CA. AAAI.

Richard Eckart de Castilho, Eva Mujdricza-Maydt, Seid Muhie Yimam, Silvana Hartmann, Iryna Gurevych, Anette Frank, and Chris Biemann. 2016. A web-based tool for the integrated annotation of semantic and syntactic structures. In *Proceedings of the Workshop on Language Technology Resources and Tools for Digital Humanities (LT4DH)*, pages 76–84.

Nathanael Chambers and Daniel Jurafsky. 2008. Unsupervised learning of narrative event chains. In *ACL 2008, Proceedings of the 46th Annual Meeting of the Association for Computational Linguistics, June 15-20, 2008, Columbus, Ohio, USA*, pages 789–797.

Nathanael Chambers and Daniel Jurafsky. 2009. Unsupervised learning of narrative schemas and their participants. In *Proceedings of 47th Annual Meeting of the ACL and the 4th IJCNLP of the AFNLP*, pages 602–610, Suntec, Singapore.

Danqi Chen and Christopher Manning. 2014. A fast and accurate dependency parser using neural networks. In *Proceedings of the 2014 conference on empirical methods in natural language processing (EMNLP)*, pages 740–750.

François Chollet et al. 2015. Keras. https://github.com/fchollet/keras.

Cuong Xuan Chu, Niket Tandon, and Gerhard Weikum. 2017. Distilling task knowledge from how-to communities. In *Proceedings of the 26th International Conference on World Wide Web*, WWW '17, pages 805–814, Republic and Canton of Geneva, Switzerland. International World Wide Web Conferences Steering Committee.

Jacob Cohen. 1960. A coefficient of agreement for nominal scales. *Educational and psychological measurement*, 20(1):37–46.

Andrew Gordon and Reid Swanson. 2009. Identifying personal stories in millions of weblog entries. In *International Conference on Weblogs and Social Media, Data Challenge Workshop, May 20, San Jose, CA*.

Andrew S. Gordon. 2001. Browsing image collections with representations of common-sense activities. *Journal of the American Society for Information Science and Technology.*, 52:925.

Andrew S. Gordon. 2010. Mining commonsense knowledge from personal stories in internet weblogs. In *Proceedings of the First Workshop on Automated Knowledge Base Construction*, Grenoble, France.

Herbert Paul Grice. 1975. Logic and conversation. In Peter Cole and Jerry L. Morgan, editors, *Syntax and Semantics: Vol. 3: Speech Acts*, pages 41–58. Academic Press, New York.

Rakesh Gupta and Mykel J. Kochenderfer. 2004. Common sense data acquisition for indoor mobile robots. In *Proceedings of the 19th National Conference on Artifical Intelligence*, AAAI'04, pages 605–610. AAAI Press.

Marti A Hearst. 1994. Multi-paragraph segmentation of expository text. In *Proceedings of the 32nd annual meeting on Association for Computational Linguistics*, pages 9–16. Association for Computational Linguistics.

Niels Kasch and Tim Oates. 2010. Mining script-like structures from the web. In *Proceedings of the NAACL HLT 2010 First International Workshop on Formalisms and Methodology for Learning by Reading*, FAM-LbR '10, pages 34–42, Stroudsburg, PA, USA. Association for Computational Linguistics.

Boyang Li, Stephen Lee-Urban, D. Scott Appling, and Mark O. Riedl. 2012. Crowdsourcing narrative intelligence. volume vol. 2. Advances in Cognitive Systems.

M Manshadi, R Swanson, and AS Gordon. 2008. Learning a probabilistic model of event sequences from internet weblog stories. FLAIRS Conference.

Ashutosh Modi, Tatjana Anikina, Simon Ostermann, and Manfred Pinkal. 2016. Inscript: Narrative texts annotated with script information. In *Proceedings of the 10th International Conference on Language Resources and Evaluation (LREC 16)*, Portorož, Slovenia.

Nasrin Mostafazadeh, Nathanael Chambers, Xiaodong He, Devi Parikh, Dhruv Batra, Lucy Vanderwende, Pushmeet Kohli, and James Allen. 2016. A corpus and cloze evaluation for deeper understanding of commonsense stories. In *Proceedings of the 2016 Conference of the North American Chapter of the Association for Computational Linguistics: Human Language Technologies*, pages 839–849, San Diego, California. Association for Computational Linguistics.

Erik T. Mueller. 1999. A database and lexicon of scripts for thoughttreasure. *CoRR*, cs.AI/0003004.

Simon Ostermann, Ashutosh Modi, Michael Roth, Stefan Thater, and Manfred Pinkal. 2018a. MCScript: A Novel Dataset for Assessing Machine Comprehension Using Script Knowledge. In *Proceedings of the 11th International Conference on Language Resources and Evaluation (LREC 2018)*, Miyazaki, Japan.

Simon Ostermann, Michael Roth, Ashutosh Modi, Stefan Thater, and Manfred Pinkal. 2018b. SemEval-2018 Task 11: Machine Comprehension using Commonsense Knowledge. In *Proceedings of International Workshop on Semantic Evaluation (SemEval-2018)*, New Orleans, LA, USA.

Simon Ostermann, Michael Roth, and Manfred Pinkal. 2019. MCScript2.0: A Machine Comprehension Corpus Focused on Script Events and Participants. *Proceedings of the 8th Joint Conference on Lexical and Computational Semantics (*SEM 2019)*.

Simon Ostermann, Michael Roth, Stefan Thater, and Manfred Pinkal. 2017. Aligning script events with narrative texts. *Proceedings of *SEM 2017*.

Simon Ostermann, Hannah Seitz, Stefan Thater, and Manfred Pinkal. 2018c. Mapping Texts to Scripts: An Entailment Study. In *Proceedings of the Eleventh International Conference on Language Resources and Evaluation (LREC 2018)*, Miyazaki, Japan. European Language Resources Association (ELRA).

Fabian Pedregosa, Gaël Varoquaux, Alexandre Gramfort, Vincent Michel, Bertrand Thirion, Olivier Grisel, Mathieu Blondel, Peter Prettenhofer, Ron Weiss, Vincent Dubourg, et al. 2011. Scikit-learn: Machine learning in Python. *Journal of machine learning research*, 12(Oct):2825–2830.

Lev Pevzner and Marti A Hearst. 2002. A critique and improvement of an evaluation metric for text segmentation. *Computational Linguistics*, 28(1):19–36.

Karl Pichotta and Raymond J. Mooney. 2014. Statistical Script Learning with Multi-Argument Events. In *Proceedings of the 14th Conference of the European Chapter of the Association for Computational Linguistics (EACL 2014)*, pages 220–229, Gothenburg, Sweden.

James Pustejovsky and Amber Stubbs. 2012. *Natural Language Annotation for Machine Learning - a Guide to Corpus-Building for Applications.* O'Reilly.

Elahe Rahimtoroghi, Ernesto Hernandez, and Marilyn Walker. 2016. Learning fine-grained knowledge about contingent relations between everyday events. In *Proceedings of the 17th Annual Meeting of the Special Interest Group on Discourse and Dialogue*, pages 350–359.

Susanne Raisig, Tinka Welke, Herbert Hagendorf, and Elke Van der Meer. 2009. Insights into knowledge representation: The influence of amodal and perceptual variables on event knowledge retrieval from memory. *Cognitive Science*, 33(7):1252–1266.

Michaela Regneri. 2013. *Event Structures in Knowledge, Pictures and Text*. Ph.D. thesis, Saarland University.

Michaela Regneri, Alexander Koller, and Manfred Pinkal. 2010. Learning script knowledge with web experiments. In *Proceedings of the 48th Annual Meeting of the Association for Computational Linguistics*, pages 979–988, Uppsala, Sweden.

Radim Rehurek and Petr Sojka. 2010. Software framework for topic modelling with large corpora. In *In Proceedings of the LREC 2010 Workshop on New Challenges for NLP Frameworks*.

Martin Riedl and Chris Biemann. 2012. Topictiling: a text segmentation algorithm based on lda. In *Proceedings of ACL 2012 Student Research Workshop*, pages 37–42. Association for Computational Linguistics.

Rachel Rudinger, Pushpendre Rastogi, Francis Ferraro, and Benjamin Van Durme. 2015. Script induction as language modeling. In *Proceedings of the 2015 Conference on Empirical Methods in Natural Language Processing*, pages 1681–1686.

Jihee Ryu, Yuchul Jung, Kyung-min Kim, and Sung Hyon Myaeng. 2010. Automatic extraction of human activity knowledge from method-describing web articles. In *Proceedings of the 1st Workshop on Automated Knowledge Base Construction*, page 16. Citeseer.

Gerard Salton and Michael J McGill. 1986. Introduction to modern information retrieval.

Roger C. Schank and Robert P. Abelson. 1977. Scripts, plans, goals and understanding, an inquiry into human knowledge structures. *Hillsdale: Lawrence Erlbaum Associates,*, 3(2):211 – 217.

Push Singh, Thomas Lin, Erik T Mueller, Grace Lim, Travell Perkins, and Wan Li Zhu. 2002. Open mind common sense: Knowledge acquisition from the general public. In Robert Meersman and Zahir Tari, editors, *On the Move to Meaningful Internet Systems 2002: CoopIS, DOA, and ODBASE*, pages 1223–1237. Springer, Berlin / Heidelberg, Germany.

Niket Tandon, Gerard de Melo, Fabian M. Suchanek, and Gerhard Weikum. 2014. Webchild: harvesting and organizing commonsense knowledge from the web. In *Seventh ACM International Conference on Web Search and Data Mining, WSDM 2014, New York, NY, USA, February 24-28, 2014*, pages 523–532.

Niket Tandon, Gerard de Melo, and Gerhard Weikum. 2017. Webchild 2.0: Fine-grained commonsense knowledge distillation. *Proceedings of ACL 2017, System Demonstrations*, pages 115–120.

Lilian D. A. Wanzare, Alessandra Zarcone, Stefan Thater, and Manfred Pinkal. 2016. Descript: A crowdsourced corpus for the acquisition of high-quality script knowledge. In *The International Conference on Language Resources and Evaluation*.

Appendix

A   Annotation guidelines

You are presented with several stories. Read each story carefully. You are required to highlight segments in the text where any of our scenarios is realized.

1. A segment can be a clause, a sentence, several sentences or any combination of sentences and clauses.

2. Usually segments will cover different parts of the text and be labeled with one scenario label each.

3. A text passage is highlighted as realizing a given scenario only if several scenario elements are addressed or referred to in the text, more than just the evoking expression but some more material e.g at least one event and a participant in that scenario is referred to in the text. (see examples (A.1 to A.5)).

4. A text passage referring to one scenario does not necessarily need to be contiguous i.e. the scenario could be referred to in different parts of the same text passage, so the scenario label can occur several times in the text. If the text passages are adjacent, mark the whole span as one segment. (see examples (A.6 to A.10))

5. One passage of text can be associated with more than one scenario label.

   - A passage of text associated with two or more related scenarios i.e. scenario that often coincide or occur together. (see example A.11).
   - A shorter passage of text referring to a given scenario is nested in a longer passage of text referring to a more general scenario. The nested text passage is therefore associated with both the general and specific scenarios. (see example A.12).

6. For a given text passage, if you do not find a full match from the scenario list, but a scenario that is related and similar in structure, you may annotate it. (see example A.13).

Rules of thumb for annotation

1. Do not annotate if no progress to events is made i.e. the text just mentions the scenario but no clear script events are addressed.

Example A.1 *short text with event and participants addressed*
✓ `feeding a child`
... Chloe loves to stand around babbling just generally keeping anyone amused as long as you bribe her with a piece of bread or cheese first.

✓ `going grocery shopping`
... but first stopped at a local shop to pick up some cheaper beer . We also stopped at a small shop near the hotel to get some sandwiches for dinner .

Example A.2 *scenario is just mentioned*
✗ `cooking pasta` *And a huge thanks to Megan & Andrew for a fantastic dinner, especially their first ever fresh pasta making effort of salmon filled ravioli - a big winner.*

✗ `riding on a bus,` ✗ `flying in a plane`
and then catch a bus down to Dublin for my 9:30AM flight the next morning.

We decide to stop at at Bob Evan's on the way home and feed the children.

Example A.3 *scenario is implied but no events are addressed*
✗ `answering the phone`
one of the citizens nodded and started talking on her cell phone. Several of the others were also on cell phones

✗ `taking a photograph`
Here are some before and after shots of Brandon . The first 3 were all taken this past May . I just took this one a few minutes ago.

Example A.4 *different discourse mode that is not narration e.g. information, argumentative, no specific events are mentioned*
✗ `writing a letter`
A long time ago, years before the Internet, I used to write to people from other countries. This people I met through a program called Pen Pal. I would send them my mail address, name, languages I could talk and preferences about my pen pals. Then I would receive a list of names and address and I could start sending them letters. ...

2. When a segment refers to more than one scenario, either related scenarios or scenarios where one is more general than the other, if there is only a weak reference to one of the scenarios, then annotate the text with the scenario having a stronger or more plausible reference.

Example A.5 *one scenario is weakly referenced*
✓ `visiting a doctor,` ✗ `taking medicine`
taking medicine is weakly referenced
Now another week passes and I get a phone call and am told that the tests showed i had strep so i go in the next day and see the doc and he says that i don't have strep . ugh what the hell . This time though they actually give me some antibiotic to help with a few different urinary track infections and other things while doing another blood test and urnine test on me .

✓ `taking a shower,` ✗ `washing ones hair`
washing ones hair is weakly referenced
I stand under the pressure of the shower , the water hitting my back in fierce beats . I stand and dip my hand back , exposing my delicate throat and neck . My hair gets soaked and detangles in the water as it flows through my hair , every bead of water putting back the moisture which day to day life rids my hair of . I run my hands through my hair shaking out the water as I bring my head back down to look down towards my feet . *The white marble base of the shower shines back at me from below . My feet covered in water , the water working its way up to my ankles but it never gets there . I find the soap and rub my body all over*

3. Sometimes there is a piece of text intervening two instances (or the same instance) of a scenario, that is not directly part of the scenario that is currently being talked about. We call this a separator. Leave out the separator if it is long or talks about something not related to the scenario being addressed. The separator can be included if it is short, argumentative or a comment, or somehow relates to the scenario being addressed. When there

are multiple adjacent instances of a scenario, annotate them as a single unit.

Example A.6 *two mentions of a scenario annotated as one segment*
✓ `writing a letter`
I asked him about a month ago to write a letter of recommendation for me to help me get a library gig. After bugging him on and off for the past month, as mentioned above, he wrote me about a paragraph. I was sort of pissed as it was quite generic and short.

I asked for advice, put it off myself for a week and finally wrote the letter of recommendation myself. I had both Evan and Adj. take a look at it- and they both liked my version.

Example A.7 *a separator referring to topic related to the current scenario is included*
✓ `writing an exam`
The Basic Science Exam (practice board exam) that took place on Friday April 18 was interesting to say the least. We had 4 hours to complete 200 questions, which will be the approximate time frame for the boards as well. I was completing questions at a good pace for the first 1/3 of the exam, slowed during the second 1/3 and had to rush myself during the last 20 or so questions to complete the exam in time.

✓ separator: Starting in May, I am going to start timing myself when I do practice questions so I can get use to pacing. There was a lot of information that was familiar to me on the exam (which is definitely a good thing) but it also showed me that I have a LOT of reviewing to do.

Monday April 21 was the written exam for ECM. This exam was surprisingly challenging. For me, the most difficult part were reading and interpreting the EKGs. I felt like once I looked at them, everything I knew just fell out of my brain. Fortunately, it was a pass/fail exam and I passed.

Example A.8 *a long separator is excluded*
✓ `going to the beach`
Today , on the very last day of summer vacation , we finally made it to the beach . Oh , it 's not that we hadn 't been to a beach before . We were on a Lake Michigan beach just last

weekend . And we 've stuck our toes in the water at AJ 's and my lake a couple of times . But today , we actually planned to go . We wore our bathing suits and everything . We went with AJ 's friend D , his brother and his mom .

✗ separator: D and AJ became friends their very first year of preschool when they were two . They live in the next town over and we don 't see them as often as we would like . It 's not so much the distance , which isn 't far at all , but that the school and athletic schedules are constantly conflicting . But for the first time , they are both going back to school on the same day . So we decided to celebrate the end of summer together .

✓ `going to the beach`
It nearly looked too cold to go this morning ' the temperature didn 't reach 60 until after 9 :00. The lake water was chilly , too cool for me , but the kids didn 't mind . They splashed and shrieked with laughter and dug in the sand and pointed at the boat that looked like a hot dog and climbed onto the raft and jumped off and had races and splashed some more . D 's mom and I sat in the sun and talked about nothing in particular and waved off seagulls .

Example A.9 *a short separator is included*
✓ `throwing a party`
... My wife planned a surprise party for me at my place in the evening - I was told that we 'd go out and that I was supposed to meet her at Dhobi Ghaut exchange at 7 .

✓ separator: But I was getting bored in the office around 5 and thought I 'd go home - when I came home , I surprised her !

She was busy blowing balloons , decorating , etc with her friend . I guess I ruined it for her . But the fun part started here - She invited my sister and my cousin ...

✓ `visiting sights`
Before getting to the museum we swung by Notre Dame which was very beautiful . I tried taking some pictures inside Notre Dame but I dont think they turned out particularly well . After Notre Dame , Paul decided to show us the Crypte Archeologioue .
✓ separator: This is apparently French for

parking garage there are some excellent pictures on Flickr of our trip there .

Also on the way to the museum we swung by Saint Chapelle which is another church . We didnt go inside this one because we hadnt bought a museum pass yet but we plan to return later on in the trip

4. Similarly to intervening text (separator), there may be text before or after that is a motivation, pre or post condition for the applications of the script currently being referred to. Leave out the text if it is long . The text can be included if it is short, or relates to the scenario being addressed.

Example A.10 *the first one or two sentences introduce the topic*
✓ `getting a haircut`
I AM , however , upset at the woman who cut *his hair recently . He had an appointment with my stylist (the one he normally goes to) but I FORGOT about it because I kept thinking that it was a different day than it was . When I called to reschedule , she couldn 't get him in until OCTOBER (?!?!?!) ...*

✓ `baking a cake`
I tried out this upside down cake from Bill Grangers , Simply Bill . As I have mentioned before , I love plums am always trying out new recipes featuring them when they are in season . *I didnt read the recipe properly so was surprised when I came to make it that it was actually cooked much in the same way as a tarte tartin , ie making a caramel with the fruit in a frying pan first , then pouring over the cake mixture baking in the frypan in the oven before turning out onto a serving plate , the difference being that it was a cake mixture not pastry ....*

5. If a text passage refers to several related scenarios, e.g. "renovating a room" and "painting a wall", "laying flooring in a room", "papering a room"; or "working in the garden" and "growing vegetables", annotate all the related scenarios.

Example A.11 *segment referring to related scenarios*
✓ `growing vegetables,` ✓

The tomato seedlings Mitch planted in the compost box have done really well and we noticed flowers on them today. Hopefully we will get a good crop. It has rained and rained here for the past month so that is doing the garden heaps of good. We bought some organic herbs seedlings recently and now have some thyme, parsley, oregano and mint growing in the garden. We also planted some lettuce and a grape vine. ...

6. If part of a longer text passage refers to a scenario that is more specific than the scenario currently being talked about, annotate the nested text passage with all referred scenarios.

Example A.12 *nested segment*

I can remember the recipe, it's pretty adaptable and you can add or substitute the vegetables as you see fit!! One Pot Chicken Casserole 750g chicken thigh meat, cut into big cubes olive oil for frying 1

large onion, chopped 3 potatoes, waxy is best 3 carrots 4 stalks of celery, chopped 2 cups of chicken stock 2 zucchini, sliced large handful of beans 300 ml cream 1 or 2 tablespoons of wholegrain mustard salt and pepper parsley, chopped

##42 The potatoes and carrots need to be cut into chunks,. I used chat potatoes which are smaller and cut them in half, but I would probably cut a normal potato into quarters. Heat the oil; in a large pan and then fry the chicken in batches until it is well browned...

7. If you do not find a full match for a text segment in the scenario list, but a scenario that is related and similar in its structure, you may annotate it.

Example A.13 *topic similarity*

- *Same structure in scenario e.g. going fishing for leisure or for work, share the same core events in going fishing*
- *Baking something with flour (baking a cake, baking Blondies,)*

B   List of Scenarios

	scenario	# docs	# sents.		scenario	# docs	# sents.
1	eating in a restaurant	21	387	101	receiving a letter	5	27
2	going on vacation	16	325	102	taking a shower	4	27
3	going shopping	34	276	103	taking a taxi	4	27
4	taking care of children	15	190	104	going to the playground	3	25
5	reviewing movies	8	184	105	taking a photograph	5	25
6	shopping for clothes	11	182	106	going on a date	3	24
7	working in the garden	13	179	107	making a bonfire	2	23
8	preparing dinner	14	155	108	renting a movie	3	23
9	playing a board game	8	129	109	buying a house	2	22
10	attend a wedding ceremony	9	125	110	designing t-shirts	2	22
11	playing video games	6	124	111	doing online banking	3	22
12	throwing a party	10	123	112	planting flowers	4	22
13	eat in a fast food restaurant	9	113	113	taking out the garbage	4	22
14	adopting a pet	7	111	114	brushing teeth	3	21
15	taking a child to bed	9	108	115	changing bed sheets	3	21
16	shopping online	7	102	116	going bowling	2	21
17	going on a bike tour	6	93	117	going for a walk	4	21
18	playing tennis	5	91	118	making coffee	2	21
19	renovating a room	9	87	119	serving a drink	5	20
20	growing vegetables	7	82	120	taking children to school	3	20
21	listening to music	8	81	121	taking the underground	2	20
22	sewing clothes	6	79	122	feeding a cat	4	19
23	training a dog	3	79	123	going to a party	5	19
24	moving into a new flat	8	78	124	ironing laundry	2	19
25	answering the phone	11	75	125	making tea	3	18
26	going to a concert	5	74	126	sending a fax	3	18
27	looking for a job	5	74	127	sending party invitations	3	18
28	visiting relatives	12	73	128	planting a tree	3	17
29	checking in at an airport	5	71	129	setting up presentation equipment	2	17
30	making a camping trip	5	71	130	visiting a museum	2	17
31	painting a wall	8	71	131	calling 911	2	16
32	planning a holiday trip	12	71	132	changing a light bulb	3	16
33	baking a cake	3	69	133	making toasted bread	1	16
34	going to the gym	6	69	134	playing a song	2	16
35	attending a court hearing	3	66	135	washing clothes	3	16
36	going to the theater	6	66	136	putting up a painting	2	15
37	going to a pub	4	65	137	serving a meal	5	15
38	playing football	3	65	138	washing dishes	3	15
39	going to a funeral	5	64	139	cooking pasta	2	14
40	visiting a doctor	7	64	140	moving furniture	4	14
41	paying with a credit card	6	63	141	put a poster on the wall	2	13
42	settling bank transactions	5	63	142	cleaning up toys	1	12
43	paying bills	6	62	143	preparing a picnic	2	12
44	taking a swimming class	3	62	144	repairing a bicycle	2	12
45	looking for a flat	6	61	145	cooking meat	4	11
46	attending a church service	3	60	146	drying clothes	3	11
47	making soup	3	60	147	give a medicine to someone	3	11
48	flying in a plane	5	57	148	feeding an infant	4	10
49	going grocery shopping	13	57	149	telling a story	2	10
50	walking a dog	5	57	150	unloading the dishwasher	1	10
51	going to the swimming pool	5	56	151	putting away groceries	3	9
52	preparing a wedding	3	56	152	deciding on a movie	1	7
53	writing a letter	5	54	153	going to a shopping centre	1	7
54	buy from a vending machine	3	53	154	loading the dishwasher	2	7
55	attending a job interview	3	52	155	making a bed	1	7
56	visiting sights	9	52	156	making a dinner reservation	1	7
57	attending a football match	4	51	157	making scrambled eggs	1	7
58	cleaning up a flat	6	51	158	playing piano	2	7
59	washing ones hair	6	49	159	wrapping a gift	1	7
60	writing an exam	5	49	160	chopping vegetables	3	6
61	watching a tennis match	3	48	161	cleaning the floor	1	6
62	going to the dentist	3	47	162	getting the newspaper	1	6
63	making a sandwich	4	47	163	making fresh orange juice	1	6
64	playing golf	3	47	164	checking if a store is open	2	5
65	taking a driving lesson	2	44	165	heating food on kitchen gas	1	4
66	going fishing	4	43	166	locking up the house	2	4

	scenario	# docs	# sents.		scenario	# docs	# sents.
67	having a barbecue	4	43	167	cleaning the bathroom	2	3
68	riding on a bus	6	43	168	mailing a letter	1	3
69	going on a train	4	42	169	making a hot dog	1	3
70	going skiing	2	42	170	playing a movie	1	3
71	packing a suitcase	5	42	171	remove and replace garbage bag	1	3
72	vacuuming the carpet	3	41	172	taking copies	2	3
73	order something on the phone	6	40	173	unclogging the toilet	1	3
74	ordering a pizza	3	39	174	washing a cut	1	3
75	going to work	3	38	175	applying band aid	2	2
76	doing laundry	4	37	176	change batteries in an alarm clock	1	2
77	cooking fish	3	36	177	cleaning a kitchen	1	2
78	learning a board game	1	36	178	feeding the fish	1	2
79	fueling a car	3	35	179	setting an alarm	1	2
80	going dancing	3	35	180	getting ready for bed	1	1
81	laying flooring in a room	4	35	181	setting the dining table	1	1
82	making breakfast	2	35	182	change batteries in a camera	0	0
83	paying for gas	3	34	183	buying a tree	0	0
84	taking a bath	3	34	184	papering a room	0	0
85	visiting the beach	4	34	185	cutting your own hair	0	0
86	borrow a book from the library	3	33	186	watering indoor plants	0	0
87	mowing the lawn	3	33	187	organize a board game evening	0	0
88	changing a baby diaper	3	32	188	cleaning the shower	0	0
89	driving a car	9	32	189	canceling a party	0	0
90	making omelette	3	32	190	cooking rice	0	0
91	play music in church	2	32	191	buying a DVD player	0	0
92	taking medicine	5	31	192	folding clothes	0	0
93	getting a haircut	3	30	193	buying a birthday present	0	0
94	heating food in a microwave	3	30	194	Answering the doorbell	0	0
95	making a mixed salad	3	30	195	cleaning the table	0	0
96	going jogging	2	28	196	boiling milk	0	0
97	going to the sauna	3	28	197	sewing a button	0	0
98	paying taxes	2	28	198	reading a story to a child	0	0
99	sending food back	2	28	199	making a shopping list	0	0
100	making a flight reservation	2	27	200	emptying the kitchen sink	0	0

Personality Traits Recognition in Literary Texts

Daniele Pizzolli
University of Trento / Trento, Italy
daniele.pizzolli@studenti.unitn.it

Carlo Strapparava
FBK-irst / Trento, Italy
strappa@fbk.eu

Abstract

Interesting stories often are built around interesting characters. Finding and detailing what makes an interesting character is a real challenge, but certainly a significant cue is the character personality traits. Our exploratory work tests the adaptability of the current personality traits theories to literal characters, focusing on the analysis of utterances in theatre scripts. And, at the opposite, we try to find significant traits for interesting characters. Our preliminary results demonstrate that our approach is reasonable. Using machine learning for gaining insight into the personality traits of fictional characters can make sense.

1 Introduction

The availability of texts produced by people using the modern communication means can give an important insight in personality profiling. And computational linguistic community has been quite active in this topic. In this paper we want to explore the use of the techniques and tools nowadays used for user generated content, for the analysis of literary characters in books and plays. In particular we will focus on the analysis of speech utterances in theatre scripts. Dialogues in theatre plays are quite easy to collect (i.e. the characters are explicitly stated in the scripts) without the need of lengthy and costly manual annotation.

Of course the style of the language in social media is very different. For example, usually the user generated content is quite short in length, not always with the correct spelling and correct in syntax, and nowadays full of emoticons. On the other hand we can expect that authors of great theatre masterpieces (e.g. Shakespeare) had exceptional skill in rendering the personality traits of the characters, just only through dialogues among them.

Computational linguistics exploits different frameworks for the classification of psychological traits. In particular the Five Factor Model (Big5) is often used. Advantages and drawbacks of those frameworks are well-known. A good reference on this is the work by Lee and Ashton (2004). We are interested in a broad, exploitative classification and do not endorse a model over the others. We choose to use the Big Five model because the gold labeled dataset we exploited was built using this framework.

1.1 Literature review

To our knowledge, there is little ongoing research on personality traits recognition in literary texts. Most of the works in literary text is focused on other aspects such as author attribution, stylometry, plagiarism detection. Regarding personality traits recognition, the used datasets are often collected from modern communication means, e.g. messages posted in social media.

Indeed there is interest in using modern NLP tools in literary texts, for example Grayson et al. (2016) use word embeddings for analyzing literature, Boyd (2017) describes the current status and tool for psychological text analysis, Flekova and Gurevych (2015) profile fictional characters, Liu et al. (2018) conduct a traits analysis of two fictional characters in a Chinese novel.

The use of the Five Factor Model for literature is explained in McCrae et al. (2012).

Bamman et al. (2014) consider the problem of automatically inferring latent character types in a collection of English novels. Bamman et al. (2013) present a new dataset for the text-driven analysis of film. Then they present some latent variable models for learning character types in movies.

Vala et al. (2015) propose a novel technique for character detection, achieving significant improvements over state of the art on multiple datasets.

Proceedings of the Second Storytelling Workshop, pages 107–111
Florence, Italy, August 1, 2019. ©2019 Association for Computational Linguistics

2 Model Building and Evaluation

We approached the problem as a supervised learning problem, using a labeled dataset and then transferring the result to our dataset.

In literary studies it is difficult to find a classification of characters according to some model of personality. Literary critics often prefer to go deeper into analyzing a character rather than putting her/him in an simple categories.

At the basis of our model, and in general in the framework we mentioned there is a lexical hypothesis: we are, at least to some extent, allowed to infer personality traits from the language and from words. From a psychological point of view, a support to the lexical hypothesis is in Ashton and Lee (2005). Our concern is also if those models can be applied to theatrical scripts, where everything is faked (and thus false) to be real (true). A crucial role is played by author's expertise in knowing how to render in the scripts the psychological traits of the characters.

2.1 Big5 Dataset with Gold Labels

As a labelled dataset, we used "essays", originally from Pennebaker and King (1999). "Essays" is a large dataset of stream-of-consciousness texts (about 2400, one for each author/user), collected between 1997 and 2004 and labelled with personality classes. Texts have been produced by students who took the Big5 questionnaires. The labels, that are self-assessments, are derived by z-scores computed by Mairesse et al. (2007) and converted from scores to nominal classes by Celli et al. (2013) with a median split[1].

The main reason behind the usage of this dataset is that is the only one containing gold labels suitable for our task. For sure the fact that the material does not match perfectly with literary text can pose some issues, discussed later in Section 3.

2.2 Literary Dataset Building and Validation

The proposed task is to recognize the personality of a character of a literary text, by the word s/he says. Theatre play scripts is probably the easiest type of literary text from which to extract characters' dialogues.

The name of the character speaking, following an old established convention, is at the start of the line, usually in a bold typeface, and after a colon ":" or a dot "." the text of the utterance follows until another character takes the turn or the play, act or scene ends.

An excerpt from William Shakespeare, *Hamlet, Act III, Scene 4* shows the patterns:

[…]

Hamlet. Do you see nothing there?

Gertrude. Nothing at all; yet all that is I see.

Hamlet. Nor did you nothing hear?

Gertrude. No, nothing but ourselves.

[…]

Our first candidate dataset was the Shakespeare Corpus in NLTK by Bird et al. (2009) that consist of several tragedies and comedies of Shakespeare well formatted in the XML format. However the the Shakespeare Corpus in NLTK is only a fraction of Shakespeare's plays. To collect more data we looked for a larger corpus. Open Source Shakespeare (OSS) contains all the 38 works[2] (some split in parts) commonly attributed to William Shakespeare[3], in a format good enough to easily parse dialogue structure

In our model a character is associated to all her/his turns as a single document. This is a simplified view but good enough as a starting point. One of the main consequences of this is a sort of flattening of the characters and the missing of the utterances said together at the same time by two characters. A quick check did not spot this type of event for two or more named characters. Very seldom, there are some references to the character "All" that mean all the characters on the stage together.

We know in advance that our models to be based on common words between the corpora, so we quickly checked the total lemma in commons that is 6755 over the two different corpora with roughly 60000 words each.

---

[1] We recall the five factors in Big5 model: Extroversion (EXT), Agreeableness (AGR), Conscientiousness (CON), Neuroticism (NEU), and Openness to experience (OPN).

[2] See: https://opensourceshakespeare.org/views/plays/plays_alpha.php.

[3] We acknowledge the fact that the works of William Shakespeare are routinely used for the classical NLP task of authorship recognition and that some attribution are still controversial. But this is not in our scope. The OSS includes the 1864 Globe Edition of Shakespeare works.

2.3 Modeling

We started working on our model using the Scikit-learn toolkit to do Machine Learning in Python (Pedregosa et al., 2011).

The initial task was to get reasonable performance on the "essay" dataset.

The problem falls in the class of multi-output labels. For simplicity each label (corresponding to a personal trait) can be treated as independent, partitioning the problem in 5 classification problems.

Starting from a simple bag of words model, we added to the features the output of TextPro (Pianta et al., 2008) for the columns: pos, chunk, entity, and tokentype[4].

The possible values of those columns are categorical variables that can be counted for each character in order to build a feature for the model.

Following the suggestion from (Celli et al., 2013, 2014), our model was built as a pipeline incorporating both the bag of word model and the output of TextPro.

We acknowledge that a lot of tweaking is possible for improving the performance of a model (such as building a different model for each trait, or use different features or classifier). However that was not our primary scope.

2.4 Testing the model

The OSS dataset missed some features used in the training and testing of the original model. We solved the issue by adding the required features with the initial value of 0. Since the feature are related to countable occurrences or related to ratios, this operation is safe.

We briefly discuss a couple of models. In Table 1 are reported the results for a simple model that uses the bag-of-word concept and with some POS tagging extracts the lemmas.

Table 1: Model: NLTK Lemma

trait	model	classifier	f1-score
AGR	NLTK Lemma	Linear SVC	0.45
CON	NLTK Lemma	Linear SVC	0.46
EXT	NLTK Lemma	Linear SVC	0.45
NEU	NLTK Lemma	Random Forest	0.53
OPN	NLTK Lemma	Multinomial NB	0.61

By adding the features obtained with TextPro as described in subsection 2.3 we gained some score for most of the traits, for the weighted average of each trait our results are comparable to the ones reported by Celli et al. (2013).

The results shown in Table 2 report the best results.

Table 2: Model: NLTK Lemma + TextPro (both truncated and weighted) for Random Forest Classifier

trait	model	f1-score
AGR	NLTK Lemma + TextPro	0.59
CON	NLTK Lemma + TextPro	0.45
EXT	NLTK Lemma + TextPro	0.54
NEU	NLTK Lemma + TextPro	0.54
OPN	NLTK Lemma + TextPro	0.66

Going deeper into commenting the feature engineering and comparing the models should give us insight for understanding the linguistic features related to personality. This requires further knowledge beyond the scope of the current work and it leaves the path open to future explorations.

3 Results and Discussion

As with our models on a known dataset we got state_of_the_art performance, we tried to apply the classifier on the Shakespeare's plays dataset. Table 3 reports the results for the most verbose speakers of a selected list of plays.

Table 3: Personality Trait Attribution Selected List

Play	Name	AGR	CON	EXT	NEU	OPE
Hamlet	Hamlet	0	1	0	0	1
	Claudius	0	1	0	0	1
	Polonius	0	1	0	0	1
	Horatio	0	1	0	0	1
	Laertes	0	0	0	0	1
Macbeth	Macbeth	0	0	0	0	1
	Lady Macbeth	0	1	0	1	1
	Malcolm	0	0	0	0	1
	Macduff	0	0	0	0	1
	Ross	0	0	0	0	1
Merchant of Venice	Portia	0	1	0	0	1
	Shylock	0	0	0	1	1
	Bassanio	0	1	0	0	1
	Launcelot Gobbo	0	0	0	0	1
	Antonio	0	1	0	0	1
Othello	Iago	0	1	0	0	1
	Othello	0	0	0	0	1
	Desdemona	0	1	0	0	1
	Cassio	0	1	0	0	1
	Emilia	0	0	0	0	1
Romeo and Juliet	Romeo	0	0	0	0	1
	Juliet	0	0	0	0	1
	Friar Laurence	0	0	0	0	1
	Nurse	0	1	0	1	1
	Capulet	0	0	0	1	1

We do not have a gold labeled dataset to confront with. But a quick look at the result table for the best known (at least to us) characters of the

---

[4] A brief description of TextPro usage and the meaning of the annotations is available at: `http://textpro.fbk.eu/annotation-layers`.

Shakespeare's plays reveals some traits in common for characters that are at the opposite, like the protagonist and the antagonist. This is the case for "Hamlet", the most verbose characters seem to have similar traits. We are glad that Portia and Antonio in "Merchant of Venice" display conscientiousness and Shylock neuroticism, as our shallow knowledge of the play remind us. A vertical look reveals low variability for the Agreeableness, Extraversion and Openness traits. Intuitively we acknowledge that something strange is happening here. Those traits are for sure related to the self-expression, something that a character is forced to do in a play. A model with numerical scores instead of boolean values would have offered some guidance here. In general we think that there are some reasons for the drawbacks of the model. We detail them in the following paragraphs.

A possible explanation is that the Big Five model, and/or our implementation does not capture the personality traits of the characters that are at the level that is needed. In other words, the model is too broad. Indeed, the Big Five Model has also the sub-classification for "Facets", but we do not know any public available gold standard dataset labeled at facet level.

The idea that the Big 5 is quite limited is not new. For example Paunonen and Jackson (2000) sustain that the following categories are to be considered outliers of the Big 5: a) Religious, devout, reverent; b) Sly, deceptive, manipulative; c) Honest, ethical, moral; d) Sexy, sensual, erotic; e) Thrifty, frugal, miserly; f) Conservative, traditional, down-to-earth; g) Masculine-feminine; h) Egotistical, conceited, snobbish; i) Humorous, witty, amusing; j) Risk-taking or Thrill-seeking.

Indeed those categories seem more appropriate to describe some of the characters in Shakespeare's scripts.

The essays dataset does not matches the OSS dataset along a number of dimensions. The most relevant ones that come to our mind are: purpose, grammar and mistakes and language diacronicity. Purpose: the essay is stream of consciousness, written once, probably never checked, by the author, the OSS is high quality writing, mostly where people speak with others. Grammar and mistakes: we think that the OSS corpus contains low rate of spelling errors, and the formulation of the sentences should be almost always correct, due to the nature of the corpus, but of course is another thing

to check. For sure also English grammar changed, so additional caveats may apply. Language diacronicity: Shakespeare's English is not today's English. To what extended this has an impact need to be verified.

Usually the personality traits are considered stable. But the need of creating tension and drama in a play may also imply some evolution in the personality of the character. A possible insight on this could come from a dispersion plot of the character traits all along the play, maybe with different granularity (one for each utterance, one for each scene). The dispersion plot should highlight such changes.

By following the Aristotle's Rules (Aristoteles, 1998) the playwright may set the dramatic tone for an entire scene, and the personality traits coherence may be sacrificed for this. The previously mentioned dispersion plot could show if such changes are aligned with the scenes or the acts. Since the acts usually are situated in distant time settings is reasonable to expect a change in personality traits due to the development of the character.

Our assumption that the characters' words capture the personality traits could be not always correct. Especially for plays where there are a lot of lies, alliances and breakages. Additional analysis taking care of the persons whom the speech is directed may discover that the personality traits change in relation of the recipient.

For sure there are different ways to write and perform a play. We choose Shakespeare's scripts because they are a classical resource and they rely a lot on the dialogues. But discarding the actions may have caused the loss of information, hindering the discover of the personality trait. Indeed, an advice for newcomers in drama writing is to build characters by showing their actions.

Two different characters (e.g., a king and a jester) can say the same thing, with a total different meaning. What differentiates them is the reaction of the others on the stage. A thorough modelling should take into account also this type of event. Intuitively this is used in comedies. Two different characters say the same thing to a third person in a short span of time. The second time the audience will anticipate the utterance in mind and will be delighted of the effect. In general a more detailed investigation has to be done to highlight different traits characterization in comedies and tragedies.

In conclusion the present work describes a first step towards capturing the personality traits of the characters in literary texts, in particular in the Shakespeare's theatre scripts. We discussed the results and the limitation of our approach and envisioned possible mitigations or solutions that require more research and dedication.

References

Aristoteles. 1998. *Poetica*. GLF editori Laterza, Roma.

Michael C. Ashton and Kibeom Lee. 2005. A defence of the lexical approach to the study of personality structure. *European Journal of Personality*, 19(1):5–24.

David Bamman, Brendan O'Connor, and Noah A. Smith. 2013. Learning latent personas of film characters. In *ACL (1)*, pages 352–361. The Association for Computer Linguistics.

David Bamman, Ted Underwood, and Noah A. Smith. 2014. A bayesian mixed effects model of literary character. In *Proceedings of the 52nd Annual Meeting of the Association for Computational Linguistics (Volume 1: Long Papers)*, pages 370–379, Baltimore, Maryland. Association for Computational Linguistics.

S. Bird, E. Klein, and E. Loper. 2009. *Natural Language Processing with Python: Analyzing Text with the Natural Language Toolkit*. O'Reilly Media.

Ryan L Boyd. 2017. Psychological text analysis in the digital humanities. In *Data analytics in digital humanities*, pages 161–189. Springer.

Fabio Celli, Bruno Lepri, Joan-Isaac Biel, Daniel Gatica-Perez, Giuseppe Riccardi, and Fabio Pianesi. 2014. The workshop on computational personality recognition 2014. In *The Workshop on Computational Personality Recognition 2014*.

Fabio Celli, Fabio Pianesi, David Stillwell, and Michal Kosinski. 2013. Workshop on computational personality recognition: Shared task. In *AAAI Workshop - Technical Report*.

Lucie Flekova and Iryna Gurevych. 2015. Personality profiling of fictional characters using sense-level links between lexical resources.

Siobhán Grayson, Maria Mulvany, Karen Wade, Gerardine Meaney, and Derek Greene. 2016. Novel2vec: characterising 19th century fiction via word embeddings. In *24th Irish Conference on Artificial Intelligence and Cognitive Science (AICS'16), University College Dublin, Dublin, Ireland, 20-21 September 2016*.

Kibeom Lee and Michael C Ashton. 2004. Psychometric properties of the hexaco personality inventory. *Multivariate Behavioral Research*, 39(2):329–358. PMID: 26804579.

Mingming Liu, Yufeng Wu, Dongdong Jiao, Michael Wu, and Tingshao Zhu. 2018. Literary intelligence analysis of novel protagonists' personality traits and development. *Digital Scholarship in the Humanities*.

François Mairesse, Marilyn Walker, Matthias Mehl, and Roger Moore. 2007. Using linguistic cues for the automatic recognition of personality in conversation and text. *Journal of Artificial Intelligence Research (JAIR)*, 30:457–500.

Robert R. McCrae, James F. Gaines, and Marie A. Wellington. 2012. *The Five-Factor Model in Fact and Fiction*, chapter 4. American Cancer Society.

Sampo V. Paunonen and Douglas N. Jackson. 2000. What is beyond the big five? plenty! *Journal of Personality*, 68(5):821–835.

F. Pedregosa, G. Varoquaux, A. Gramfort, V. Michel, B. Thirion, O. Grisel, M. Blondel, P. Prettenhofer, R. Weiss, V. Dubourg, J. Vanderplas, A. Passos, D. Cournapeau, M. Brucher, M. Perrot, and E. Duchesnay. 2011. Scikit-learn: Machine learning in Python. *Journal of Machine Learning Research*, 12:2825–2830.

James Pennebaker and Laura A. King. 1999. Linguistic styles: Language use as an individual difference. *Journal of Personality and Social Psychology*, 77(6):1296–1312.

Emanuele Pianta, Christian Girardi, Roberto Zanoli, and Fondazione Bruno Kessler. 2008. The textpro tool suite. In *In Proceedings of LREC, 6th edition of the Language Resources and Evaluation Conference*.

Hardik Vala, David Jurgens, Andrew Piper, and Derek Ruths. 2015. Mr. bennet, his coachman, and the archbishop walk into a bar but only one of them gets recognized: On the difficulty of detecting characters in literary texts. In *Proceedings of the 2015 Conference on Empirical Methods in Natural Language Processing*, pages 769–774, Lisbon, Portugal. Association for Computational Linguistics.

"Winter is here": Summarizing Twitter Streams related to Pre-Scheduled Events

Anietie Andy
andyanietie@gmail.com
University of Pennsylvania

Derry Wijaya
wijaya@bu.edu
Boston University

Chris Callison-Burch
ccb@cis.upenn.edu
University of Pennsylvania

Abstract

Pre-scheduled events, such as TV shows and sports games, usually garner considerable attention from the public. Twitter captures large volumes of discussions and messages related to these events, in real-time. Twitter streams related to pre-scheduled events are characterized by the following: (1) spikes in the volume of published tweets reflect the highlights of the event and (2) some of the published tweets make reference to the characters involved in the event, in the context in which they are currently portrayed in a sub-event. In this paper, we take advantage of these characteristics to identify the highlights of pre-scheduled events from tweet streams and we demonstrate a method to summarize these highlights. We evaluate our algorithm on tweets collected around 2 episodes of a popular TV show, Game of Thrones, Season 7.

1 Introduction

Every week, pre-scheduled events, such as TV shows and sports games capture the attention of vast numbers of people. The first episode of the seventh season of Game of Thrones (GOTS7), a popular fantasy show on HBO, drew in about 10 million viewers during its broadcast[1].

During the broadcast of a popular pre-scheduled event, Twitter users generate a huge amount of time-stamped tweets expressing their excitements/frustrations, opinions, and commenting about the characters involved in the event, in the context in which they are currently portrayed in a sub-event. For example, the following are some tweets that were published during a three minute time period of an episode of GOTS7:

- Bend the knee... Jon snow #gots7

- finally Jon and Dany meet and i'm freaking out #gots7
- Daenerys: have you not come to bend the knee? Jon Snow: i have not Daenerys.

These tweets reflect a part of or the whole scene that happened during this time period on the show i.e. Jon Snow meeting with Daenerys.

Monitoring tweet streams - related to an event, for information related to sub-events can be time consuming partly because of the overwhelming amount of data, some of which are redundant or irrelevant to the sub-event. In this paper, we propose a method to summarize tweet streams related to pre-scheduled events. We aim to identify the highlights of pre-scheduled events from tweet streams related to the event and automatically summarize these highlights. Specifically we evaluate our algorithm on tweets we collected around a popular fantasy TV show, Game of Thrones. We will make this dataset available to the research community[2]. This paper makes the following contributions:

- Identify the highlights of pre-scheduled events from tweets streams related to the event and identify the character that had the most mentions in tweets published during the highlight.
- Identify the context in which this character was being discussed in tweets published during the highlight and summarize the highlight by selecting the tweets that discuss this character in a similar context.

2 Related Work

Some approaches to summarizing tweets related to an event adapt or modify summarization techniques that perform well with documents from news articles and apply these adaptations to tweets. In Sharifi et al. (2010a); Shen et al.

---

[1] https://en.wikipedia.org/wiki/Game_of_Thrones_(season_7)#Ratings

[2] https://anietieandy.github.io

Proceedings of the Second Storytelling Workshop, pages 112–116
Florence, Italy, August 1, 2019. ©2019 Association for Computational Linguistics

(2013) a graph-based phrase reinforcement algorithm was proposed. In Sharifi et al. (2010b) a hybrid TF-IDF approach to extract one-or-multiple-sentence summary for each topic was proposed. In Liu et al. (2011) an algorithm is proposed that explores a variety of text sources for summarizing twitter topics. In Harabagiu and Hickl (2011) an algorithm is proposed that synthesizes content from multiple microblog posts on the same topic and uses a generative model which induces event structures from the text and captures how users convey relevant content. In Marcus et al. (2011), a tool called "Twitnfo" was proposed. This tool used the volume of tweets related to a topic to identify peaks and summarize these events by selecting tweets that contain a desired keyword or keywords, and selects frequent terms to provide an automated label for each peak. In Takamura et al. (2011); Shen et al. (2013) a summarization model based algorithm was proposed based on the facility location problem. In Chakrabarti and Punera (2011) a summarization algorithm based on learning an underlying hidden state representation of an event via hidden Markov models is proposed. Louis and Newman (2012) proposed an algorithm that aggregates tweets into subtopic clusters which are then ranked and summarized by a few representative tweets from each cluster (Shen et al., 2013). In Nichols et al. (2012) an algorithm was proposed that uses the volume of tweets to identify subevents, then uses various weighting schemes to perform tweet selection. Li et al. (2017) proposed an algorithm for abstractive text summarization based on sequence-to-sequence oriented encoder-decoder model equipped with a deep recurrent generative decoder. Nallapati et al. (2016) proposed a model using attentional endoder-decoder Recurrent Neural Network.

Our algorithm is different from the previous work in that it identifies the character that had the most mentions in tweets published in a highlight and identifies the context in which this character was being discussed in this highlight; it then summarizes the highlight by selecting tweets that discuss this character in a similar context.

3 Dataset

Our dataset consist of tweets collected around 7 episodes of a popular TV show, GOTS7. We algorithmically identify points of elevated drama or

highlights from this dataset and summarize these highlights.

Each episode of GOTS7 lasted approximately an hour. We used the Twitter streaming API to collect time-stamped and temporally ordered tweets containing "#gots7", a popular hashtag for the show, while each episode was going on. We note that filtering by hashtag gives us only some of the tweets about the show–we omit tweets that used other GOTS7 related hashtags or no hashtags at all. Our dataset consists of the tweet streams for seven episodes of GOTS7; we collected the following number of tweets: 32,476, 9,021, 4,532, 8,521, 6,183, 8,971, and 17,360 from episodes 1,2,3,4,5,6, and 7 respectively.

3.1 Highlight Identification

To identify the highlights of each episode, we plot the number of tweets that were published per minute for each minute of an episode. Since data at the minute level is quite noisy and to smooth out short-term fluctuations, we calculated the mean of the number of tweets published every 3 minutes as shown by the red line in Figure 1, which forms peaks in the tweet volume. We observed the following: (1) the spikes in the volume of tweets correspond to some exciting events/scenes during the show and (2) when there is a spike in the volume of tweets, the characters involved in the subevents (around that time period) spike in popularity as well in the published tweets. For example, in episode 1, when the character Arya Stark wore Walder Freys face and poisoned all of house Frey, there was a spike in the volume of tweets at this time period; also Arya Stark and Walder Frey spiked in popularity in tweets published in this time period.

Several studies have suggested that a peak needs to rise above a threshold to qualify it as a highlight in a given event. Hence, similar to Shamma et al. (2009); Gillani et al. (2017), we identify highlights of the events by selecting the peaks using the mean and standard deviation of the peaks in all the tweets collected around the 7 episodes of GOTS7.

3.2 Character Identification

To identify the characters involved in GOTS7, we select all the character names listed in the GOTS7 Wikipedia page. It is common for tweets to mention nicknames or abbreviations rather that character full names. For example, in tweets col-

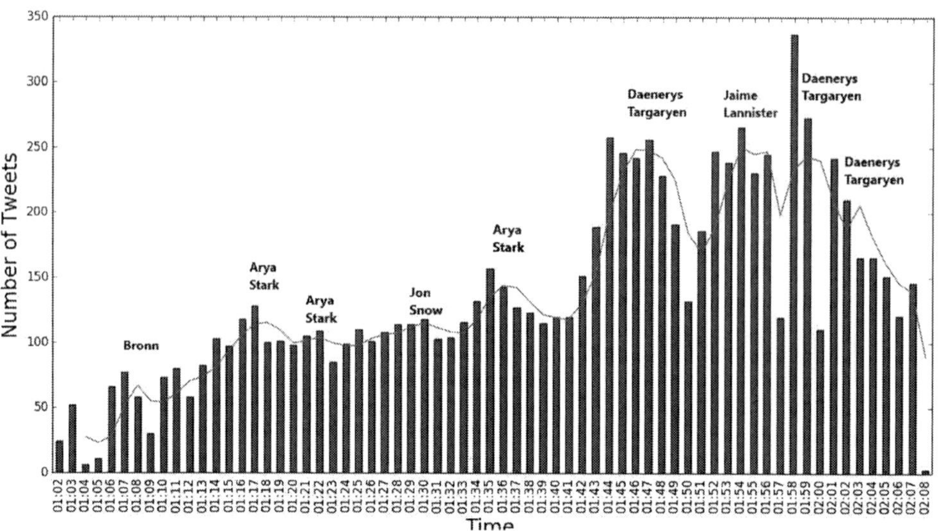

Figure 1: Histogram of number of tweets published per minute during an episode of Game of Thrones. The red line, which forms peaks, shows the mean of the number of tweets published every 3 minutes. The names of the character that had the most mentions during each peak in tweet volume are also shown.

lected around GOTS7 episode 1, the character Sandor Clegane is mentioned 22 times by his full name and 61 times by his nickname "the hound." Therefore, for each character, we assemble a list of aliases consisting of their first name (which for GOTS7 characters is unique), and the nicknames listed in the first paragraph of the character's Wikipedia article. All characters end up having at most 2 aliases i.e. their first name and/or a nickname. For example, the nicknames for Sandor Clegane are Sandor and the hound.

To identify the character(s) involved in a highlight from the tweets published during the highlight, we do the following: (1) given the highlight (section 3.1) we count the frequency of mentions of characters in tweets published during the highlight. We select the character with the most mentions. The intuition here is that the character with the most mentions in tweets published in each highlight played a major role in the sub-event that occurred during the highlight.

4 Our Model

We use context2vec Melamud et al. (2016) to create a vector representation for the tweets in each highlight. Context2vec uses an unsupervised neural model, a bidirectional LSTM, to learn sentential context representations that result in comparable or better performances on tasks such as

sentence completion and lexical substitution than popular context representation of averaged word embeddings. Context2vec learns sentential context representation around a target word by feeding one LSTM network with the sentence words around the target from left to right, and another from right to left. These left-to-right and right-to-left context word embeddings are concatenated and fed into a multi-layer perceptron to obtain the embedding of the entire joint sentential context around the target word. Finally, similar to word2vec, context2vec uses negative sampling to assign similar embeddings to this sentential context and its target word. This process indirectly results in sentential contexts, which are associated with similar target words, being assigned similar embeddings.

Given the tweets that mention the character that had the most mentions in tweets published during the time period of a highlight, we want vector representations of tweets that represent the context in which this character is discussed in these tweets. Tweets that discuss the character in a similar context should have similar vector representations. The sentential context representation learned by context2vec is used to find the tweets that best summarize the highlight.

We cluster the context2vec vectors using K-Means. To identify the number of clusters for

Episode	Scene Description	Tweet Summary
Episode 3	Daenerys Targaryen meets Jon Snow	(1) Jon snow telling Daenerys about the white walkers (2) Davos keeping it straight and simple for team Jon snow, the king in the north! (3) Daenerys Targaryen and Jon snow... in the same. room.
Episode 4	Arya displays superb fencing skills as Littlefinger and Sansa watch	(1) Arya got Sansa and Littlefinger shook! (2) Arya and Brienne fighting each other, marvellous piece of telly. (3) so what i'm getting from this is that Arya can beat the hound.

Table 1: Example highlight summaries of Game of Thrones episode 3 and 4

tweets published during the time period of a highlight, we use the elbow method (Kodinariya and Makwana, 2013). For each cluster we choose the five tweets closest to their respective cluster centroids as the tweets that summarize the highlight; these five tweets were concatenated together. We varied the number of tweets we concatenated and five gave the optimal results.

5 Experiments

We evaluate our algorithm on tweets collected around 2 episodes of GOTS7 i.e. episodes 3 and 4. The plot summaries of these GOTS7 episodes are available on the IMDB website. We collected the plot summaries for GOTS7 episodes 3 and 4 from the IMDB website. We compared the summaries from our model to the plot summaries of these episodes from IMDB using the ROUGE metric (Lin, 2004). We compared our model to 5 competitive summarization algorithms and our model performed better than all the baselines in both episodes 3 and 4 as shown int tables 2 and 3. Table 1 shows some of the summaries from our model for a highlight in both episodes 3 and 4.

6 Baselines

LexRank: Computes the importance of textual units using eigenvector centrality on a graph representation based on the similarity of the units (Erkan and Radev, 2004).

TextRank: A graph based extractive summarization algorithm (Mihalcea and Tarau, 2004).

LSA: Constructs a terms-by-units matrix, and estimates the importance of the textual units based on SVD on the matrix (Gong and Liu, 2001)

Luhn: Derives a significance factor for each textual unit based occurrences and placements of frequent words within the unit (Luhn, 1958)

Most Retweeted: We select the tweet with the most number of re-tweets in an highlight as a summary of the highlight.

Algorithms	Rouge-1	Rouge-2	Rouge-L
Our Model	**38**	**10**	**31.5**
Luhn	14.4	5	12.3
Most Re-tweets	10	3	10
TextRank	15	2	11.7
LexRank	10	2	10
LSA	10	0	10

Table 2: ROUGE-F1 scores on tweets from highlights in Episode 3

Algorithms	Rouge-1	Rouge-2	Rouge-L
Our Model	**33**	**19.4**	**25.2**
Luhn	16.5	0	13
Most Re-tweets	10	4	10
TextRank	10.5	4	10
LexRank	10	5	10
LSA	11.3	5	10

Table 3: ROUGE-F1 scores on tweets from highlights in Episode 4

7 Conclusion and Future Work

We proposed a model to summarize highlights of events from tweet streams related to the events and showed that our model outperformed several baselines. In the future, we will test our model on tweets collected around other events such as Presidential debates. There were a few cases where our algorithm generated summaries that are somewhat similar, for example: "Arya got Sansa and Littlefinger shook!" and "Littlefinger is shook by Aryas fighting skills". In the future, we will improve the diversity of the generated summaries.

References

Deepayan Chakrabarti and Kunal Punera. 2011. Event summarization using tweets. *ICWSM*, 11:66–73.

Günes Erkan and Dragomir R Radev. 2004. Lexrank: Graph-based lexical centrality as salience in text summarization. *Journal of artificial intelligence research*, 22:457–479.

Mehreen Gillani, Muhammad U Ilyas, Saad Saleh, Jalal S Alowibdi, Naif Aljohani, and Fahad S Alotaibi. 2017. Post summarization of microblogs of sporting events. In *Proceedings of the 26th International Conference on World Wide Web Companion*, pages 59–68. International World Wide Web Conferences Steering Committee.

Yihong Gong and Xin Liu. 2001. Generic text summarization using relevance measure and latent semantic analysis. In *Proceedings of the 24th annual international ACM SIGIR conference on Research and development in information retrieval*, pages 19–25. ACM.

Sanda M Harabagiu and Andrew Hickl. 2011. Relevance modeling for microblog summarization. In *ICWSM*.

Trupti M Kodinariya and Prashant R Makwana. 2013. Review on determining number of cluster in k-means clustering. *International Journal*, 1(6):90–95.

Piji Li, Wai Lam, Lidong Bing, and Zihao Wang. 2017. Deep recurrent generative decoder for abstractive text summarization. *arXiv preprint arXiv:1708.00625*.

Chin-Yew Lin. 2004. Rouge: A package for automatic evaluation of summaries. *Text Summarization Branches Out*.

Fei Liu, Yang Liu, and Fuliang Weng. 2011. Why is sxsw trending?: exploring multiple text sources for twitter topic summarization. In *Proceedings of the Workshop on Languages in Social Media*, pages 66–75. Association for Computational Linguistics.

Annie Louis and Todd Newman. 2012. Summarization of business-related tweets: A concept-based approach. *Proceedings of COLING 2012: Posters*, pages 765–774.

Hans Peter Luhn. 1958. The automatic creation of literature abstracts. *IBM Journal of research and development*, 2(2):159–165.

Adam Marcus, Michael S Bernstein, Osama Badar, David R Karger, Samuel Madden, and Robert C Miller. 2011. Twitinfo: aggregating and visualizing microblogs for event exploration. In *Proceedings of the SIGCHI conference on Human factors in computing systems*, pages 227–236. ACM.

Oren Melamud, Jacob Goldberger, and Ido Dagan. 2016. context2vec: Learning generic context embedding with bidirectional lstm. In *CoNLL*, pages 51–61.

Rada Mihalcea and Paul Tarau. 2004. Textrank: Bringing order into text. In *Proceedings of the 2004 conference on empirical methods in natural language processing*.

Ramesh Nallapati, Bowen Zhou, Caglar Gulcehre, Bing Xiang, et al. 2016. Abstractive text summarization using sequence-to-sequence rnns and beyond. *arXiv preprint arXiv:1602.06023*.

Jeffrey Nichols, Jalal Mahmud, and Clemens Drews. 2012. Summarizing sporting events using twitter. In *Proceedings of the 2012 ACM international conference on Intelligent User Interfaces*, pages 189–198. ACM.

David A Shamma, Lyndon Kennedy, and Elizabeth F Churchill. 2009. Tweet the debates: understanding community annotation of uncollected sources. In *Proceedings of the first SIGMM workshop on Social media*, pages 3–10. ACM.

Beaux Sharifi, Mark-Anthony Hutton, and Jugal Kalita. 2010a. Summarizing microblogs automatically. In *Human Language Technologies: The 2010 Annual Conference of the North American Chapter of the Association for Computational Linguistics*, pages 685–688. Association for Computational Linguistics.

Beaux Sharifi, Mark-Anthony Hutton, and Jugal K Kalita. 2010b. Experiments in microblog summarization. In *Social Computing (SocialCom), 2010 IEEE Second International Conference on*, pages 49–56. IEEE.

Chao Shen, Fei Liu, Fuliang Weng, and Tao Li. 2013. A participant-based approach for event summarization using twitter streams. In *Proceedings of the 2013 Conference of the North American Chapter of the Association for Computational Linguistics: Human Language Technologies*, pages 1152–1162.

Hiroya Takamura, Hikaru Yokono, and Manabu Okumura. 2011. Summarizing a document stream. In *European conference on information retrieval*, pages 177–188. Springer.

WriterForcing: Generating more interesting story endings

Prakhar Gupta[*]   **Vinayshekhar Bannihatti Kumar**[*]   **Mukul Bhutani**[*]   **Alan W Black**
School of Computer Science
Carnegie Mellon University
Pittsburgh, PA
{prakharg, vbkumar, mbhutani, awb}@cs.cmu.edu

Abstract

We study the problem of generating interesting endings for stories. Neural generative models have shown promising results for various text generation problems. Sequence to Sequence (Seq2Seq) models are typically trained to generate a single output sequence for a given input sequence. However, in the context of a story, multiple endings are possible. Seq2Seq models tend to ignore the context and generate generic and dull responses. Very few works have studied generating diverse and interesting story endings for a given story context. In this paper, we propose models which generate more diverse and interesting outputs by 1) training models to focus attention on important keyphrases of the story, and 2) promoting generation of non-generic words. We show that the combination of the two leads to more diverse and interesting endings.

1 Introduction

Story ending generation is the task of generating an ending sentence of a story given a story context. A story context is a sequence of sentences connecting characters and events. This task is challenging as it requires modelling the characters, events and objects in the context, and then generating a coherent and sensible ending based on them. Generalizing the semantics of the events and entities and their relationships across stories is a non-trivial task. Even harder challenge is to generate stories which are non-trivial and interesting. In this work, we focus on the story ending generation task, where given a story context - a sequence of sentences from a story, the model has to generate the last sentence of the story.

Context
My friends and I did not know what to do for our friends birthday. We sat around the living room trying to figure out what to do. We finally decided to go to the movies. We all drove to the theatre and bought tickets.
Specific response (ground truth) The movie turned out to be terrible but our friend had a good time. **Generic response (seq2seq output)** We were so happy to see that we had a good time.

Table 1: For a given story context there can be multiple possible responses. The ones which are more specific to the story are more appealing to the users.

Seq2seq models have been widely used for the purpose of text generation. Despite the popularity of the Seq2seq models, in story generation tasks, they suffer from a well known issue of generating frequent phrases and generic outputs. These models when trained with Maximum Likelihood Estimate (MLE), learn to generate sequences close to the ground truth sequences. However, in story generation tasks, there can be multiple possible reasonable outputs for a given input story context. MLE objective in these models results in outputs which are safe (that is more likely to be present in any output), but also bland and generic. Some examples of such generic outputs in story ending generation task are - "He was sad", "They had a great time", etc. Table 1 shows an example story from the ROC stories corpus (Mostafazadeh et al., 2017) and the corresponding specific and generic responses.

Proceedings of the Second Storytelling Workshop, pages 117–126
Florence, Italy, August 1, 2019. ©2019 Association for Computational Linguistics

There have been many attempts to solve the issue of generation of generic responses. They can be broadly categorized into two categories:

1. Use conditionals such as emotions, sentiments, keywords, etc. that work as factors to condition the output on (Li et al., 2016b; Hu et al., 2017a). When the models focus on these conditionals given as additional input features, they tend to generate outputs which are more relevant and specific to the conditionals, which leads to less generic outputs. In our models, we use the keyphrases present in the story context as conditionals.

2. Modify the decoding procedure (Vijayakumar et al., 2018) with beam search or other variants, or the loss of the decoder (Baheti et al., 2018; Li et al., 2016a) to encourage the model to generate more diverse outputs. Our proposed model uses the ITF loss function suggested by Nakamura et al. (2018) to encourage the decoder to produce more interesting outputs.

We show that our proposed models can generate diverse and interesting outputs by conditioning on the keyphrases present in the story context and incorporating a modified training objective. Apart from human judgement based evaluation, we measure performance of the models in terms of 1) Diversity using DISTINCT-1,2,3 metrics and 2) Relevance by introducing an automatic metric based on Story Cloze loss. Experiments show that our models score higher than current state of the art models in terms of both diversity and relevance.

For reproducibility purposes we are making our codebase open source [1].

2 Related Work

There has been a surge in recent years to tackle the problem of story generation. One common theme is to employ the advances in deep learning for the task. Jain et al. (2017) use Seq2Seq models (Sutskever et al., 2014) to generate stories from descriptions of images. Huang et al. (2018) leverage hierarchical decoding where a high-level decoder constructs a plan by generating a topic and a low-level decoder generates

sentences based on the topic. There have been a few works which try to incorporate real world knowledge during the process of story generation. Guan et al. (2018) use an incremental encoding (IE) scheme and perform one hop reasoning over the ConceptNet graph ConceptNet in order to augment the representation of words in the sentences. Chen et al. (2018) also tackle the problem in a similar way by including "commonsense knowledge" from ConceptNet as well. Several prior work focus on generating more coherent stories. Clark et al. (2018) model entity representations explicitly by combining it with representations of the previous sentence and Martin et al. (2018) model events representations and then generate natural language sentences from those events (event2sentence). Li et al. (2018) use adversarial training to help the model generate more reasonable endings.

A common problem with such neural approaches in general is that the generated text is very "safe and boring". There has been a lot of recent efforts towards generating diverse outputs in problems such as dialogue systems, image captioning, story generation, etc., in order to alleviate the safe or boring text generation problem. Methods include using self-attention Shao et al. (2017), Reinforcement Learning (Li et al., 2017), GANs etc. Xu et al. (2018) proposed a method called Diversity-Promoting Generative Adversarial Network, which assigns low reward for repeatedly generated text and high reward for novel and fluent text using a language model based discriminator. Li et al. (2016a) propose a Maximum Mutual Information (MMI) objective function and show that this objective function leads to a decrease in the proportion of generic response sequences. Nakamura et al. (2018) propose another loss function for the same objective. In our models we experiment with their loss function and observe similar effects.

Recent works have also made advances in controllable generation of text based on constraints to make the outputs more specific. Peng et al. (2018) have a conditional embedding matrix for valence to control the ending of the story. Hu et al. (2017b) have a toggle vector to introduce constraint on the output of text generation models using Variational Auto Encoders(Doersch, 2016). Generating diverse responses based on conditioning has been done

---

[1]https://github.com/witerforcing/WriterForcing

extensively in the field of dialogue systems. Xing et al. (2016); Zhou et al. (2018); Zhang et al. (2018) propose conditioning techniques by using emotion and persona while generating responses. Conditioned generation has also been studied in the field of story generation to plan and write (Yao et al., 2018; Huang et al., 2018) stories.

In this work, we focus on generating more diverse and interesting endings for stories by introducing conditioning on keyphrases present in the story context and encouraging infrequent words in the outputs by modifying the training objective, thus leading to more interesting story endings.

3 Background

3.1 Sequence-to-Sequence with Attention

We use a Seq2Seq model with attention as our baseline model. Words (w_i) belonging to the context of the story are fed one by one to the encoder (uni-directional but multi-layer) which produces the corresponding hidden representations h_i^{enc}. Finally, the hidden representation at the final timestep (T) is passed on to the decoder. During training, for each step t, the decoder (a unidirectional GRU) receives the word embedding of the previous word(x_{t-1}) and the hidden state (h_{t-1}^{dec}). At training time, the word present in the target sentence at timestep $t-1$ is used and at test time, the actual word emitted by the decoder at the time step $t-1$ is used as input in the next time step.

However, to augment the hidden representation that is passed from encoder to the decoder, one can use the mechanism of attention (Bahdanau et al., 2014). The attention weights at time step t during decoding, denoted as a^t, can be calculated as:

$$e^t = v^T \tanh\left(W_{dec}\, h_t^{dec} + W_{enc}\, h_{1:T_{src}}^{enc}\right) \quad (1)$$

$$a_i^t = \mathrm{softmax}\left(e_i^t\right) \quad (2)$$

where W_{dec}, W_{enc} and v^T are learnable parameters and a_i^t denotes the ith component of the attention weights. The attention weights can be viewed as a probability distribution over the source words, that tells the decoder where to look to produce the next word. Next, the attention weights are used to produce a weighted sum

of the encoder hidden states, known as the context vector(c_t):

$$c_t = \sum_{i=1}^{T_{src}} a_i^t h_i^{enc} \quad (3)$$

This context vector is then concatenated with the embedding of the input word. It is used by the decoder to produce a probability distribution. P_t^{vocab} over the whole vocabulary:

$$P_t^{vocab} = Decoder_t([x_{t-1} : c_t]; h_t) \quad (4)$$

During training, the loss for timestep t is the negative log likelihood of the target word w_t^* for that timestep.

$$\mathrm{loss}_t = -\log P\left(w_t^*\right) \quad (5)$$

Thus, the overall averaged loss of the whole sequence becomes:

$$\mathrm{loss} = \frac{1}{T_{dec}} \sum_{t=1}^{T_{dec}} \mathrm{loss}_t \quad (6)$$

4 Model Overview

We now describe our model and its variations. We hypothesize that conditioning on the keyphrases present in the story context leads to more specific and interesting outputs. We experiment with several variants for incorporating keyphrases in our base model. We further adapt the loss suggested by Nakamura et al. (2018) to encourage the model to generate infrequent tokens.

4.1 Keyphrase Conditioning

In this section we briefly describe four different variants used for incorporating keyphrases from the story context. We first extract top k keyphrases from the story context using the RAKE algorithm (Rose et al., 2010). RAKE determines the keyphrases and assigns scores in the text based on frequency and co-occurrences of words. We then sort the list of keyphrases by their corresponding scores and take the top-k of those. Note, each of the keyphrases can contain multiple words. Each of the word in a multi-word key phrase is assigned the same score as the keyphrase.

We use the top-k keyphrases and ignore the rest. For that, we explicitly set the score of 0 to all the keyphrases which couldn't get to the top-k list. Next, the scores of these top-k keyphrases are normalized so that the total score sums to 1. We call this set keyphrases and its corresponding score vector p. p is a vector with length equal to the length of the story context, and the value of every element j is equal to score of the keyphrase to which the word w_j belongs.

In all the four model variants described next, we incorporate the score vector p to encourage the model to condition on the keyphrases.

4.1.1 Keyphrase Addition

In a Seq2Seq model with attention, for every timestep t during decoding, the model generates a distribution a_i^t which is the weight given for a given source context word w_i. In this variant, the model is provided an additional keyphrase attention score vector p along with the self-learnt attention weight vector a^t. To combine the two vectors, we simply add the values of the two vectors for each encoder position i and normalize the final vector $a_i^{'t}$.

$$a_i^{'t} = \sum_i a_i^t + p_i$$

$$a_i^{'t} = \frac{a_i^{'t}}{|a_i^{'t}|}$$

Now at each time step t of the decoder, we compute the new context vector as follows:

$$c_t^{'} = \sum_{i=1}^{T_{src}} a_i^{'t} h_i^{enc} \qquad (7)$$

4.1.2 Context Concatenation

This variation calculates two separate context vectors - one based on attention weights learnt by the model, and another based on the keyphrase attention score vector. Then both these context vector are concatenated. The intuition for this method comes from multi-head attention (Vaswani et al., 2017), where different attention heads are used to compute attention on different parts of the encoder states. Similarly we also expect the model to capture salient features from both types of context vectors.

$$k_t = \sum_i p_i h_i^{enc} \qquad (8)$$

$$c_t^{'} = [k_t; c_t] \qquad (9)$$

We use this new context vector to calculate our probabilities over the words as described in equation 4.

4.1.3 Coverage Loss

This is a variant which implicitly encourages the model to pay attention to all words present in the context. We adapt the attention coverage based loss proposed by See et al. (2017). It also helps in avoiding repeated attention across different timesteps while decoding. Due to this constraint, the model should focus on different words in the story and generate outputs conditioned on these words. The loss function which is presented in the paper is :

$$\text{loss}_t = -\log P\left(w_t^*\right) + \lambda \sum_i \min\left(a_i^t, s_i\right) \qquad (10)$$

Here s_i is the sum of attention weight vectors till i time steps and a_i^t is the attention weight vector for the current time step i.

4.1.4 Keyphrase Attention Loss

In this variant, instead of explicitly forcing the model to attend on the keyphrases, we provide additional guidance to the model in order for it learn to attend to keyphrases. We introduce an attention similarity based loss. We first create a coverage vector q, which is the sum of the attention weights across all the decoders time steps. We then calculate Mean Squared Error loss between this vector and our keyphrase score vector p. This loss is calculated once per story after the whole decoding of the generated ending has finished. Unlike the first two variants, this method only nudges the model to pay more attention to the keyphrases instead of forcing attention on them. While backpropagating into the network, we use two losses. One is the original reconstruction loss which is used in Seq2Seq models and the other is this keyphrase based attention loss. This can be summarised by the following set of equations.

$$q = \sum_t^{T_{dec}} a^t \qquad (11)$$

$$\text{loss}_{keyphrase} = \text{MSE}(q, p) \qquad (12)$$

Where MSE is the mean squared error between the coverage vector and the probability distribution produced by the RAKE algorithm. This loss is weighted by a factor λ and added to the cross-entropy loss.

	Train Set	Dev set	Test Set
ROC Stories	90,000	4,081	4,081

Table 2: The number of train, dev and test stories in each of the ROCStories corpus.

4.2 Inverse Token Frequency Loss

As mentioned earlier, Seq2Seq models tend to generate frequent words and phrases, which lead to very generic story endings. This happens due to the use of conditional likelihood as the objective, especially in problems where there can be one-to-many correspondences between the input and outputs. MLE loss unfairly penalizes the model for generating rare words which would be correct candidates, but are not present in the ground truth. This holds for our problem setting too, where for the same story context, there can be multiple possible story endings. Nakamura et al. (2018) proposed an alternative Inverse Token Frequency (ITF) loss which assigns smaller loss for frequent token classes and larger loss for rare token classes during training. This encourages the model to generate rare words more frequently compared to cross-entropy loss and thus leads to more interesting story ending outputs.

5   Experimental Setup

5.1   Dataset

We used the ROCStories (Mostafazadeh et al., 2017) corpus to generate our story endings. Each story in the dataset comprises of five sentences. The input is the first four sentences of the story and output is the last sentence of the story. The number of stories which were used to train and test the model are shown in Table 2.

5.2   Baselines and Proposed Methods

For the evaluation of story ending generation, we compare the following baselines and proposed models:

Seq2Seq: Seq2Seq model with attention trained with vanilla Maximum likelihood Estimate(MLE) loss.

IE + GA: model based on Incremental Encoding (IE) and Graph Attention (GA) (Guan et al., 2019).

Seq2Seq + ITF: Seq2Seq model with attention trained with ITF loss.

Keyphrase Add + ITF: Our model variant de-

scribed in section 4.1.1.

Context Concat + ITF: Our model variant described in section 4.1.2.

Coverage Loss + ITF: Our model variant described in section 4.1.3 based on (See et al., 2017).

Keyphrase Loss + ITF: Our model variant described in section 4.1.4.

Keyphrase Loss: Our model variant described in section 4.1.4 without the ITF loss.

5.3   Experiment Settings

All our models use the same hyper-parameters. We used a two layer encoder-decoder architecture with 512 GRU hidden units. We train our models using Adam optimizer with a learning rate of 0.001. For the Keyphrase Attention Loss model we assign the weight of 0.9 to Keyphrase loss and 0.1 to reconstruction loss. We use the best win percent from our Story-Cloze metric (described in the next section) for model selection. For ITF loss we use the hyperparameters mention in the original paper.

5.4   Automatic Evaluation Metrics

In this section, we briefly describe the various metrics which were used to test our models. We did not use perplexity or BLEU as evaluation metric, as neither of them is likely to be an effective evaluation metric in our setting. This is since both these metrics measure performance based on a single reference story ending present in the test dataset, however there can be multiple valid possible story endings for a story. Therefore, we

DIST (Distinct): Distinct-1,2,3 calculates numbers of distinct unigrams, bigrams and trigrams in the generated responses divided by the total numbers of unigrams, bigrams and trigrams. We denote the metrics as DIST-1,2,3 in the result tables. Higher Distinct scores indicate higher diversity in generated outputs.

Story-Cloze: Since it is difficult to do human evaluation on all the stories, we use the Story-Cloze task (Mostafazadeh et al., 2017) to create a metric in order to pick our best model and also to evaluate the efficacy of our model against Seq2Seq and its variants. This new proposed metric measures the semantic relevance of the generated ending with respect to the context. In the Story-Cloze task, given two endings to a story the task is to pick the correct ending. We can use this task to identify the better of two endings.

Model	DIST-1	DIST-2	DIST-3
Seq2Seq	0.039	0.165	0.335
IE + GA	0.026	0.130	0.263
Seq2Seq + ITF	0.063	0.281	0.517
Keyphrase Add + ITF	0.065	0.289	0.539
Context Concat + ITF	0.065	0.294	0.558
Coverage Loss + ITF	0.066	0.315	**0.590**
Keyphrase Loss	0.055	0.243	0.443
Keyphrase Loss + ITF	**0.068**	**0.318**	0.588

Table 3: Model comparison based on automatic metrics DIST-1, DIST-2 and DIST-3.

Model	Story-cloze
Seq2Seq	49.8
Seq2Seq + ITF	54.1
Keyphrase Add + ITF	52.9
Context Concat + ITF	55.8
Coverage Loss + ITF	54.7
Keyphrase Loss	53.4
Keyphrase Loss + ITF	**55.9**

Table 4: We measure the performance of the models using an automated Story-Cloze classifier which compares the outputs of model with the outputs of IE model.

Number of keyphrases	DIST-1	DIST-2	DIST-3	Story-Cloze
1	0.069	0.309	0.569	53.3
3	0.067	0.305	0.569	**55.2**
5	0.066	**0.315**	**0.590**	54.7
7	**0.072**	0.315	0.575	53.9
All	0.072	0.307	0.558	51.8

Table 5: Results for automatic metrics with varying number of keyphrases. Diversity is measured using DIST-1, DIST-2 and DIST-3 metrics. Story-Cloze loss measures relevance in comparison to IE model.

In order to do so, we fine-tune BERT (Devlin et al., 2018) to identify the true ending between two story candidates. The dataset for this task was obtained using the Story-Cloze task. Positive examples to BERT are obtained from the Story-Cloze dataset while the negative examples are obtained by randomly sampling from other story endings to get false ending for the story. We fine tune BERT in the two sentence setting by providing the context as the first sentence and the final sentence as the second. We pick the ending with a greater probability (from BERT's output head) of being a true ending as the winner. With this approach we were able to get a Story-Cloze test accuracy of 72%.

We now use this pre-trained model to compare the IE + GA model with our models. We select the winner based on the probability given by the pre-trained Bert model.

5.5 Results

We measure the performance of our models through automatic evaluation metrics as well as human evaluation. We use Distinct1, Distinct2 and Distinct3 to measure the diversity of our outputs. Additionally, we have built an automatic evaluation system using BERT and the Story-Cloze task following Fan et al. (2018) in order to compare our model against the state of the art models like the IE model. We also perform human evaluation on the stories generated by our model to get a overall sense of the model's performance.

5.5.1 Model Comparison and Ablation Study

From the Table 3, we observe that the Seq2Seq model and the incremental encoding + graph attention (IE + GA) model have the worst performance in diversity. Although it has been shown that the IE + GA model achieves a good BLEU score, we observe that the model does not do as well on our automated metrics like DIST-1, 2 and 3 because the model has learnt to generate endings which match the distribution as a whole instead of generating story specific endings.

As expected, Seq2Seq + ITF loss model greatly outperforms the vanilla Seq2Seq model. As does the Keyphrase loss, showing that these models are indeed able to focus on different context words resulting in more diverse generations.

The Story-Cloze based performance of the models is presented in Table 4. The Keyphrase + ITF loss model outperforms all models on both the diversity and Story-Cloze metrics. Hence, we select Keyphrase + ITF loss model as the best model in further discussions. As an *ablation* study, we run the Keyphrase loss model with the MLE loss instead of the ITF loss. We find that this model performs poorly than then its version with the ITF loss but still performs quite better than the Seq2Seq model. Also we note that the diversity obtained in Keyphrase + ITF loss model is greater than the Seq2Seq + ITF model and the Keyphrase loss model without ITF. It shows that a combination of both, Keyphrase attention loss and ITF loss, achieves better performance than these components by themselves.

Example 1	**Context**	megan was new to the pageant world . in fact , this was her very first one . she was really enjoying herself , but was also quite nervous . the results were in and she and the other contestants walked out .
	Seq2Seq Model	she was disappointed that she couldn't have to learn how to win . the next day , she was happy to have a new friend .
	IE Model	
	Our Best Model	megan won the pageant competition .
	Ground Truth	they read off the names and megan had won !
Example 2	**Context**	alicia was going on a trip to disney . she was very excited . yet when she got there she did not like it . she thought it was too childish .
	Seq2Seq Model	she had to go home .
	IE Model	thankfully she got a call .
	Our Best Model	alicia decided to watch the movie instead .
	Ground Truth	she decided to never go back.
Example 3	**Context**	katie found out her husband was cheating on her . she tried to make it work , but he wasn't interested . he took all her money and divorced her . a few weeks later , his mistress dumped him
	Seq2Seq Model	katie was so happy , he helped her to help her out .
	IE Model	he was so upset , he decided to go home .
	Our Best Model	katie was devastated by himself and dumped her boyfriend .
	Ground Truth	she is much happier for being rid of him .
Example 4	**Context**	tom had a cat . he noticed the litter wasn't being used . after a while he started noticing a bad smell . he looked around and found a corner under the sofa .
	Seq2Seq Model	he was able to get it back .
	IE Model	he was able to get it out and clean it .
	Our Best Model	tom cleaned the catnip smell up and cleaned it outside .
	Ground Truth	it was full of cat poop that he had to clean up .

Table 6: Qualitative analysis of the outputs produced by our model. For each context of the story, we show the endings generated by various models. It can be seen from the outputs that our model is able to generate specific outputs for a context.

5.5.2 Effect of varying number of keyphrases

In order to better understand the effect of keyphrases on the diversity and relevance of story endings, we ran the Coverage Loss model with varying number of keyphrases. Table 5 shows the results of the experiment. We see that both Story-Cloze loss and DIST-1,2,3 are low when we use 1 keyphrase and also when we use all the keyphrases. This is expected, since in the case of 1 keyphrase, the model has very little keyphrase related information. In the other extreme case, providing all keyphrases covers a large proportion of the original context itself, and thus does not provide any extra benefit. We see good performance within the range of 3-5 keyphrases, where using 5 keyphrases gives the best diversity and 3 keyphrases gives the best Story-Cloze score. Informed by this experiment, we use 5 keyphrases in all our other experiments.

5.6 Human Evaluation

Since automatic metrics are not able to capture all qualitative aspects of the models, we performed a human evaluation study to compare our models. We first randomly selected 50 story contexts from the test set, and show them to three annotators. The annotators see the story context, and the story endings generated by our best model and the baseline IE+GA model in a random order. They are asked to select a better ending among the two based on three criteria -

1) *Relevance* - Story ending should be appropriate and reasonable according to the story context. 2) *Interestingness* - More interesting story ending should be preferred 3) *Fluency* - Endings should be natural english and free of errors. We found that both models were preferred *50%* of the time, that is, both model was picked for 25 stories each. From a manual analysis of human evaluation, we found that our model was selected over the baseline in many cases for generating interesting endings, but was also equivalently penalized for losing the relevance in some of the story endings. We discuss this aspect in more detail in section 5.7.

5.7 Qualitative Analysis

In Table 6, we show some example generations of our model and baselines. From example 1 and 2, it can be seen that the baseline models produce generic responses for story endings without focusing much on the context and keyphrases in the story. However, our model conditions on words like "pageant" in the story context, and includes it in the output even though it is a rare word in the corpus. Another point to note is that our model tends to include more proper nouns and entities in its output, like *alicia* and *megan* instead of using generic words like "he" and "she". However, our model is penalised a few times for being too adventurous, because it tends to generate more rare outputs based on the context. For example, in example 3, it got half of the output correct till "katie was devastated", but the other half "dumped her boyfriend" although is more interesting than the baseline models, is not relevant to the story context. The model incorrectly refers to katie with the pronoun "himself". In example 4, our model's generated output is quite relevant and interesting, apart from the token "catnip", for which it is penalized in human evaluation. Hence, although our model generates more interesting outputs, further work is needed to ensure that 1) The generated outputs entail the story context at both semantic and token level. 2) The generated output is logically sound and consistent.

6 Conclusion

In this paper we have presented several models to overcome the generic responses produced by the state of the art story generation systems. We have both quantitatively and qualitatively shown that our model achieved meaningful improvements over the baselines.

References

Dzmitry Bahdanau, Kyunghyun Cho, and Yoshua Bengio. 2014. Neural machine translation by jointly learning to align and translate. *arXiv preprint arXiv:1409.0473*.

Ashutosh Baheti, Alan Ritter, Jiwei Li, and Bill Dolan. 2018. Generating more interesting responses in neural conversation models with distributional constraints. In *Proceedings of the 2018 Conference on Empirical Methods in Natural Language Processing*, pages 3970–3980, Brussels, Belgium. Association for Computational Linguistics.

J. S. Chen, Jiaao Chen, and Zhou Yu. 2018. Incorporating structured commonsense knowledge in story completion. *CoRR*, abs/1811.00625.

Elizabeth Clark, Yangfeng Ji, and Noah A Smith. 2018. Neural text generation in stories using entity representations as context. In *Proceedings of the 2018 Conference of the North American Chapter of the Association for Computational Linguistics: Human Language Technologies, Volume 1 (Long Papers)*, pages 2250–2260.

Jacob Devlin, Ming-Wei Chang, Kenton Lee, and Kristina Toutanova. 2018. Bert: Pre-training of deep bidirectional transformers for language understanding. *arXiv preprint arXiv:1810.04805*.

Carl Doersch. 2016. Tutorial on variational autoencoders. *arXiv preprint arXiv:1606.05908*.

Angela Fan, Mike Lewis, and Yann Dauphin. 2018. Hierarchical neural story generation. *arXiv preprint arXiv:1805.04833*.

Jian Guan, Yansen Wang, and Minlie Huang. 2018. Story ending generation with incremental encoding and commonsense knowledge. *arXiv preprint arXiv:1808.10113*.

Jian Guan, Yansen Wang, and Minlie Huang. 2019. Story ending generation with incremental encoding and commonsense knowledge. *CoRR*, abs/1808.10113.

Zhiting Hu, Zichao Yang, Xiaodan Liang, Ruslan Salakhutdinov, and Eric P. Xing. 2017a. Toward controlled generation of text. In *Proceedings of the 34th International Conference on Machine Learning*, volume 70 of *Proceedings of Machine Learning Research*, pages 1587–1596, International Convention Centre, Sydney, Australia. PMLR.

Zhiting Hu, Zichao Yang, Xiaodan Liang, Ruslan Salakhutdinov, and Eric P Xing. 2017b. Toward controlled generation of text. In *Proceedings of the 34th International Conference on Machine Learning-Volume 70*, pages 1587–1596. JMLR. org.

Qiuyuan Huang, Zhe Gan, Asli Celikyilmaz, Dapeng Wu, Jianfeng Wang, and Xiaodong He. 2018. Hierarchically structured reinforcement learning for topically coherent visual story generation. *arXiv preprint arXiv:1805.08191.*

Parag Jain, Priyanka Agrawal, Abhijit Mishra, Mohak Sukhwani, Anirban Laha, and Karthik Sankaranarayanan. 2017. Story generation from sequence of independent short descriptions. *arXiv preprint arXiv:1707.05501.*

Jiwei Li, Michel Galley, Chris Brockett, Jianfeng Gao, and Bill Dolan. 2016a. A diversity-promoting objective function for neural conversation models. In *Proceedings of the 2016 Conference of the North American Chapter of the Association for Computational Linguistics: Human Language Technologies*, pages 110–119, San Diego, California. Association for Computational Linguistics.

Jiwei Li, Michel Galley, Chris Brockett, Georgios Spithourakis, Jianfeng Gao, and Bill Dolan. 2016b. A persona-based neural conversation model. In *Proceedings of the 54th Annual Meeting of the Association for Computational Linguistics (Volume 1: Long Papers)*, pages 994–1003, Berlin, Germany. Association for Computational Linguistics.

Jiwei Li, Will Monroe, Tianlin Shi, Sébastien Jean, Alan Ritter, and Dan Jurafsky. 2017. Adversarial learning for neural dialogue generation. In *Proceedings of the 2017 Conference on Empirical Methods in Natural Language Processing*, pages 2157–2169, Copenhagen, Denmark. Association for Computational Linguistics.

Zhongyang Li, Xiao Ding, and Ting Liu. 2018. Generating reasonable and diversified story ending using sequence to sequence model with adversarial training. In *Proceedings of the 27th International Conference on Computational Linguistics*, pages 1033–1043, Santa Fe, New Mexico, USA. Association for Computational Linguistics.

Lara J Martin, Prithviraj Ammanabrolu, Xinyu Wang, William Hancock, Shruti Singh, Brent Harrison, and Mark O Riedl. 2018. Event representations for automated story generation with deep neural nets. In *Thirty-Second AAAI Conference on Artificial Intelligence.*

Nasrin Mostafazadeh, Michael Roth, Annie Louis, Nathanael Chambers, and James Allen. 2017. Lsdsem 2017 shared task: The story cloze test. In *Proceedings of the 2nd Workshop on Linking Models of Lexical, Sentential and Discourse-level Semantics*, pages 46–51.

Ryo Nakamura, Katsuhito Sudoh, Koichiro Yoshino, and Satoshi Nakamura. 2018. Another diversity-promoting objective function for neural dialogue generation. *arXiv preprint arXiv:1811.08100.*

Nanyun Peng, Marjan Ghazvininejad, Jonathan May, and Kevin Knight. 2018. Towards controllable story generation. In *Proceedings of the First Workshop on Storytelling*, pages 43–49.

Stuart Rose, Dave Engel, Nick Cramer, and Wendy Cowley. 2010. *Automatic Keyword Extraction from Individual Documents*, pages 1 – 20.

Abigail See, Peter J. Liu, and Christopher D. Manning. 2017. Get to the point: Summarization with pointer-generator networks. In *Proceedings of the 55th Annual Meeting of the Association for Computational Linguistics (Volume 1: Long Papers)*, pages 1073–1083, Vancouver, Canada. Association for Computational Linguistics.

Yuanlong Shao, Stephan Gouws, Denny Britz, Anna Goldie, Brian Strope, and Ray Kurzweil. 2017. Generating high-quality and informative conversation responses with sequence-to-sequence models. In *Proceedings of the 2017 Conference on Empirical Methods in Natural Language Processing*, pages 2210–2219, Copenhagen, Denmark. Association for Computational Linguistics.

Ilya Sutskever, Oriol Vinyals, and Quoc V Le. 2014. Sequence to sequence learning with neural networks. In *Advances in neural information processing systems*, pages 3104–3112.

Ashish Vaswani, Noam Shazeer, Niki Parmar, Jakob Uszkoreit, Llion Jones, Aidan N Gomez, Łukasz Kaiser, and Illia Polosukhin. 2017. Attention is all you need. In *Advances in neural information processing systems*, pages 5998–6008.

Ashwin K. Vijayakumar, Michael Cogswell, Ramprasaath R. Selvaraju, Qing Sun, Stefan Lee, David J. Crandall, and Dhruv Batra. 2018. Diverse beam search for improved description of complex scenes. In *Proceedings of the Thirty-Second AAAI Conference on Artificial Intelligence, (AAAI-18), the 30th innovative Applications of Artificial Intelligence (IAAI-18), and the 8th AAAI Symposium on Educational Advances in Artificial Intelligence (EAAI-18), New Orleans, Louisiana, USA, February 2-7, 2018*, pages 7371–7379.

Chen Xing, Wei Wu, Yu Wu, Jie Liu, Yalou Huang, Ming Zhou, and Wei-Ying Ma. 2016. Topic augmented neural response generation with a joint attention mechanism. *arXiv preprint arXiv:1606.08340, 2(2).*

Jingjing Xu, Xuancheng Ren, Junyang Lin, and Xu Sun. 2018. Diversity-promoting gan: A cross-entropy based generative adversarial network for diversified text generation. In *Proceedings of the 2018 Conference on Empirical Methods in Natural Language Processing*, pages 3940–3949.

Lili Yao, Nanyun Peng, Weischedel Ralph, Kevin Knight, Dongyan Zhao, and Rui Yan. 2018. Plan-and-write: Towards better automatic storytelling. *arXiv preprint arXiv:1811.05701.*

Saizheng Zhang, Emily Dinan, Jack Urbanek, Arthur Szlam, Douwe Kiela, and Jason Weston. 2018. Personalizing dialogue agents: I have a dog, do you have pets too? *arXiv preprint arXiv:1801.07243.*

Hao Zhou, Minlie Huang, Tianyang Zhang, Xiaoyan Zhu, and Bing Liu. 2018. Emotional chatting machine: Emotional conversation generation with internal and external memory. In *Thirty-Second AAAI Conference on Artificial Intelligence.*

Prediction of a Movie's Success From Plot Summaries Using Deep Learning Models

You-Jin Kim
Department of Applied Data Science
Sungkyunkwan University
Suwon-si, South Korea
k01077679687@gmail.com

Jung-Hoon Lee
College of Computing
Sungkyunkwan University
Suwon-si, South Korea
vhrehfdl@gmail.com

Yun-Gyung Cheong
College of Computing
Sungkyunkwan University
Suwon-si, South Korea
aimecca@skku.edu

Abstract

As the size of investment for movie production grows bigger, the need for predicting a movie's success in early stages has increased. To address this need, various approaches have been proposed, mostly relying on movie reviews, trailer movie clips, and SNS postings. However, all of these are available only after a movie is produced and released. To enable a more earlier prediction of a movie's performance, we propose a deep-learning based approach to predict the success of a movie using only its plot summary text. This paper reports the results evaluating the efficacy of the proposed method and concludes with discussions and future work.

1 Introduction

Movie industry is a huge sector within the entertainment industry. The global movie box office revenue is predicted to reach nearly 50 billion U.S dollars in 2020 (Sachdev et al., 2018). With huge capital investments, the movie business is a high-risk venture (De Vany and Walls, 1999). Therefore, an early prediction of a movie's success can make a great contribution to the film industry, when post-production factors are unknown before the film's release. This task is extremely challenging, as the success of the movie should be determined based on the scenario or plot of the movie without using the post-production drivers such as actor, actress, director, MPAA rating and etc.

To address this issue, our work attempts to predict a movie's success from its textual summary. We used the CMU Movie Summary Corpus [1], which contains crowd-sourced summaries from the real users. The success of a movie is assessed with the review scores of Rotten Tomatoes [2], an American review-aggregation website

for film and television. The scoring system utilizes two scores: the tomato-meter and the audience score. The tomato-meter score is estimated by hundreds of film and television critics, appraising the artistic quality of a movie. The audience score is computed by the collective scores from regular movie viewers.

In this paper we present a deep-learning based approach to classify a movie popularity and quality labels using the movie textual summary data. The primary hypothesis that we attempted to answer is to predict a movie's success in terms of popularity and artistic quality by analyzing only the textual plot summary.
The contributions of our research are as follows:

- To prepare a data set to define a movie's success

- To incorporate sentiment score in predicting a movie's success

- To evaluate the efficacy of ELMO embedding in predicting a movie's success

- To evaluate merged deep learning models (CNN and residual LSTM) in predicting a movie's success

2 Our Approach

Figure 1 illustrates the system architecture that classifies an input text as successful or non-successful based on the critics score and the audience score.

The pre-processing step tokenizes the summary text into sentences. Then, the list of sentences are given to the ELMO embedding and the sentiment score extraction modules. The ELMO embedding module converts the sentences into word vectors. The sentiment score extractor generates a sentiment score that combines the positive and negative sentiment score of each sentence. Lastly, the two

---

[1] http://www.cs.cmu.edu/~ark/personas/
[2] https://www.rottentomatoes.com/

Proceedings of the Second Storytelling Workshop, pages 127–135
Florence, Italy, August 1, 2019. ©2019 Association for Computational Linguistics

Genre/Audience	Train		Test		
	Not popular(0)	Popular(1)	Not popular(0)	Popular(1)	Total
All genre	11,635 (62%)	7,122 (38%)	1,292 (62%)	793 (38%)	20,842
Drama	4,506 (51%)	4,375 (49%)	502 (50%)	485 (50%)	9,868
Thriller	2,639 (70%)	1,123 (30%)	295 (70%)	124 (30%)	4,181
Comedy	3,254 (65%)	1,746 (35%)	358 (64%)	198 (36%)	5,556
Romance	1,811 (57%)	1,336 (43%)	196 (56%)	154 (44%)	3,497
Genre/Critics	Not Well-made(0)	Well-made(1)	Not Well-made(0)	Well-made(1)	Total
All genre	5,493 (50%)	5,324 (50%)	590 (49%)	612 (51%)	12,019
Drama	2,416 (42%)	3,306 (58%)	273 (42%)	363 (58%)	6,358
Thriller	1,349 (55%)	1,078 (45%)	142 (52%)	128 (48%)	2,697
Comedy	1,898 (57%)	1,389 (43%)	222 (60%)	144 (40%)	3,653
Romance	1,103 (52%)	1,015 (48%)	107 (45%)	129 (55%)	2,354
Genre/Compound	Not Successful (0)	Successful(1)	Not Successful(0)	Successful(1)	Total
All genre	3,812 (51%)	3,586 (49%)	440 (53%)	383 (47%)	8,221

Table 1: Training and test data set proportion. Class 1 denotes movies with scores greater than 75. Class 0 denotes movies with scores less than 65.

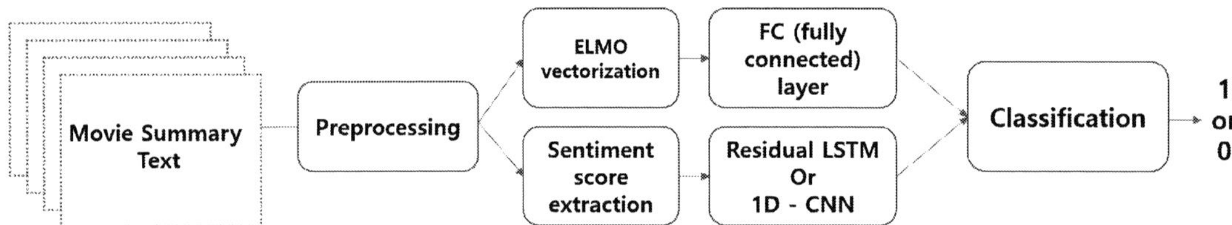

Figure 1: The overall classification procedure

outputs are merged to classify a movie summary into the success or non-success classes.

2.1   Data

To evaluate our approach, we used the CMU Movie Summary Corpus (Bamman et al., 2013), which contains crowd-sourced summaries from the real users.

The corpus contains 42,306 movie plot summaries and their metadata such as genre, release date, cast, character traits, etc. However, we use only the plot summary text feature and the genre. The following example summary which consists of 36 sentences and 660 words, shows a part of the plot summary of 'The Avengers' (released in 2012) directed by Joss Whedo.

> The Asgardian Loki encounters the Other,the leader of an extraterrestrial race known as the Chitauri. In exchange for retrieving the Tesseract, a powerful energy source of unknown potential,
> ...
> In the first of two post-credits scenes, the Other confers with his master about the attack on Earth and humanity's resistance; in the second, the Avengers eat

in silence at a shawarma restaurant.

We created the classification labels based on the Rotten tomato scores that we crawled from Rotten Tomatoes' website with the Selenium [3] and Beautiful Soup python packages (Richardson, 2013). These scores serve as a credible indicator of a movie's success (Doshi et al., 2010). We classify movies following the Rotten Tomato rule; if the review score is greater than 75, the corresponding movie is classified fresh (1); if its score is less than 60, the movie is classified not fresh (0).

As some movies do not have both the audience and the critics score, we collected 20,842 and 12,019 movie plot summary data for the audience score and for the critic score respectively. The audience score is assessed by ordinary people, we regard the class 1 as representing 'popular' movies and the class 0 as representing 'not popular' movies. Likewise, since the critics score is assessed by professionals in the industry, we consider class 1 as representing 'well-made' movies and class 0 as representing 'not well-made' movies. Since these scores indicate the popularity and quality of a movie, we define a successful movie as having the combination of

---
[3] https://www.seleniumhq.org/

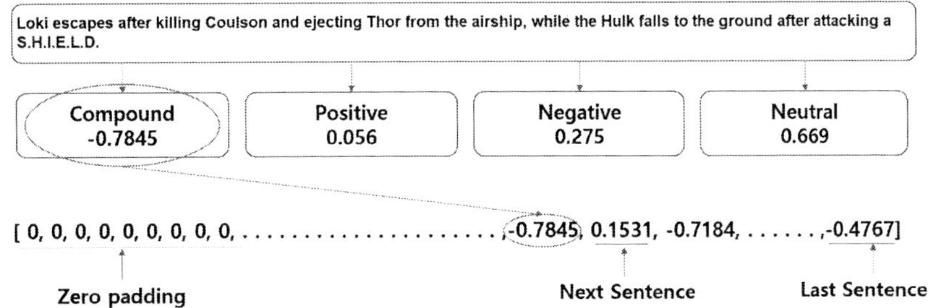

Figure 2: The sentiment vector representation of the movie 'The Avengers'.

these score greater than 75. Finally, we prepared the third data set considering both of the audience and the critics scores. We define movies with each audience and critics score greater than 75 as 'successful' and less than 60 as 'not successful'.

There are two reasons that the number of instances in the prepared data is less than the number of summaries in the CMU Movie summary corpus. First, movies that have received review scores above 60 and below 75 are filtered out. Second, some movies in the CMU Movie summary corpus have no scores at the Rotten Tomato site.

Table 1 shows the statistics of the data set. The ratio between class 1 and 0 is approximately 6:4 for the audience score and 5:5 for the critics score and the combination of both scores.

The data sets were also divided into different genres, to test whether the genre of a movie has an impact on the prediction of a performance. The table shows the ratios between class 1 and 0 are balanced except for the thriller and comedy genres in the audience score. Since each movie is tagged with multiple genres, the sum of all the number of summaries of each genre is greater than the total number of summaries.

A simple statistical analysis shows that the maximum number of sentences in the longest summary in the train set is 198, the minimum is 1, and the average is 18.3. The number of words in the largest summary is 4,264, while that of the shortest summary is 10. The average is 361.2 words.

2.2 ELMO embedding

When the list of sentences representing a movie summary is given as input, the module creates its corresponding word embedding vectors. Traditional word embedding schemes such as Word2vec (Mikolov et al., 2013) and Glove (Pennington et al., 2014) produce a fixed vector for each word. While those embedding methods have been shown effective in many NLP applications, they do not deal with words which mean differently as their contexts vary such as homophones. Thus, We applied a contextualized embedding method that can generate different word vectors depending on the context. ELMO (Peters et al., 2018) is a popular contextualized embedding method, which uses two bidirectional LSTM networks for constructing the vector.

In this work, we utilized the TensorFlow Hub implementation[4] to represent the word vector. We then fine-tuned the weight for ELMO embedding to gain better performance for the classification task (Perone et al., 2018).

Since the length of the summary varies, we need to set a maximum number of sentences in a summary. We set the maximum number at 198, as it is the number of sentences in the longest summary found in the train set.

2.3 Sentiment score extraction

To extract the sentiment score of each sentence, we applied the NLTK's Vader sentiment analyzer (Hutto and Gilbert, 2014) to each sentence. Figure 2 illustrates a part of the sentiment vector representation of the movie 'The Avengers'. A summary is represented as a 198 dimensional vector, where each denotes the sentiment score of a single sentence. A summary shorter than 198 sentences is zero-padded. The highlight of the story (i.e., the conflict and resolution stages) is usually located towards the end of the story. So, we reversed the order as the vector is given as input to the LSTM deep learning model in the next stage which better remember the recent input.

The VADER(Valence Aware Dictionary for sentiment Reasoning) module computes four scores for each sentence: negative, positive, neutral, and compound scores. In this research, we use the

---

[4]https://tfhub.dev/google/elmo/2

129

compound score ranging from -1 (most negative) to 1 (most positive).

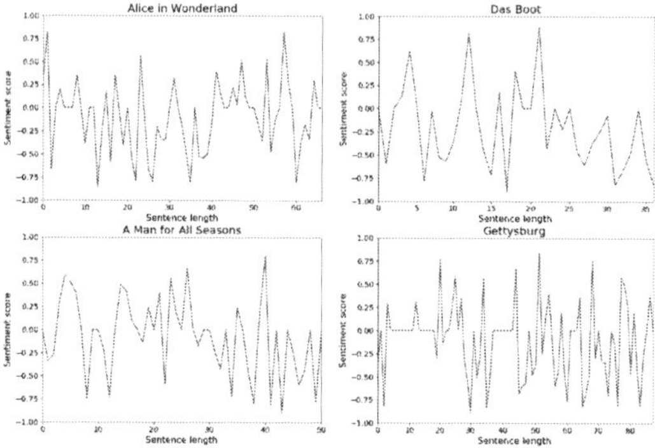

Figure 3: Sentiment flow graphs of successful movies. X axis denotes the sentence index, and the Y axis denotes the sentiment score of a sentence normalized between -1 and 1.

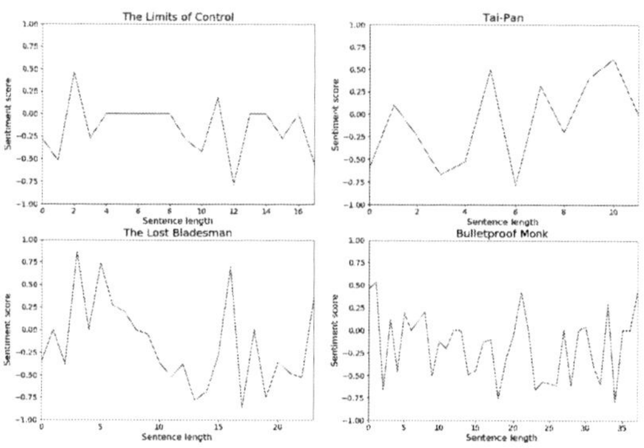

Figure 4: Sentiment flow graphs of unsuccessful movies. X axis denotes the sentence index, and the Y axis denotes the sentiment score of a sentence normalized between -1 and 1.

Figure 3 and Figure 4 depict the sentiment plots of successful movies and unsuccessful movies respectively. The 4 graphs shown in Figure 3 exhibit various patterns of successful movies' sentiment flows. The movie *Alice in Wonderland* begins and ends positively. On the other hand, the movies *Das Boot* and *A Man for All Seasons* begin and end with negatively. The movie *Gettysburg* shows the reversal of fortune pattern which begins negatively and ends positively. It is commonly noted that these successful movies have frequence sentiment fluctuations. On the other hand, the graphs in Figure 4 illustrate unsuccessful movies' sentiment flows, which exhibit less frequent sentiment fluctuations. Both the movie *The Limits of Control* and *The Lost Bladesman* have negative beginning and ending. The movie *Tai-Pan* begins negatively

and ends positively. The movie *Bluetproof Monk* begins and ends positively, however, its majority sentiment scores are negative while the story is being developed. Therefore, it suggests that the frequency of sentiment changes may signal the success of films. Yet, the polarity of sentiment have a little impact on predicting a movie's success.

2.4 Classification Models

We built an ELMO, a merged 1D CNN (Figure 5), and a merged residual LSTM (Figure 6) networks. We establish our baseline by calculating a majority class baseline for comparison.

First, we use deep contextualized word representations created by the ELMO embedding. This network consists of a character embedding layer, a convolutional layer, two highway networks, and two LSTM layers. Each token is converted to a character embedding representation, which is fed to a convolutional layer. Then, it goes through two highway networks to help the deep learning network training. Then, the output is fed to the LSTM layer as input data. The weights of each LSTM hidden layer are combined to generate the ELMO embedding. Finally, a 1024 dimensional ELMO embedding vector is constructed for each sentence, which is put into the 256 dimensional dense network. RELU (Nair and Hinton, 2010) is used as its activation function.

Figure 5 shows the 1D CNN merged network, where the sentiment score vector is given as input to the CNN network. The model consists of two 1D convolutional layers, with 64-size filters and 3-size kernels. The second CNN layer includes a dropout layer. The next max-pooling layer reduces the learned features to 1/4 of their size. The final flatten layer constructs a single 100-dimensional vector. Then, the output from the ELMO embedding and the output from the CNN model is concatenated and given to the last 1-dense classification layer.

Figure 6 employs two bidirectional LSTM layers which have 128 memory units. The outputs of these layers are added and flattened to create a 50,688 dimensional vector. 50,688 was obtained as the length of the sentences (198) times the size of the vector (256). Then, the next 128 dense layer reduces the vector for the final binary classification. We employed the binary cross-entropy as the loss function and the Adam optimizer.

Score	Genre	Model	Recall		Precision		F1	
			1	**0**	**1**	**0**	**1**	**0**
Audience	All	ELMO	0.54	0.81	0.64	0.74	**0.58**	0.78
		CNN	0.38	0.90	0.70	0.70	0.49	**0.79**
		LSTM	0.56	0.67	0.51	0.71	0.53	0.69
	Drama	ELMO	0.62	0.73	0.69	0.67	0.66	**0.70**
		LSTM	0.79	0.39	0.56	0.66	0.65	0.49
		CNN	0.77	0.48	0.59	0.68	**0.67**	0.56
	Thriller	ELMO	0.39	0.91	0.65	0.78	0.48	**0.84**
		CNN	0.41	0.79	0.45	0.76	0.43	0.77
		LSTM	0.60	0.70	0.45	0.80	**0.52**	0.75
	Comedy	ELMO	0.31	0.94	0.73	0.71	0.43	**0.81**
		CNN	0.41	0.83	0.57	0.72	0.48	0.77
		LSTM	0.62	0.63	0.48	0.75	**0.54**	0.68
	Romance	ELMO	0.63	0.68	0.61	0.70	**0.62**	**0.69**
		CNN	0.57	0.67	0.58	0.67	0.58	0.67
		LSTM	0.55	0.71	0.60	0.67	0.57	**0.69**

Table 2: The evaluation results for the audience score. The best performances in F1 score are in bold.

Score	Genre	Model	Recall		Precision		F1	
			1	**0**	**1**	**0**	**1**	**0**
Critics	All	ELMO	0.72	0.60	0.65	0.68	0.69	0.63
		CNN	0.76	0.56	0.64	0.69	**0.70**	0.62
		LSTM	0.71	0.63	0.66	0.68	0.69	**0.65**
	Drama	ELMO	0.79	0.47	0.66	0.63	**0.72**	**0.53**
		CNN	0.79	0.46	0.66	0.62	**0.72**	**0.53**
		LSTM	0.71	0.50	0.65	0.57	0.68	**0.53**
	Thriller	ELMO	0.65	0.72	0.67	0.69	0.66	0.71
		CNN	0.68	0.77	0.73	0.73	**0.70**	**0.75**
		LSTM	0.64	0.76	0.71	0.70	0.67	0.73
	Comedy	ELMO	0.61	0.77	0.63	0.75	**0.62**	0.76
		CNN	0.52	0.82	0.65	0.73	0.58	**0.77**
		LSTM	0.49	0.80	0.62	0.71	0.55	0.75
	Romance	ELMO	0.64	0.62	0.67	0.58	0.65	**0.60**
		CNN	0.64	0.61	0.66	0.59	0.65	**0.60**
		LSTM	0.71	0.50	0.63	0.59	**0.67**	0.54

Table 3: The evaluation results for the critics score. The best performances in F1 score are in bold.

Score	Genre	Model	Recall		Precision		F1	
			1	**0**	**1**	**0**	**1**	**0**
Audience&Critics	**All genre**	ELMO	0.67	0.74	0.69	0.72	**0.68**	**0.73**
		CNN	0.68	0.70	0.64	0.67	0.66	0.69
		LSTM	0.68	0.67	0.64	0.71	0.66	0.69

Table 4: The evaluation results for the audience & critics score. The best performances in F1 score are in bold.

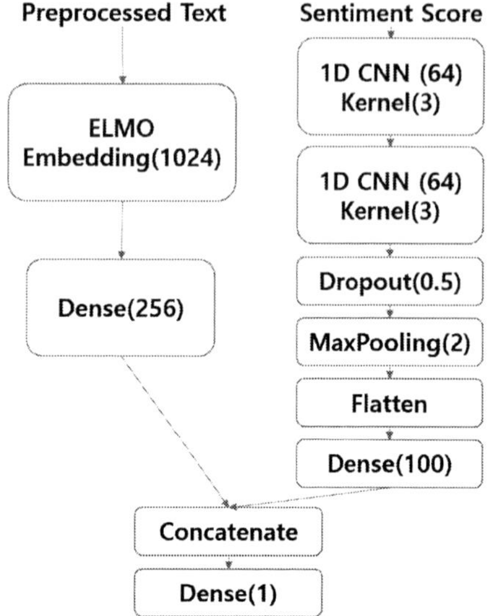

Figure 5: A merged 1D CNN

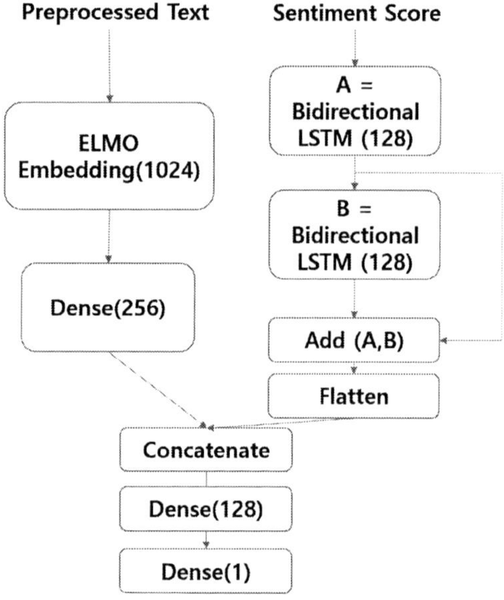

Figure 6: A merged bidirectional residual LSTM

3 Evaluation Results

We evaluated the classification performance of our approach for the audience score and for the critics score. We also inspected the performance based on the movie genre. We report the performance in terms of recall, precision, and F1 scores.

3.1 The Results

Table 2 shows the performance result for the audience score. We use the F1 score as the primary metric for comparison as it is the harmonic means of recall and precision. Overall, the classification performance of 'not popular ' movies better than that of 'popular ' ones. The CNN model performed best in 'all genre ' with F1 of 0.79, which is 0.17 higher than the majority class baseline (F1 of 0.62). The ELMO model outperformed best in the genres of drama, thriller, comedy, and romance. On the contrary, the ELMO model had the highest performance for 'popular' at 0.58 and 0.62 in overall and romance genre respectively, while LSTM and CNN had the highest performance in the rest of the genre

Table 3 summarizes the evaluation results for the critics score.

For all the genres, the deep learning models outperform the majority class baseline (F1 score=0.51) for predicting 'well-made ' movies producing its highest F1 of 0.70. The CNN model achieved the highest F1 score of 0.72 in predicting 'well-made' drama movies when its majority class baseline performance is 0.58. In the thriller, the CNN model also outperformed the baseline (F1 score=0.52) producing an F1 score of 0.75. The LSTM model achieved the best performance in predicting 'not well-made' movies, and yet the score is low–0.65.

Inspection of the genre-specific F1 score shows that the best performance was obtained from CNN model when predicting 'not well-made' movies for the comedy genre (F1 score of 0.77).

Finally, Table 4 shows the results when our approach is applied to the combined score. The ELMO embedding model outperforms the majority class baseline and the other models, achieving F1 scores of 0.68 and 0.73 when predicting 'successful' and 'not successful' movies respectively.

3.2 Discussions

Overall, the results suggest that the merged deep learning models proposed in this paper outperform the majority class baseline.

For the audience score, the performance results of predicting 'not popular' movies outperform that of predicting 'popular' movies. This may suggest that using the textual summary only is limited in predicting 'popular' movies. When inspecting the results genre-wise, the precision of predicting 'not popular' movies for the thriller and the comedy genres yields the best performance when the LSTM model is used along with the sentiment score. On the other hand, the ELMO model outperforms the merged deep learning models that employ the sentiment score in predicting 'popular' movies with significant difference.

The CNN model produces a F1 score higher than ELMo does in the thrillers and comedy genres and in the drama genre for 'popular' movies.

In case of the critics score, the overall performance was inferior to that of the audience score. Inspection of the F1 score of each genre shows that predicting 'not well-made' movies in the thriller and the comedy genre achieved the best performance (0.75 and 0.77 respectively) when the CNN model was used along with the sentiment score. Generally, the CNN or LSTM models have shown F1 scores higher than the ELMO models at predicting well-made movies using the critics score except the drama genre.

Then, employing the ELMO model outperforms other models that used the sentiment score as well. This may suggest that words are the primary determiner of predicting a movie' success.

The research work by Eliashberg et al. Eliashberg et al. (2007) is most similar to our work. Their evaluation achieved the F1 score of 0.5 (recomputed from the evaluation metrics reported) in predicting a movie's success using the CART (Bootstrap Aggregated Classification and Regression Tree) model and the movie spoiler text which is 4-20 pages long. Although our result appear to be superior to their work in terms of yielding higher F1 score, it is not directly comparable since the data sets and the evaluation metrics are different.

4 Related work

The prediction of movie box office results has been actively researched (Rhee and Zulkernine, 2016; Eliashberg et al., 2007, 2010, 2014; Sharda and Delen, 2006; Zhang et al., 2009; Du et al., 2014).

Most researches predict a movie's success using various factors such as SNS data, cost, critics ratings, genre, distributor, release season, and the main actors award history, etc (Mestyán et al., 2013; Rhee and Zulkernine, 2016; Jaiswal and Sharma, 2017). This means that the prediction is made in the later stages of movie production, when the movie has already been produced and released.

The evaluation carried out in (Jaiswal and Sharma, 2017) achieved the highest performance with F1 score of 0.79, which is recomputed from the evaluation metrics reported. However, this performance is not directly comparable to our result, since their work employed a small data set which consists of 557 movies and was based on a different genre (i.e., Bollywood movie). Their work employs rich feature such as YouTube statistics, lead actor, actress and director ratings, critics reviews, which are mostly available only after the movie is produced. Therefore, movie distributors and investors cannot rely on this approach when they need to make an investment decision.

To overcome this problem, our approach relies on only the plot summary, which can assist the investors in making their invest decisions in the very early stages when they only have the written movie script.

5 Conclusions

In this paper, we propose a deep learning based approach utilizing the ELMO embedding and sentiment scores of sentences for predicting the success of a movie, based only on a textual summary of the movie plot. To test the efficacy of our approach, we prepared our evaluation data sets: movie plot summaries gathered from the CMU Movie Summary Corpus and their review scores from a movie review website.

Since these plot summaries were obtained from Wikipedia, where the data are crowd sourced voluntarily. Hence, some movie summaries may have been written by people who like or value the movie. This may complicate our task to predict the movie's success only from the summary. We built three deep learning models: an ELMO embedding and two merged deep learning models (a merged 1D CNN network and a merged residual bidirectional LSTM network).

The evaluation results show that our deep learning models outperform the majority class baseline.

For the combination of the audience and the critics scores, the majority class baseline is F1 of 0.53 for 'not successful' , and 0 for 'successful '. Our best model obtained the highest F1 score of 0.68 for predicting 'successful' movies and that of 0.70 for predicting 'not successful' movies were obtained.

Considering that only textual summaries of the movie plot are used for the predictions, the study results are promising. Forecasting the popularity and success of movies only with their textual descriptions of the plot, will aid the decision-making in funding movie productions.

It seems that predicting 'not popular' or 'not successful' movies performs better than that of predicting 'popular' or 'successful' movies. Predicting unsuccessful movies can be useful for the Internet Protocol television (IPTV) content providers such as Netflix. Whereas tens of thousands of TV contents are made available, only a small portion of them are actually consumed (Reformat and Yager, 2014). Therefore, our approach can be used to filter out such contents that are not appealing to the content viewers.

For future work, we will further investigate the efficacy of our approach in the thriller and the comedy genes, which presented the best performances. In addition, we will extend our model to deal with the magnitude of a movie's success. For this, linear regression models can be applied to predict different levels of success.

Acknowledgement

This work was supported by the National Research Foundation of Korea(NRF) grant funded by the Korea government(MEST) (No. 2019R1A2C1006316). This research was supported by Basic Science Research Program through the National Research Foundation of Korea(NRF) funded by the Ministry of Education(No. 2016R1D1A1B03933002).

References

David Bamman, Brendan OConnor, and Noah A Smith. 2013. Learning latent personas of film characters. In *Proceedings of the 51st Annual Meeting of the Association for Computational Linguistics (Volume 1: Long Papers)*, volume 1, pages 352–361.

Arthur De Vany and W David Walls. 1999. Uncertainty in the movie industry: Does star power reduce the terror of the box office? *Journal of cultural economics*, 23(4):285–318.

Lyric Doshi, Jonas Krauss, Stefan Nann, and Peter Gloor. 2010. Predicting movie prices through dynamic social network analysis. *Procedia-Social and Behavioral Sciences*, 2(4):6423–6433.

Jingfei Du, Hua Xu, and Xiaoqiu Huang. 2014. Box office prediction based on microblog. *Expert Systems with Applications*, 41(4):1680–1689.

Jehoshua Eliashberg, Sam K Hui, and Z John Zhang. 2007. From story line to box office: A new approach for green-lighting movie scripts. *Management Science*, 53(6):881–893.

Jehoshua Eliashberg, Sam K Hui, and Z John Zhang. 2014. Assessing box office performance using movie scripts: A kernel-based approach. *IEEE Transactions on Knowledge and Data Engineering*, 26(11):2639–2648.

Jehoshua Eliashberg, SK Hui, and SJ Zhang. 2010. *Green-lighting Movie Scripts: Revenue Forecasting and Risk Management*. Ph.D. thesis, Ph. D. thesis, University of Pennsylvania.

Clayton J Hutto and Eric Gilbert. 2014. Vader: A parsimonious rule-based model for sentiment analysis of social media text. In *Eighth international AAAI conference on weblogs and social media*.

Sameer Ranjan Jaiswal and Divyansh Sharma. 2017. Predicting success of bollywood movies using machine learning techniques. In *Proceedings of the 10th Annual ACM India Compute Conference on ZZZ*, pages 121–124. ACM.

Márton Mestyán, Taha Yasseri, and János Kertész. 2013. Early prediction of movie box office success based on wikipedia activity big data. *PloS one*, 8(8):e71226.

Tomas Mikolov, Kai Chen, Greg Corrado, and Jeffrey Dean. 2013. Efficient estimation of word representations in vector space. *arXiv preprint arXiv:1301.3781*.

Vinod Nair and Geoffrey E Hinton. 2010. Rectified linear units improve restricted boltzmann machines. In *Proceedings of the 27th international conference on machine learning (ICML-10)*, pages 807–814.

Jeffrey Pennington, Richard Socher, and Christopher Manning. 2014. Glove: Global vectors for word representation. In *Proceedings of the 2014 conference on empirical methods in natural language processing (EMNLP)*, pages 1532–1543.

Christian S Perone, Roberto Silveira, and Thomas S Paula. 2018. Evaluation of sentence embeddings in downstream and linguistic probing tasks. *arXiv preprint arXiv:1806.06259*.

Matthew E Peters, Mark Neumann, Mohit Iyyer, Matt Gardner, Christopher Clark, Kenton Lee, and Luke Zettlemoyer. 2018. Deep contextualized word representations. *arXiv preprint arXiv:1802.05365*.

Marek Z Reformat and Ronald R Yager. 2014. Suggesting recommendations using pythagorean fuzzy sets illustrated using netflix movie data. In *International Conference on Information Processing and Management of Uncertainty in Knowledge-Based Systems*, pages 546–556. Springer.

Travis Ginmu Rhee and Farhana Zulkernine. 2016. Predicting movie box office profitability: a neural network approach. In *2016 15th IEEE International Conference on Machine Learning and Applications (ICMLA)*, pages 665–670. IEEE.

Leonard Richardson. 2013. Beautiful soup. *Crummy: The Site*.

Shaiwal Sachdev, Abhishek Agrawal, Shubham Bhendarkar, Bakshi Rohit Prasad, and Sonali Agarwal. 2018. Movie box-office gross revenue estimation. In *Recent Findings in Intelligent Computing Techniques*, pages 9–17. Springer.

Ramesh Sharda and Dursun Delen. 2006. Predicting box-office success of motion pictures with neural networks. *Expert Systems with Applications*, 30(2):243–254.

Li Zhang, Jianhua Luo, and Suying Yang. 2009. Forecasting box office revenue of movies with bp neural network. *Expert Systems with Applications*, 36(3):6580–6587.

Author Index

Ammanabrolu, Prithviraj, 46
Andy, Anietie, 112

Bannihatti Kumar, Vinayshekhar, 117
Bhutani, Mukul, 117
Black, Alan W, 11, 117

Callison-Burch, Chris, 112
Chandu, Khyathi, 11
Cheong, Yun Gyung, 127
Cheung, Wesley, 46

Demberg, Vera, 34

Flor, Michael, 75

Gupta, Prakhar, 117

Jo, Yohan, 22

Kim, Evgeny, 56
Kim, You Jin, 127
Klinger, Roman, 56

Lee, Jung Hoon, 127
Luo, Zhaochen, 46

Ma, William, 46
Martin, Lara, 46

Naik, Aakanksha, 22

Pinkal, Manfred, 90
Pizzolli, Daniele, 107
Prabhumoye, Shrimai, 11

Qi, Xiaoyu, 1
Qureshi, Mohammed Rameez, 81

Rajkumar, Rajakrishnan, 81
Ranjan, Sidharth, 81
Riedl, Mark, 46
Rose, Carolyn, 22
Roth, Michael, 90

Sakai, Tetsuya, 1
Salakhutdinov, Ruslan, 11
Sayeed, Asad, 34

Shah, Kushal, 81
Shi, Wei, 34
Shkadzko, Pavel, 34
Somasundaran, Swapna, 75
Song, Ruihua, 1
Strapparava, Carlo, 107

Theune, Mariët, 65
Tien, Ethan, 46

van Stegeren, Judith, 65

Wang, Chunting, 1
Wanzare, Lilian Diana Awuor, 90
Wijaya, Derry Tanti, 112

Yan, Xinru, 22

Zhai, Fangzhou, 34
Zhou, Jin, 1

Association for Computational Linguistics
209 N. Eighth Street
Stroudsburg, Pennsylvania 18360

ISBN 978-1-5108-9110-4